Come to the X

First published by Galileo Press in 2020
ISBN 987-0-913123-37-9

A portion of the proceeds from this book will go to the Permanently Disabled Jockeys
Fund, a public charity that provides financial assistance to former jockeys who have
suffered catastrophic on-track injuries.

Grateful acknowledgment to the following journals, in which some of the poems first
appeared, in somewhat different form.

"Cut It Down, They Said" *Revolution John*
"The Art of Falling" *Poet Lore*
"Gift Horse" *The Notebook*
"After a Night of Almost Making Love" *JMWW*
"Riding In Hitchcock Woods" *Muse/A Journal*
"Dieting" *Take This Spoon* (Main Street Rag Press, 2014)
"Glads" *Muse/A Journal*

This book is memoir. It reflects the author's present recollections of experiences over time.
Some names and characteristics have been changed, some events have been compressed,
and some dialogue has been recreated.

Author painting by Kelli Plitz
Book design by Adam Robinson
The map on the cover was provided by the Historical Society of Baltimore County

Come to the X

a memoir

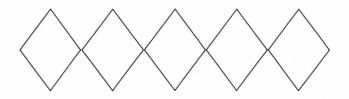

Julia Wendell

GALILEO
PRESS

Also by Julia Wendell

Take This Spoon (Main Street Rag Press, 2014)

The Sorry Flowers (Word Tech Editions, 2009)

Finding My Distance: A Year in the Life of a Three-day Event Rider (Galileo Press, 2009)

Restalrig (Finishing Line Press, 2007)

Dark Track (Word Tech Editions, 2005)

Scared Money Never Wins (Finishing Line Press, 2004)

Wheeler Lane (Igneus Press, 1998)

Fires at Yellowstone (Bacchae Press, 1993)

An Otherwise Perfect History (Ithaca House Press, 1988)

For Caitlin

Contents

The soul's joy lies in doing.

—Percy Bysshe Shelley

The things you have caused
Me most to want
Are those that furthest elude me.

—Jane Hirshfield, "A Person Protests to Fate"

Chapter One

Look in His Mouth

LAST SUMMER, THERE WAS AN EARTHQUAKE IN GUILFORD SIDING, Pennsylvania, that measured 2.1 on the Richter scale. All the buzzing world went silent in the moments after the tremors and before the aftershock, except for the chinking of the shimmering metal on Calvin's bit rack.

As a tall, slender woman, I could only manage a horse like Calvin with the right bit. I have an entire wall shellacked with his dried spit: loose rings and D rings; eggbutts and elevators; pelhams, gags, and kimberwickes of every kind; slow twists and corkscrews; two, three, and four rings; plus long-shanked and filigreed western bits used for team penning, roping, barrel racing, turning on a dime—or stopping Calvin. He has run off with me in every context, blown through every bit I've tried. The only rig that can hold him is a three-ring Waterford with a chain tightened to the last hole around his chin. It digs into his velvety lips like a surgical curette, and he comes off a cross-country gallop with red foam at the corners of his mouth.

MY FATHER'S HORSE SEEMED LIKE THE BIGGEST ON EARTH. IN REALity, he was about a hand smaller than Calvin. Big Horse had a penchant for running away from my father's noisy hands and badly balanced riding, and would often deposit him in the woodpile upon galloping out of control back to the barn, all lathered up, sides heaving.

"There goes Jack, showing off again," my grandmother would scoff, as my father and Big Horse careened by.

COME TO THE X

Only now do I empathize with my father's plight. He was too busy holding on for dear life and too proud to contradict my grandmother's judgment.

A FRIEND COMES OUT TO THE FARM TO HELP ME FIND ANOTHER BIT for Calvin. Hope has the slowly disappearing visage of an aging blond, countered by an ebullient personality, especially concerning Myler bits. The moment Calvin feels the soft mouth of the Myler and realizes it isn't going to bite him back, he puts his head down and goes to work. For the first time in almost a decade, my horse is going right.

But I'm still thinking of my father. And Big Horse running off with him. The horse, always running off with him.

AT THE PLANTATION FIELD FOUR-STAR EVENT, I PUT CALVIN BACK in the double bridle for dressage, not trusting that I can get him to change his leading canter leg in the flying changes with the Myler. I am not unhappy with the test. The judges feel differently. Our 78.6 spills over the lip of a qualifying score.

I've had it.

"I'LL TRY CALVIN," THE DIRT GUY SAYS. HE HAS ASKED TO BORROW one of my horses for a family hack. I'm reluctant, but at the same time I can't say no. Maybe he'll take Calvin off my hands for good.

Tall and goofy-lanky, with a Walrus moustache, Edwin Forrest has pushed all the dirt there is to push at An Otherwise Perfect Farm over the last twenty years—leveling ground, installing our riding arenas, building the water jump, and burying our horses. He rents an old barracks barn we rebuilt as a party space for our kids, John and Chance, when they were growing up, that morphed into a tenant house once they had moved away.

I find Ed hand-grazing Calvin by the round pen next to the mare barn.

4

"Actually, would you mind riding Patrick instead?" I ask, having already changed my mind about Goliath. My young horse Patrick, whose show name is Planet of Joy, is another nightmare ride. Should have named him Planet of Pain instead.

"I'm sorry, Julia, I hate to bother you."

Hate? Apology? In twenty years, I haven't had a single conversation with Edwin in which he didn't unnecessarily apologize for something. I always wonder what he's hiding, his apologies cousins to something darker.

"No worries," I say, grabbing the rope before my Four-Star horse can teach him to gallop out of control. "I love being bothered."

Maybe I'll stay home from South Carolina this winter and foxhunt Calvin instead. Experiment with more bits. Which means I better keep up his fitness. I hurry him back to the barn, grab his tack, and get going. Calvin seems relieved that I've rescued him from the hole digger. He rests his chin on my shoulder for a moment in his stall before I saddle him.

It is a brilliant fall day in Maryland. I can't help myself. I work on Calvin's flying changes on the trail. I jump a log or two on my way from Point A to Nowhere. My lips part and I'm smiling. Calvin's retirement has lasted exactly twenty-four hours.

"I'm so glad you're not going to event Calvin again," my husband, Barrett, says. We are on our way to a poetry reading.

I grunt vaguely into my lap. Yellow leaves pell-mell our windshield, furious and ghostly, as we pull up to the Ivy Bookshop.

Calvin came into my life a few months after my father died. As his health care agent, I made the decision to end life support. I thought if I just kept going, I wouldn't feel so bad. Old wounds and new ones— perpetual motion, my answer to grief. I competed two weeks after my father's funeral, determined to soldier through.

Calvin was 17 hands tall when I bought him at age four and grew another two inches in the first year of our partnership. I stopped sticking

COME TO THE X

him at 17.3; I didn't want to know. Kind of like not getting on scales. Calvin is as sensitive and fragile minded as he is huge, doubtfully strong enough mentally to handle the upper level pressures of my sport. We'd bought a second horse, a gray thoroughbred—Houston Galaxy—at the same time as Calvin, who spiral-fractured his ankle three months later and had to be put down.

I had a dead horse and the wrong horse. And no father.

BLASTING RAIN FOR THE FIRST TIME IN A MONTH. DIEHARDS, CALVIN and I hack across Mt. Zion Road to the Menzies' secret field.

When I was growing up in the Allegheny Forest, there was a field, enclosed on all sides by woods, with a narrow trail leading to it. The Secret Field—my favorite haunt to hack to with my pony, Tommy. I'd pack a peanut butter sandwich and thermos of milk in my saddlebags—one for me and one for Tommy, and later for Billy and the quarter horses Maggie and Jim—and spend my days there, fantasizing that I was in charge of a herd of hundreds, on a cattle drive from central Texas to the railyards in Kansas.

My cattle drive today bypasses the Menzies'. Recently felled trees and brush surround the field and conceal the space from view. "A forest is a garden, you have to prune it," my father once said. I pick up a quick canter, swap a couple of leads, and call it a day for my flatwork, which I might otherwise have spent a half hour practicing without censorious eyes to judge me. Calvin is relaxed and happy not to have to work too hard. My gray Lab, Georgia, waits by the side of the field. She picks up a trot. As we get closer to home, she disappears, her usual trick, when her pal Simon was alive. I call and call, but without her Virgil, she is deaf to my pleas. She's headed off into the dark harbor, where she'll exhaust herself darting between rows of high corn to find a stray bone.

THREE LESSONS IN THE POURING RAIN WITH THE GHOST. CALVIN first. Weighted boots, a skimpy Myler bit in his mouth, and a hundred doxycycline pills on board.

Calvin loves to push one shoulder, hip, or hind off to one side or the other. I have to feel it before the Dublin Express derails. If so much as an ear falls outside the line of the imaginary track, then hundreds of pounds ensue. If I don't nip the deviation before it starts, I might as well be falling from a trestle.

I funnel, channel, dance on the tightrope of that three-foot-wide lane.

"It's great news he's got Lyme's," the Ghost says. I look quizzically at my trainer. The Ghost is one to want a medical excuse for poor performance. I would rather point to training issues. Riding mistakes are rarely the rider's fault in his own daybook. One of the best jump riders in the world, he works hard chasing his own demons: seven days a week, no letup, as if almost inhuman. Both of us keeping busy so as not to have to look too hard inside.

"I guess so," I reply. The vet had said that Calvin's Lyme titer was only slightly elevated. His white blood cell count was low, indicative of chronic Lyme, but not a full-blown case of it. Might be the reason for one of those rails at Plantation—but seven?

Calvin doesn't touch the rails, feels relaxed and looser in his body, and stretches his head and neck over the fences. Perhaps the long-shanked hackamore with its Annie Oakley leverage sets him too much in a frame and interferes with the freedom and form of his jump. Or maybe he's just a horse that likes to train but not compete—a morning glory.

I catch myself looking back over my shoulder, thinking I hear the distinctive rattle of Simon's collar. What can Georgia comprehend about death? She gets a little needier, a little more confused—not heeding my calls, wandering around the house, whining with her night toy, a noodle-legged giraffe, in her mouth, searching in all the nooks where Simon would likely be hiding—on the couch, under my desk. Time doesn't seem to be doing a thing for her yet. What is grief like for a dog? I wonder. Barrett takes her to the Gunpowder River for walks and swims; I get her out on hacks with the horses. We try to make her sadness smaller by making her world larger.

But she keeps searching for Simon under the bed.

MY MOTHER WAS A SELF-PROCLAIMED ANIMAL LOVER. FIRST, THERE were Siberian Huskies. Niki was like most Huskies; he lived to run and was never attached to his owners. The instinct to run and kill was his driving force. My father refused to keep him penned up or on a leash. "Dogs should be allowed to run," he always said. We got a phone call one day from a neighbor. Niki had singled out a sheep from its herd and was in the process of devouring it without killing it first, craving the taste of adrenaline. The farmer was nice enough to call my parents rather than simply shoot the dog. But the dog got shot anyway, when he turned on my father as he was trying to pull the animal off the dying ewe. The farmer had his rifle trained on the dog, and shot him before he could maul my father.

My stubborn father kept letting the second Husky out, until the dog ran into an oil tanker on Jackson Run Road. There were two Sheepdogs, one of whom also got hit. An Otterhound had to be put down for biting anyone who rang the doorbell. Two German Shepherds were also allowed to run, until one of them disappeared. The other got into rat poison. We found what was left of her come spring in nearby woods. There were two Labs: one died of an eye disorder; the other got killed on the road when my father let him out against my mother's wishes. By the time the Standard Poodles came along, my father was too old and tired to see to those dogs' freedom. They stayed penned up their entire lives and were only brought into the house at dinnertime. "Why is he always licking me?" my mother would complain. It wouldn't have occurred to her that dogs lick to be affectionate, not having hands or arms to hold or hug with. My mother may have been an animal lover, but she never went out of her way to understand her dogs, or to try to work with their disobediences.

Dogs do bad things for a reason. Same with horses.

A SCREECH OF TIRES ON BLACKROCK. THE TEAPOT AND I RUN TOWARD the road. It's clear neither of us does much sprinting. My joints explode. At 4'10", the Teapot's legs are the length of baseball bats.

"There's Georgia," she says.

"What do you mean?" I panic.

"No, no, coming out the door," she explains.

As I get closer, I see the white belly of a deer, flopping its head and neck, trying to hoist itself up with its broken body. But it will never do that.

I run to the house to fetch Barrett's shotgun. "How do you use this thing?" I ask helplessly.

"I'll do it," the Teapot offers. The Teapot is a woman who loves to take control. And she craves to help in a crisis. Since we have so many of them at the farm, we see a lot of each other and have become quite close.

I hand her the gun, and we head back to the road. The deer has gone still in the westbound lane. I cross the road to check for life, then pull myself back, as a dark SUV barrels around the corner and smacks the carcass head on. "You motherfucking idiot," I scream, shaking my fist at the driver, who careens into an anonymous future. The Teapot is in the middle of the road, slowing traffic with the shotgun. Barrett pulls up in the tin can and drags the deer into the ditch by the side of the road. I know how much this must hurt his bad hand.

"We'll get it tomorrow," he reassures.

The Teapot waves the stopped cars onward with the barrel of the gun. To one woman who leans out her passenger-side window the Teapot hisses, "Slow the fuck down."

Barrett and I walk back to the house. "Please tell me it was quicker than that for Simon," I say. "Did you see the agony in the doe's face? Brown Dog's expression didn't look like that."

"It was quicker," he reassures. "You could see it in his eyes. Instantaneous."

As I pulled down the tarp over Simon, the velvety eyelids were closed. I put my palm there, hoping to feel twitching underneath—but they had a clammy stillness about them.

HEAVY RAIN AT THE MARYLAND HORSE TRIALS. A BAD FENCE AT 12. Planet of Joy overruns his distance and gets underneath the corner. Startled, I tone down the canter exactly when I need more. We come over the rise to a hut on a knoll, which introduces the water jump. Neither of us can see what's on the other side, and because he's cantering at a snail's pace, the horse stops. I smack him with the crop, turn him around, re-present, and he canters on through.

I'm ready for the second water. I spur and cluck and growl and tap him on the shoulder as we approach the blurry steeplechase fence into water through the deep muck of saturated footing. Planet of Joy launches over and in. My wet gloves slip on slick reins. I land on the buckle, regather the reins, but can't make it to the second element out of the water in time. We circle. Ouch. A second stop.

Somewhere, Barrett is muttering, "If you punish a horse for his first effort, he'll overdo the next one."

The Ghost might blame our problems on the weather and throw out the whole run, and that's probably what I should do. Was it Aeolus's fault, unlocking his storm winds? Something is lessening my drive to get to the other side. Today, I misread the amount of leg required to negotiate the first water obstacle.

I got Patrick from a friend as a resale project, then kept him when he couldn't pass a vetting. This one attacks other horses as well as cross-country fences. Not exactly the nicest guy to date—definitely not one you'd take home to meet the parents—but he's a talented and game hoodlum, so I've put in the time and gotten him as far as Preliminary, despite bad feet and a fascist personality. "Never give up on a horse," my father used to say. "This one could be president one day."

I decide not to run the greener Shiva in the pouring muck, and we pack up and go home. Having helped pull the lanky chestnut out of his mother six years ago, I'm more protective of Shiva. I don't want him to get hurt in lousy conditions. Maybe I just don't want another failure on my hands.

Calvin is waiting for me at home, head hanging over his stall guard, watching as I lead Shiva and Patrick down the barn aisle. He's had two days off, and his own daily internal rhythms are feeling the lack of attention. No worries, Calvin. Your job today: clearing Julia's mind.

We hack out with the Teapot and her pony. Calvin adores the 13-hand Ego, and they stroll shoulder-to-knee down the split between pastures and into the back field, and beyond.

I'VE NEVER LIKED BAMBOO. OPPRESSIVE, JUNGLELIKE, GLUTTONOUS. It's so creepy the way it devours a space. Way worse than wisteria or spearmint. Impossible to control.

"Going to touch him with it next time," the Ghost says. I figure-eight the four-foot panel. He picks up a bamboo pole. I repeat the exercise. Calvin rocks back to leave the ground, and the Ghost taps him lightly on his hocks with the fishing rod. Calvin lifts his withers and balloons over the jump, transforming his vertical arc to clear the panel. He's a little feisty on landing, reacting to the encouragement. The Ghost and I look at each other, drop-jawed. When it comes to horse-training gadgets, the Ghost is usually not standing in line. I'm surprised he even owns a bamboo rod. He *had* hidden it among the other lumber in the ring, as if embarrassed to reveal his arsenal.

"I'm surprised how rideable he stayed," he says.

The Ghost places heavy pipes as rails to form a wide hogsback oxer. As he heaves them up from the footing, one falls out of its skewed placing in the jump cup and lands on a toe. The Ghost bends over with a couple of muffled expletives.

"You've got to be kidding," I say.

"Don't change your ride," he gasps.

Calvin jumps the steel rails without a rub. He's a smart horse; he knows what hurts and what doesn't. The Ghost and I have a staring match.

"I wouldn't tell anybody about this," he advises, "and I wouldn't try it on your own."

My guess is that an ostrich feather tickling Calvin's hocks would have produced the same impressive jump.

"Write this down," the Ghost advises. "Keep track of what we've tried."

Apparently, the Ghost didn't read my last book.

I'M A HYPOCRITICAL NURSE, SOOTHING THE DAMAGE I'VE INFLICTED.

Calvin's mouth is small in comparison to the rest of his bulk. I balm the sides of the mouth twice a day. I've experimented with Desitin, Preparation H, Lanisol, and even Kama Sutra gel hidden in the depths of my grooming bag. I settled on a German product that comes by way of Canada—Effol Melkfett with calendula, the best healer for Calvin's mouth sores.

I cut apples into small crescents for him to manage the bites.

Calvin loves to train in his long-shanked hackamore, but without using a bit while his mouth heals, I lose the feel of *any* bit. The less I use a bit, the more he resents it when I do. What does horsewoman Sally O'Connor say about horses suffering mouth problems? *Sell them.*

Calvin reminds me so much of myself—I love to train but become defensive when being judged. I've stuck with him so long not because he's a mini me, but because he's a mighty me.

Many have seen Calvin drop his back, pin his ears, rear, spin, run sideways, bolt out of the ring. They called him difficult, incorrigible, untrainable. But no one ever thought to look in his mouth. Not even the vets. They were too busy ogling his bad behavior and examining his enormous body, missing the subtler details. It took me years to discover the deep raw grooves in the fleshy corners of his mouth caused by the bits. In reality, Calvin is as sensitive as he is enormous. He is desperate to be good and needs a soft bit to encourage his best efforts. Once he panics, barbed wire can't hold him. He runs away from the pain in his mouth by running into it.

Faulkner wrote, before he was killed falling from a horse, "We cling to that which has robbed us."

I comprehend so little. I'm so focused on the sun, I overlook answers that bloom only at night.

Last winter, I made a pact with myself to use my winter training time in Aiken to find another bit besides the three-ring Waterford, which rips Calvin's lips. I landed on a western bit—a long-shanked Myler with a two-inch port. The Myler could stop him, all right, but it also had little influence on turning him. It was not going to be much help in the more intricate combinations on Intermediate and Advanced tracks.

That's the rub—any bit that controls forward motion takes away steering. Any bit that helps turn takes away forward control. At some point, it's up to the horse, and to the troubled rider who comes to him every day, saying, "Heal me, heal me."

IN MY MIND, IT'S ALWAYS THE END OF SEPTEMBER.

Barrett and I woke at dawn to head back up to Unionville. Simon and Georgia joined us in the barn, though Simon soon retreated to the house. As we booted Calvin for the trip, there was commotion on the road—a squeal of tires and a line of horse trailers in tandem, on their way to Saturday morning's foxhunt, slowing and coming to a brief stop in the half light. Barrett hopped in the gator and came back to report that it must have been a deer leaping across the road and cutting off traffic. All was quiet.

Calvin was on his toes in warm-up—relaxed, in good form, and not touching the rails. We cantered into the arena, waiting for the buzzer to begin our round. As I negotiated the lines of jumps, I could feel Calvin jumping well, though a bit lackadaisically. I hoped I hadn't shoved one too many tubes of quieting magnesium down his gullet. I could hear an annoying ticking underneath me. I hadn't panicked yet.

"That's twenty-eight jump and twelve time faults," the announcer blasted through the sound system, in case anyone was hard of hearing.

"What happened?" I asked the Ghost when I dragged myself out of the ring, eyes riveted to the horse's withers.

He shook his head. "We need to regroup." This was the first time he hadn't encouraged me to go on with the horse, the first implication that our problems might not be solvable.

"Well, I'm not going to run him tomorrow, that's for sure. In fact, I'm never going to run him again. That's it. He's done."

The Ghost nodded, and a dark shadow crossed his face.

WE GET UP AT 2:30 TO DRIVE TO REMINGTON, VIRGINIA, CHASING Shiva's first Preliminary run at Kelly's Ford. It has taken me nearly four years to get Shiva to this level, which might have taken a stouter horse half that time. Our rig crawls down a dark suburban lane—the destination definitely not on our left. I've mistakenly keyed into my GPS the secretary's home address rather than the event address. Our diesel engine has surely awakened everyone in this tiny neighborhood. I find the correct address, punch a few keys, and we struggle for another hour, back in the direction from whence we'd come, passing Spotsylvania, Manassas, and Fredericksburg battlefields before arriving at Kelly's Ford. Just enough time before dressage to jog around half of the cross-country course in the tumescent light.

He smells the beefers before he sees them, their shit pies splatting the dressage warm-up area. Shiva tiptoes across the fouled triangle of space allotted for our practice circles. He comes to a sliding stop when he spies the herd of Angus strolling along the fence line in the adjacent field. The cows are both curious and nearsighted. They lower their heads to get a better view. I feel my horse's heart thumping through his chest, his sides quivering between my knees.

I've apparently left my horse at home along with my sense of direction. Whether it is the cows, the show jumps decorated in a zombie apocalypse motif, or Shiva's unfocused mind, who knows? In show jumping, I power-lift him over the rails. He nearly stops at one vertical set unusually on a mound, plowing through rather than jumping it. Technically it isn't a stop, so I keep going. Cross-country fares worse. With a lot of coaxing from my crop, voice, and leg, I cowboy him through half of the course as he climbs over the oxers and shies at all the bright decorations. Approaching fence 8, my eye catches Barrett off to the side. We have to negotiate a small mound and jump a vertical, take two strides, and jump off a bank. Shiva stops at the vertical. I clock him with my whip, flip him around, and he climbs over the jump. I announce to the judge my intent to retire. The horse veers into the flag, breaking it and sending me to the ground.

Maybe Shiva also has Lyme disease. If Calvin has the nasty tick-borne virus maybe Shiva does, too. They do, after all, share the same leaves of grass.

Barrett thinks we need to get a cow. "We could let him graze in the splits between paddocks," he suggests. I scrunch my face into a negative. "Would cut down on the mowing," he offers like a swindler, as if saving money would convince me. "I love cows," he finally says, appealing to my desire to please him.

"I don't," I reply.

THE FARM, ALWAYS BUSY ON A WEEKEND. CALVIN LEANS OUT HIS stall door. He hates having a day off. His eyes follow me around the barn as I unpack, clean up, put away. When I go into his stall to rub his ears, he rests his head on my shoulder.

Sounds like you've had a rough day, my partner says.

Barrett returns to the house for a much-needed rest. His insides have been acting up. In short order, he's back at the barn.

"The Ghost just fell and is still down," he says as he ducks out of the tin can. Today is also cross-country day at Fair Hill International.

I call the Teapot, who is at Fair Hill as a spectator. "They are helicoptering him."

The horse hit the final element of the coffin jump, rotated, went down, landed partially on his rider, and kicked him in the head as it got up. The Ghost was knocked out for over fifteen minutes. Half of the Four-Star division either fell, were eliminated, or retired.

On the Teapot's next report twenty minutes later, the Ghost is awake and groaning.

Next year, I tell myself. Since my success with Redmond over the Four-Star track at Fair Hill ten years ago, I have been trying to repeat that run.

I'M NO LONGER SURE OF MY GOALS. "THERE'S SOMETHING GOING ON with me," I say to Barrett.

"I know," he says. "And it's making you beautiful."

"How can I be beautiful if I don't have a goal?"

"Look at me," he says. "I've never had a goal, and I'm gorgeous."

He rolls his belly to the other side of the bed and begins the three-step process of getting up, bracing his weight against the exercise bike.

CALVIN AND I WERE ON OUR WAY TO FAIR HILL INTERNATIONAL LAST fall. We jumped around clean at a Four-Star event in Quebec earlier that year. I should have known better. Horses change after they've completed an international competition. Completing the long-format Two Star at Morven Park in 2006 woke up the tiger. He got his first taste of what his gigantic body feels like at speed in the steeplechase phase. After Morven, everything that scared him provoked his flight response.

It took a long time for Calvin to feel comfortable at speed, and he still has a tendency to bolt when he's afraid. Overcoming obstacles and attaining goals can be so stressful on horses, undoing them in the very attainment. I learned to train horses against their natures in order to better balance them. If their tendency is to gallop, then teach them to canter slowly; if they are sluggish, then show them some speed; if spooky, hack them; easily winded, then miles of trotting. But how to train an animal against his inherent nature, and not train his instincts and initiative out of him entirely? Solve that riddle, and you can open the door to past and future.

A few years before, Calvin and I were qualified for the Four Star at Fair Hill, but we probably shouldn't have gone. Just because you qualify doesn't mean your horse and you are ready. At the event, Calvin's dressage was unsalvageable; lots of hopping up and down and rearing after he lost his counter-canter somewhere in warm-up. On cross-country, we landed in the middle of fence 3, twisted badly over fence 4, and finally stopped at the water, fence 5. I then had the good sense to retire. The Ground Jury called me into a trailer for a meeting. They were putting me on the watch list for dangerous riding. "But why?" I croaked. "I retired."

My inclusion on the watch list meant just that: officials would watch my performance at six Advanced horse trials. If there were no further "infractions," then I could petition to be taken off the list. This is not something to brag about.

I LOUNGE ON A NAVAL OFFICER'S TRUNK OUTSIDE CALVIN'S STALL, enjoying the sun flooding the barn's west end. Calvin seems happy to me there, either standing along his stall wall, one hip cocked, doz- r hanging his head over the red rubber spaghetti-strap stall guard, *beautiful*

rummaging with his nose over the top of my head, as if there might be a peppermint embedded in my hair. I could happily spend the rest of my life right here, warming and being warmed, alongside Calvin.

You could tell time by the lines accumulating in your sleep, lost on waking. Men look right through you, bone on bone. Nothing adds up. Stuck in the middle of your life, you don't want another Everest to stand in your way. You want to rest at sea level, put the conch to your ear, listen to yourself live.

THREE ON THE RIG TO LOCH MOY'S CROSS-COUNTRY FIELD. I'M mainly interested in showing Shiva a mix of black- and green-flagged fences. Something has to give with that one.

I met Stephen Bradley nearly twenty years ago on a One-Star course walk at Morven Park—back when I was still doing half-mile workouts on Stormy Fling at Pimlico. Just seeing him makes me feel younger.

"How's the eye?" Stephen asks.

"Clear as a bell," I say.

Shiva is game to his fences, though short strided and bouncy. Stephen wants me to find the middle stride out of which I'll have more options—either moving up or holding to the fences. The first serious combination is downhill to a narrow brush fence situated in the crotch of a tree, then uphill several strides to a rolltop. Shiva plants his front legs under the jump and vomits over the lip, backs up, whips around, and I'm pitched in front of the saddle, which explodes my air vest. I wiggle back in the tack as the horse commences a toe spin. I try to catch my breath as my lungs get squashed by the inflated vest.

Shiva rears and runs sideways. I turn to Stephen: "Now what," I pant.

"We stay here until he jumps it," he says, smiling and bossy.

Shiva raced only five times, including two wins, two seconds, and one disaster when he "left the track" while leading in a top-shelf allowance race. Barreling into the home stretch, he spied his exit at a gap and went for it. He came home for a while after that race, so I could teach him how to steer. His race trainer was delighted to see him leave; the horse was so ill behaved that none of the jockeys wanted to ride him in spite of his good record.

After several more attempts, I finally get him over the fence and up the hill to the rolltop. I'm exhausted but fairly certain that we've made a point to my adolescent brat, more interested in smoking a blunt behind the barn with Barrett than doing his geometry homework. I've at least driven home the value of repetition.

A fellow schooler insists on loaning me her spare air vest for the remainder of my ride, now that my CO_2 cartridge is spent. Things go smoothly after that, until Shiva catches a toe in the first ditch and stutters on through. He doesn't seem to understand he's supposed to jump over it rather than in it. Unfortunately, that misunderstanding catches up to us at the end of the school. As we are negotiating our last jumping effort—a larger ditch in the woods—Shiva puts a front foot in the ditch, catapulting himself into a face plant, all 1,200 pounds of him going down and me with him. I count to ten and hoist myself up. I'm ok, he's ok. I yank myself back up into the saddle and come again. Shiva jumps the ditch correctly this time. When I get back to the trailer, I gulp a handful of pills, trying to head off the inevitable. Two cartridges down and none to go.

Next up is Planet of Pain. On a good day, Patrick is hard for me to sit. He is an extravagant jumper, and his gaits are uncomfortable. Thankfully, he's in a quieter jumping mood and earns a gold star.

Calvin has been waiting for his race number to be called. We jump a couple of straightforward single fences, then head to the water. The Intermediate water obstacle involves negotiating a hut, taking one stride, then jumping down a brush bank into the water. First time through, he hesitates but goes; on the second attempt, we don't have enough power. He jumps the house too quietly and stops at the bank. I hit him, come again with a little more pizzazz, and he jumps it fine. We repeat the water until I feel he has it. I decide we need to build a steeplechase bank into our own water back home, and that Calvin needs to jump it every day until whatever demons still lurking have gotten bored and gone home. I'm not upset with him, though—he is alert, happy to be on the cross-country course, game, ratable, and jumping well, despite his elephant's memory of our fall into the water at Jersey Fresh, as well as the debacle at Fair Hill last year. Like Icarus, jumping into water for Calvin is a form of flying and drowning in one spectacular moment.

The Ghost shows up limping, his face looking milled. "I don't remember any of it," he says. "The horse was on top of me."

My horses go well in their lessons. They always go well in lessons with the Ghost, especially at home, in part because they're comfortable in their surroundings, and also because the clinic patterns are geared for the majority of novice students. He brings out the bamboo for Calvin, tapping him on the shins a couple of times as he's pushing off.

Only once does the Ghost pause to search his memory bank for a certain word that has already been spent. The word is *oxer*, which is kind of like a gymnast forgetting what a balance beam is called. "Are you riding?" I ask him stupidly. Of course he is riding, and planning to compete this weekend. The way opposites often attract in love relationships, so teachers and students should perhaps strive to be different. If it's important to train horses against their natures, then it stands to reason that a woman who is driven to be perpetually in motion might be better off training with someone a bit more placid than the Ghost.

"I know how to come back from a crash," he explains. "When I broke my leg, I had to sit on it all winter, and that did me no favors come spring. I'm not that badly hurt this time."

The Ghost has had so many injuries over the years that even his face has taken a beating—one half looks alertly at you, while the other half sags and yawns, looking like it's always on the verge of falling asleep, as if he is divided between wanting to go and wanting to stop.

So painful to sit on the couch where Simon and I used to spend early mornings, but here I sit. Barrett is on the Eastern Shore teaching at a writing conference, while I am left to oversee the farm. At 6:22, the welcomed pungency of coffee brewing. It is getting colder.

A squeal of tires. A line of horse trailers slowing.

Barrett and Calvin and I walked down the endless hill from Plantation Field's show jumping to the trailer, while I struggled to hold back the dam. Once the saddle and bridle were off, Barrett took me by the arm, diverting me from getting into a discussion with my trailer neighbor about the debacle of my show jumping.

"Julia, come walk with me a minute," Barrett said, leading Calvin to a grassier spot beyond hearing distance.

"You remember the deer this morning?" he began, tentatively. "It wasn't a deer. It was Simon. Simon was hit and killed on the road this morning. That was Marta calling to tell me the news as you were getting on. She just found him."

I looked at my husband in disbelief, choking on my own breath. A sound came out of my body I didn't recognize as I threw myself into the tack room, slamming shut the door. *Please, no, please, no. Why didn't I check on him before we left? Why didn't I go look for myself when we heard the commotion on the road? Maybe I would have found him. Maybe I should have kept life support going for a couple days longer. Maybe I could have saved him. Oh please, let it have been swift.* The jagged clawing at the chest, the no turning back, the utter vacuum.

HOPE PULLS OUT A KINDER MYLER FOR SHIVA, AND MY YOUNGSTER'S body relaxes into the bridle. His topline softens and his step lengthens. Shiva is easy-peasy on the flat, so long as he's in the safety of a ring. In the wide-open spaces, however, I can count on him to be a spaz. It doesn't help that my happiest moments on horseback are out on the trail. It has always been my time to think, as well as my best private moments with the horses. But not if I have to focus on staying alive.

Patrick, too, has been making progress on the flat. Hope concludes that the bit she originally suggested might be too strong for his current level of training. Out comes another softer correctional bit. Patrick will never be a Shiva on the flat, though; his downhill conformation won't allow it. As I'm turning Shiva back out in his field, he shies at a stick on the ground and rams into me, stomping on my right foot. I push him off and hobble to the gate, letting go of the chestnut. I lean over, head down, forearms on thighs, dizzy with pain.

As she posts another letter to the sound of five / People gather 'round her and she finds it hard to stay alive / It's just another day.

After singing to one hundred, I limp back to the barn.

I CALL UNTIL MY THROAT GETS SCRATCHY AND STRAINED. CALVIN IS patient at first, but he starts to dance in place, carving slow pirouettes in the middle of our fork to the Menzies' stream cabin, or hard right toward home. The gray dog slinks through the underbrush, head down, guilty as charged. She won't look me in the eye. I repeat her name. She looks away. I say it again. No response. I slide off Calvin in the middle of the newly cut corn field, wincing with pain, take Georgia by the scruff of her neck, and shake her, "Look at me." No response. I shake her again. Her gray wolf eyes glance sideways before they'll deign to look at me straight on.

This is how dogs express mourning. They act out, disappear, won't come when called nor look their master in the eye. *I am hurting, too*, she is telling me. Calvin flinches at my reprimands, worried that I'm mad at him. Mr. Sensitive, so panicked to do what's right it usually ends up wrong. We thread our way down the dark woods path, crossing Mt. Zion Road, with the reins of the giant horse in one hand and the collar of the bad dog in the other, Mom on sore foot, the brown phantom our guide.

THE JUDGE AT SHIP'S QUARTERS FARM HASN'T SEEN CALVIN GO SINCE a meltdown in her lesson ring about a year ago. I thought at the time she had pushed Calvin too far. She has no reason to be kind to us today.

The judge gets out of her car at the end of our Intermediate test. "His canter work is rock-solid," she says. "Counter-canter serpentines, simple changes, medium canters—all sevens or eights."

Maybe not quite Fred Astaire, but still. Now it's our trot work that needs improvement: she suggests various adjustments for Calvin's trot, as well as my position.

I've had to pull out my neck warmer and winter riding mitts on this blustery day. The wind blowing up Cal's tail gives him an excuse to be bad, but he doesn't take it. He's stone sober, too: no Perfect Prep or Chill, the usual calming chemistry. Not even our stockpile of therapies—the Respond magnetic blanket, the Equissage, the laser—are on board today. I want to clarify by taking everything away, except the new bit. I want the *tabula* as *rasa* as I can erase it.

At home, I notice sheets of stock wire that Barrett has asked Miguel to place eight inches below the existing backyard fence, so Georgia can't dig her way out. This request requires a hand-dug trench. Miguel's sense of depth obviously does not include a tape measure. It's about four inches, maximum. Barrett's Spanish is as fluent as mine is not, a source of endless frustration for me. I have to rely on him to translate. Lord knows what gets lost, which must provide him with a delicious sense of control. Barrett has a little bit of the *Ah-fuck-it* in him. As in, the horse can't be caught—*Ah-fuck-it*—just leave him out; Miguel can't measure—*Ah-fuck-it*—close enough, let's wait and see if the dog can escape. I'm just the opposite—as neurotic as he is complacent. I'll waste a morning and a bag full of carrots trying to catch the uncatchable. Moreover, Barrett has a tendency not to enforce my requests when he believes they are not in the best interests of either the farm or the horses. Rather than discussing the issue with me, sometimes it's just *Ah-fuck-it*.

El Chapo has joined us on the other side of the fence, crouched, tail wagging, dying for me to turn my back so she can begin digging. Four inches down is child's play for a Lab. This job will have to be redone.

Barrett, as usual, is the recipient of my ill-directed ire.

"It's so frustrating," I whine.

"Believe me," he counters, "your frustration is one millionth of my own." And so we repeat the old game of who-feels-most-knows-best, which never gets won between a husband and wife who have been in business together as long as they have been in love.

"Can't we just see if it holds her?" he asks.

"We've already lost one dog," I say in disgust, as if good enough could ever be just that. It certainly never is in the dressage ring. Which makes me even angrier. Barrett knows too well that laziness and laissez-faire will not be rewarded on a farm where good luck is as rare as earthquakes.

The thing about Barrett is that he will say what he feels should be done. He'll say it once. He won't argue if someone disagrees. Later, if proven right, he'll refuse to do the very thing he was right about. Twenty years ago, he suggested a perimeter stock wire fence for the farm. I said no. Now, even after Simon, he won't take a part in making it happen.

THE PAIN IN MY FOOT DISAPPEARS WHEN I AM IN THE SADDLE. WE head off into the slant light of a late afternoon, Miss Georgia trotting on ahead. It's chilly yet sunny. Georgia, surprisingly, stays close as we navigate our way around the Halles' cut cornfield, up Fenwick's hill by the enticing line of jumpable debris, and back down to Mt. Zion Road. At the Menzies' driveway, we step to the side as a police car turns in. The policeman waves. Next, a beat-up Datsun sedan slides to a stop, backs up a few, then speeds up the driveway, jamming on the brakes halfway up. A disheveled woman, sporting a housecoat and holding a cigarette between two fingers as she clutches the steering wheel, leans out the car window.

"Do you live here?" she asks. I shake my head. "We're looking for a runaway."

"Horse?" I ask.

"Girl," she says, disgustedly. "A fourteen-year-old," she adds.

"Well, I just saw a cop car pull in," I suggest. She nods affirmatively, rolls up her window, and speeds up the driveway. Georgia looks at the smoking mother and her unkempt maybe ten-year-old other daughter fidgeting in the back seat, as if contemplating hopping in and going for a joyride.

"Don't even think about it," I say to my unpredictable young Lab. "One runaway is enough for the day."

I don't have to warn her. Georgia wants to stay on my good side this afternoon. She trots ahead, stopping every hundred feet to look over her shoulder, making sure we're right behind her. We end up back at the farm, in the front field where our water jump with the new brush rolltop into water is waiting for us, thanks to Edwin Forrest. Jumping over the coop into the field, Georgia won't get out of our way, so Calvin jumps both the coop and the dog. He doesn't care. Georgia hops in the stream first, and again doesn't budge as Calvin sets sail down the bank and over the rolltop into the water. I'm manning the cantle, shoulders so far back I'm practically lying down with my feet jammed out in front. I'm not sure what part of her we jump this time, but we clear her, as well as the jump.

TWO YEARS AGO, I FELL OFF SHIVA IN OUR BACK FIELD WHEN HE spooked at an ear of corn. As I got to my feet, a swirling red mass sprouted in my eye. I could see nothing but blobs. A retinal specialist reassured me that it was "only" an eye hemorrhage, from drops of blood leaking through an old detached retina, clouding my vision. Most likely it would clear on its own. Which it did, after a couple of weeks. Vision restored, I went about my life. A year later, the vision in that eye blurred again. I took it in stride and waited for my eyesight to return. And waited. Two, three, four weeks—*nada*. My anticipated run at the Jersey Fresh Four-Star Event was fast approaching. And still, I could see nothing. I wore a patch, and when that became too distracting, I learned to close one eye so that I wouldn't become dizzy and nauseous from the disparity between the vision in each eye. Nor did I want to look like a pirate at Jersey Fresh, calling attention to myself. Surely the officials wouldn't let me compete with an eye patch.

After squinting through the dressage test, I decided to scratch from the event. There didn't seem to be much point leaving the box with another non-qualifying dressage score and a blind eye. I told the Ghost, I told the secretary, I told my groom, and then I made the mistake of telling Kittie Wilkins that I had decided not to run. Gnome-like, with a bread-bowl haircut and round glasses, Kittie is a wizard at selling horses. Though we were both scheduled to run over a Four-Star track in a couple of hours, Kittie was nonchalantly stapling sales flyers just outside the secretary's office.

"Why wouldn't you run?" she asked.

"Uh, because I can't see out of one eye," I said.

"Can you see out of the other ok?"

I unscratched.

The water complex was a tight turn off the right to a huge ditch and brush into water. Since my depth perception was catawampus, coming off the turn, my eye was as surprised by the ditch and brush as my horse was, who registered the ditch only at the last instant, stuttering our motion.

Losing momentum, he climbed over the jump, caught his front legs in the brush, twisted, and landed in the water in a heap, flinging me off the back of the saddle. I landed smack in the water on my butt. Calvin went sightseeing around the New Jersey Horse Park as I shook the stars from my head and hoisted up my dripping body. A fellow eventer caught Calvin and brought him back to me.

"I'll take him if you don't want him," he said cheerily. "This is my kind of horse."

I looked at him with my remaining eye for a few long seconds, weighing my options.

The next week, my doctor scheduled me for a vitrectomy.

Cut It Down, They Said

      Instead,
I limbed the dying
leaves and branches,
painted it yellow
to catch the sunlight,
red to fill the gash
infuriating the trunk,
where decay had set in.

I kept what I could
of the weeping cherry,
all ribs and spine,
chalice of air,
a mouth of amber tongues
beseeching the sky.
Some branches were dancers,
arms extended in fifth position.
Others writhed from crimes of excess.

Mumbling to the wind,
I pondered my new genre,
I began to laugh and entertain.
You must come see my yellow tree—
a tuft of green
sprouted like a frilly hat
from the dancer's head.

"If the horse is in balance and the rider is in balance, then the tricks are easy." Barrett has said basically the same thing to me for years. Horses hate falling down.

"Life is all about balance," my father used to say, echoing Barrett.

And so is drinking. Cocktail hour, dear to my heart. It's something I look forward to so much that I never want to abuse my love of a Chardonnay cupcake, hand frosted with a pewter blade, Barrett to smudge the icing off my pale lip.

This new dressage instructor is referring to a more subtle balance of weighting the correct seat bone, but it's really all the same thing. For years, I could hardly canter Calvin on a twenty-meter circle for fear he would tip over, the way he leaned so dramatically to the inside. He's more delicately off balance now, but it's still there.

I take my time untacking Calvin, cooling him out, letting him graze next to the farm's expanse of green paddocks, vivid hills beyond, horses being led in from turnout, the fall sun brilliant and blazing. I'm not due to meet the Ghost for another two hours.

I stop at the local tack store to kill an hour. My toe still aching, I stand weighting only one leg, staring at the exotic brow bands lining one wall.

"Hi, Julia," says a woman I vaguely recognize, fiddling with a rack of martingales. "I was so sorry to hear about your dog," she adds.

"Does this look too feminine?" I ask, diverting the conversation away from a subject I still can't talk about. I pluck a black crystal browband from the rack, hoping it might be the one to help Calvin's plain bay color be less plain, knowing all the bling in the world won't make up for his disobediences in the ring.

"Kind of," the clerk replies. "Were you thinking of putting it on a gelding?"

I move on to rubber reins. Maybe if Calvin pulls them he'll snap back to me.

THE GHOST STANDS READY WITH THE BAMBOO, BUT HE DOESN'T have to use it. Calvin has tons of push, scope, and roundness in his new glittery brow band. We wrap it up quickly, and I drive my drag queen home.

WOOFIE MADLY SWEEPS THE TACK ROOM FLOOR AS SHE WAITS FOR her daughter to finish a jump lesson. An attractive older blond, Woofie has the longest eyelashes of anyone I know, and is always perfectly coiffed in an up-flip. Today I hear her gripe about her niece, whose opportunities were handed to her by Uncle Sam after several scrapes with the law. Now she gets to go to college and have her own apartment on our tax dollars. Woofie gets more frantic with her sweeping, and her elegant eyelashes start to quiver with injustice. But it's hard to take offense; she is, after all, criticizing her own family.

Daughter Chance calls with a similar complaint. At twenty-eight, Chance is following her actor/playwright/singer/tango dancer dreams in New York, even though she has only a few ribbons to show for her passion. She had a role in Karen O's rock drama, *Stop the Virgins*, at St. Ann's Warehouse. Chance also wrote, produced, and directed an off-Broadway play, *Nesting*, about a controlling mother and her daughter who continue living on the first floor of their Baltimore row house after a fire has consumed the second floor and killed the father and brother. It's been enough success to keep from quitting, but not enough to establish a career.

Chance is working on a one-woman, one-act play starring herself. She has stalled in the writing of the new play, and in her life in general. Today she calls to complain about her unlucky demographic as a young woman playwright, which equates to zero opportunities. Her boyfriend, on the other hand, has won a number of awards for his avant-garde work, written chiefly for Latino actors. Chance has just come from an awards ceremony for his newest play, where she sat among successful starlets complaining about male superiority and the unfair literary advantages men have historically had in theater.

"There's not much you can do about it," I say, figuring why get worked up over things beyond our control.

Chance doesn't want to hear that. "So I'm just supposed to swallow it?" she says testily. I back down, knowing I'm cornered, with our boarder behind me revisiting the Diary of a Mad Housewife thing and Chance all fired up on the line. Who am I kidding? I always back down in the face of Chance's adamant opinions. Chance is as feisty as she is beautiful. At 5'2" to my 5'10", in her small jockey's frame, she has the push and personality of a giant.

"Then why don't you write an article about it for one of those theater rags?" I suggest productively. "Begin the piece at the awards ceremony, and discuss how you experienced a negative bias."

Sweep, sweep.

I can't help but give my daughter advice when she is confronted with a problem. I desperately want her to be happy, all problems solved. But that will no more be the case with Chance than with me. Twenty-eight years later, I still can't seem to accept that advice is exactly what she doesn't want.

Sweep, sweep, sweep.

"So, who are you taking to Virginia?" Woofie asks, mildly curious, after I successfully avoid answering Chance's question and end our phone conversation.

"Calvin," I say.

"What level are you running him?" Underneath this neutral question, I hear the bias I know has permeated the barn: Calvin is not an Advanced horse, and Julia should no longer be riding at that level.

"Intermediate," I say.

"Good for you," she responds, mildly patronizing. In her mind, we have appropriately stepped down.

"Well, they don't offer Advanced," I say. "And once a Four-Star horse, always a Four-Star horse."

Chapter Two

First Your Money, Then Your Clothes

DREAD ROUSES ME, WATCHES ME, FOLLOWS ME, JUDGES ME. THE long drive to Lexington, motel rooms and portable outhouses, loading and unloading, making a small nest for my next disaster. Another weekend of scores and scales. Waiting and hurrying and braiding. Having enough time but not too much for warm-up. The walking on my cranky foot. The nausea as I wait for my round in stadium jumping. And, if I'm lucky, the few moments of elation after a cross-country run.

I hit snooze.

CALVIN IS NOT DISTRACTED BY THE ELECTRIC ATMOSPHERE AT THE Virginia Horse Park. His dressage test is consistent, and, despite some tension in the walk, he gives me his most connected work to date. The organizer smiles in my direction, perhaps amused by our progress. This one has had to judge far too many of Calvin's misplaced caprioles over the last decade.

It is illegal to use over-weighted boots in show jumping—another gimmick to trick horses into picking up their feet higher over the fences. There is a scale at FEI events—with a church-lady official keeping her thumb on it. I take the weights out of the hind boots and purge the bell boots that exceed the speed limit.

I warm up for show jumping, rusty over the first couple of fences, but Calvin jumps well. I'm second to go in the Intermediate division after Down Under. Calvin twirls and dances as he waits. We canter into the arena. The bell rings, and the loudspeaker blares our disappointing dressage score. The news comes at a tricky time. I hadn't checked my score, as

31

usual, to spare myself from even harsher self-judgment. We jump the first fence well, but veer too wide to the second. Cal puts his eye on the wrong jump, and I have to squiggle back to the correct fence, which he knocks down. I become flustered by the mistake and neglect to count strides in the lines. Plus he's too strong in the Myler pelham—my failed bit selection of the day. I need to let go, but I can't. He hits four more rails. I exit the ring, head down, eyes burning.

Control freaks should use caution discovering their passion. It becomes a drug. The needle goes all the way in. They can't control their passion, and undo themselves in trying to control what they love.

I'm so, so tired of this miserable feeling. None of the tricks has worked—not weighted boots, nor bamboo rods and metal plumbing poles, nor the endless changes of mouth hardware.

"Guess the answer isn't in the gimmicks," Barrett says.

I look at my husband hard for the first time all weekend. His complexion is ashen.

CROSS-COUNTRY MORNING DAWNS COOL AND BRISK IN THE Shenandoah Valley. I fret over whether to wear a jacket under my air vest. The Ghost and I trot up to the start together—he's in a T-shirt, I'm in fleece. Every few steps, he emits a small groan.

"Are you ok?" I ask.

"Saddle is killing my leg," he says.

"You don't have to be a hero," I say.

I want to offer something more significant, but sometimes I'm at a loss with authoritative figures.

"Yes, I do," he says. "I'm not doing this for anyone else."

"What do you mean?" I respond, genuinely confused.

"I'm only doing this for myself." I'm not sure how this explanation explains anything. I'm a fine one to question motives, though—I rode Jersey Fresh with one eye.

There's a hold at the start box until another rider is scraped off the ground. I wait my turn. Olympic veteran Bruce Davidson zooms up on a scooter.

"How is it riding?" I ask, as casually as I can muster. I'm starting to perspire. God, how I wish I could shed a couple layers. I can't even dress myself right for the sport.

"No one has gotten around clean yet," he says, reassuringly.

We gallop down one of Virginia's blue mountainsides, jumping fences in our path before making a sharp right-hand turn to a big log into water, then gallop to a skinny brush oxer out. I start growling and pull on my right rein hard to get the turn done, which chokes Calvin down to a trot. But it's easy for him to trot an Intermediate log into water, as long as he wants to. We jump all the jumps clean and well the first time, which several others don't do. We accumulate a fistful of time penalties, but I don't care. I'm happy with my monster.

STEPHEN PLANS TO JOIN ME AT LOCH MOY WITH TWO OF HIS OWN, but shows up horseless. He arrived at his barn to find a flat tire on his rig. He's in a sour mood, anomalous for Stephen.

"How is it that someone who rode at the Barcelona Olympics can't change a flat tire?" Barrett asks through my cell.

I've left him at home with a tractor, fifty gallons of diesel, and eighty-five acres of orchard grass pleading, *Mow me, mow me.*

The Hindu lord of dance and light and chicanery is my first mount. My raging purple toe is taped to its neighbor for stability so that the joints in that foot feel herd bound. Shiva starts out ok, but as soon as he's asked to jump a bigger oxer, he runs out. Stephen criticizes my lack of leg-to-hand connection—my hand overpowers my leg and shuts down my horse.

"Find the distances out of a more forward, balanced canter, rather than coasting in your turns as you look for the take-off," Stephen says. Where is my outside leg today? I must have left it at the Mt. Airy Shell Station.

Things go better until we approach Neptune. Shiva jumps the Novice- and Training-level huts perched on the bank, though he's slightly backed off when he sees his reflection in the water. I ask him to jump a bigger hut on a mound with the water behind it. He hesitates, catches a leg, and almost goes down. My air vest explodes, and I smack the water like a wing-shot goose.

I hoist myself back on the horse.

"I'm impressed," Stephen says, his only compliment today.

"Don't be," I say, discouraged. "Long legs."

The sport is at least fifty percent attitude—like social media, but with ambulances involved. No one else will believe in me but me.

I come to the jump again. Shiva does a better job, and we finish our school.

I'm so tired of falling.

Stephen suggests I sell the horse with the crooked blaze. It's like suggesting I sell a wayward son. And yet I can appreciate what Stephen is trying to tell me: Shiva is an inappropriate ride. Not only is he an idiot on the trails, but he is also an inconsistent jumper.

"He's not going to do what you want to do, Julia," Stephen concludes. "He's a nice horse and he'll make a good one for somebody else at the lower levels. But he's just not a good enough jumper for you."

I cringe.

"When things are right, he's a good jumper," Stephen goes on. "But as soon as the striding is off or something else isn't quite right, his form falls apart."

Shiva is the first homebred I kept with the hopes that he might make an upper level event horse. I've started to question my assessment, both from his end and mine. He's a slow developer. By the time this one were to see Advanced—if ever he could develop the heart and form for it—I'd probably need a walker. I don't have that kind of time if I want to keep going.

My ride on Patrick fares better, although it takes me several jumps to get my mojo back. I either gun him, missing my distance, or I pick my way, cut his engine, and crawl over the fence. It isn't until I allow him to go forward that things smooth out. *Smooth* is Stephen's operative word today.

"Think smooth leg-to-hand connection," he reminds the herky-jerky marionette.

On the way home, the Ghost: *What happened to Shiva?*

I text the Ghost as smoothly as I can. I don't want him to get ouchy about my seeing Stephen. I do feel a bit like the unfaithful wife, flinging it up with Stephen, appreciating his pickiness and precision, his helpful comments and criticisms of my riding technique. He's just so damn good in bed.

Julia: *I want to sell Shiva and buy myself a talented old lady's horse who can get me through Fair Hill.*

But I don't really know. If I had to guess, I'd say Shiva got backed off his jumps after his bad experience at Kelly's Ford. He jumps as if he has excruciating pain in his back. As if he has been broken inside since birth.

Do I want to cut that tree down?

The Ghost: *We all need to stop falling off.*

I've been falling off horses all my life. I get tired of it, all right, but I also accept it as an inevitable part of the game. If you become scared of falling off, then it's the beginning of the end. There's an art to falling without getting hurt, which makes it sound like there's an art to being lucky. I've gotten pretty good at it from so much experience.

WE SEE IT SIMULTANEOUSLY, AND SHE'S OFF LIKE A ROCKET. *STRIPES.* The poor thing waddles under my rig out of Georgia's way. Georgia tries to squeeze her chubby body underneath the rig. The raccoon lunges at her, little fangs bared. I scream for the dog, who squeezes her body back out and trots to my side. Janet comes running.

"I don't think Ed's home," I say, panic in my voice. Forrest always has a pistol at the ready. I run to fetch Barrett's shotgun.

"I'll shoot it," Janet offers.

"What do you mean, *you'll* shoot it?" I say, my voice rising several octaves. Janet has spent the last three years mastering the posting trot. She looks so much more at home with a rifle in her hands than a horse between her legs.

"I used to shoot squirrels and snakes as a kid," she says. "I'm pretty good at it, too. I just don't like to pick up the mess. I was on the shooting team in high school." She adds, "The only girl on the team."

Why isn't she still shooting? I wonder. This woman, so confident with a gun yet so humble in the tack. Why have a hobby that you're afraid of? It would be like me raising rats as pets.

Rumi says: *dance the dance of death and you will live forever.* Maybe this will become true for Janet.

By the time the gun is loaded, the raccoon has waddled across the field by the mare barn and disappeared. Janet puts the gun down, clearly disappointed. I am, too. I would have loved to see her marksmanship. I crave the unexpected: bad storms, natural disasters, a timid woman with a gun.

"That's no good, seeing them in the daytime," I say. Janet nods, not needing my explanation.

I tack up Calvin, call Georgia to my side, and we mosey through the split between the front and big fields and out into the back field, where we pick up a trot. Georgia and I spy a blob on the horizon. This time it's a mangy fox sporting a rat-like hairless tail. Georgia is after it and almost pounces, but it escapes into the endless rows of Wisner's corn. My dog has developed a taste for wild critters, and there's no calling her off. She's motivated by instinct, unlike the rest of us, derailed by our minds editing our lives and telling us what we should be doing with our inappropriate horses.

WHEN SHE ISN'T SLEEPING, SHE'S CAMPED OUT BY HER WATER BOWLS, never wanting to be more than a few feet away. We've put two bowls out for Daisy, our ancient white Lab, so she'll always have plenty. On a good day last spring, she made it as far as the driveway and spent the afternoon there. I took out one water bowl, which was left behind when she came in. The next day, I smashed it with a truck tire. The Crooked Bowl has become Daisy's favorite. She always empties it first, then lies as close to it as possible, even when the other bowl is full, looking up yearningly at me. And when I fill it with fresh water again, she struggles to her feet and laps it up eagerly, an easy seventy-five times. Water. Our habits with it, our longings for it when our kidneys start to go. This is all it takes to make Daisy happy now. If only it were so easy for Shiva.

BARRETT HAS HEARD THAT THE GHOST IS PLANNING ON CELEBRATING Thanksgiving in Aiken, and running the Turkey Day Pine Top Event in Georgia. Finding out about things from Barrett is a little like playing a game of telephone—a lot of details can get lost through repeated whispers. I give the Ghost a hard time about it when I first see him.

"What, don't I get to come, too?" I tease.

He looks at me blankly.

I posit the idea to Barrett in between rides. With neither John nor Chance coming home for Thanksgiving, we envision a leisurely trip down to Aiken on the Wednesday before, maybe staying at our usual haunt, cooking for ourselves in the tiny cabin kitchen, a happy fire in the fireplace. We're already deciding between pumpkin or apple pie. If we were smart, we'd conclude that the ten-hour drive would be too much for Barrett, so close on the heels of the Virginia trip. My husband no longer travels well, and yet the routines at home are grinding him down.

"We're going down on Thursday. The event is Friday and Saturday. I'm extending the season as long as possible," the Ghost explains.

Then it hits me: this isn't about Thanksgiving in Aiken. It's about the Ghost having one more chance to feel healed and positive after his spill at Fair Hill. My excitement wanes. I rethink the interminable drive, dining out for the Thanksgiving meal at some Chinese buffet, then the concentration and energy required for yet another event—and all on a holiday weekend. Not to mention the return trip home. But Barrett is thinking about the excursion as a welcome getaway from the farm.

"How about we make a reservation at the Willcox?" he asks when I get back to the house after my chores are done. I am beat, starving, and verging on cranky.

"We'll see," I say, deep into my own reservations about the trip I've committed to.

DANIEL IS A NEW, FREQUENT PRESENCE AT OUR FARM. BARRETT HAS always been a fan of Daniel, who earns his day money at Pimlico galloping racehorses, and last year whizzed around the Rolex Five-Star course clean and within the time on his horse, Houston. He's twenty-eight years old. Tall, lanky, with a square jaw and perfect complexion.

Daniel catches me in the mare barn shed row at the end of my long barn day.

"I need to get rid of Rhapunzel," he blurts. I take a step back, catch my breath. "I wanted to talk to you first before I give her away to someone else."

A few months ago, Barrett and I gave our homebred Rhapunzel to Daniel in an attempt to winnow our herd and to give Daniel, if not another Rolex prospect, then a horse he could turn for a profit. On paper, Barrett feels Rhapunzel is the best horse he has ever bred. I can only imagine how hard it was for him to give her away. The second best was Sophie, who as a yearling kicked out viciously when we were trying to load her, shattering Barrett's right wrist and hand. Doesn't say much about our breeding instincts. He would have lost the hand, but thanks to surgical techniques discovered from doing thousands of limb reconstructions during the Iraq and Afghanistan wars, he now sports a misshapen paw with a two-inch-by-four-inch scar on the soft side, where the surgeon poured in molten skin extracted from his thigh. Sophie was a winner of five races, and Barrett was first in line to bet on her. That's my husband for you.

Daniel doesn't think he can sell Rhapunzel because she's a bit of a screwball and not quite sound behind.

"Let me talk to Barrett about it." This is what I always say when I'm too flummoxed to say anything else. You want to board your horse here? *Let me talk to Barrett.* There's a problem with the plumbing? Same. Deer carcass in the pasture, fence board missing, footing a disaster, turnout in need of rearranging, horse hurt, storm coming, tree down, stalls to muck, bills to pay—you get it—*let me talk to Barrett.* You want to get rid of Shiva's half sister? *Let's see what Barrett has to say about this.*

I call him at the house, where he has retreated after his own long day. He is not feeling well. "We've got another problem," I say. "I need you now." It's 7:30—Barrett has surely poured a glass of Cabernet by now.

He and Daniel are speaking amicably in the shed row when I barge back in. "We don't give horses away lightly," I interrupt. "What do you mean by screwball?" Daniel doesn't have much to go on besides Rhapunzel's tendency to dance at the mounting block.

"Does she have shoes on? What have you done with her? Where do you think she's unsound?" My head starts spinning on its axis with its rapid-fire questions, none receiving satisfactory answers, mainly because I don't give Daniel enough time to get the words out. Both men look startled by my sniper attack.

"I just have too many horses," Daniel lamely offers. What he doesn't admit is that Rhapunzel sent him to the hospital from a bad drop.

"Well, you should have thought of that before you took her," I say, storming out of the barn. I neglect to bite my tongue before adding, "That's the last horse you'll ever get from me," already trying to figure out where we're going to put her. I guess the horse will have to talk to Barrett.

The Art of Falling

Come off a horse enough times,
and you learn how to fall—
like snow, rain or love,
all goose-down and no elbows.

He spooks at a leaf, knocking you
sideways, the saddle slipping—
and well, you're going down again.
Relax, you'll get used to it.

Relax, you say to the lobster,
just before plopping him
into the roiling pot.
Relax, you say to a friend,

on the eve of another bender,
and to yourself,
falling off a ledge
onto a concrete floor.

It's easy, when you imagine
a soft landing.
But when your mother sinks

into her pillow in her final hour,
she knows she's not falling with grace.
Blah, blah, blah, she mouths,

flicking the back of her bruised hand,
as if brushing away a gnat,
when the priest lowers his head

to trace the thumbprint of oil,
first up and down, then sideways,
on her glistening forehead.

EXPERIMENT: NO BOOTS AND THE CROSS-COUNTRY BIT, WHICH GETS Calvin all riled up in our show jump lesson. When he feels the pressure of the long-shanked Myler, he puts two and ten together and thinks he's galloping out of the start box. In a five-stride line, I keep getting four. It feels impossible to come around the turn quietly enough to get the five, but with enough oomph to jump the 3'9" oxer off the turn. I keep getting there on a half stride and want either to push him for the long one or choke him down for the deeper distance, neither of which is desirable. On one pass, I don't see anything coming in and intentionally circle away from the first jump.

"I can't believe I just did that," I say.

The Ghost agrees.

I come again and see the same unseeable distance. Calvin gets right under the jump and plows into the fence.

"That's why we're experimenting," the Ghost says, referring to our attempts to try the cross-country bridle in a stadium format.

"Am I supposed to fret about that?" I ask as he rebuilds the demolished tower pole by pole.

"All a part of it," he says.

We try again and meet the oxer right and get the five down the line. I'm still stewing.

I hate refusals. Which is why I push my horses at their fences. Which is why Calvin has rails. My drive to get to the other side No Matter What is at the heart of the problem. My strength as a rider is also my weakness. Calvin needs the quiet waiting ride to keep his mind settled and big body organized; Julia needs the assurance of the go button. But it's the quiet ride that will get the show jumps jumped cleanly. With precision. Quiet, yet forward. A seeming oxymoron—like so much in riding—that actually works.

I WAKE IN CULPEPER, DREADING MY RUNS ON SHIVA AND PATRICK. I'd rather not have to fight Patrick's boingy jump, nor deal with Shiva's bratty attitude.

As we pull up to an open field—the venue for the event—a herd of Black Angus is grazing next to the cross-country course. You've got to be kidding.

Patrick holds himself together in dressage. Shiva is uncharacteristically nervous on the flat, probably smelling the bovines. Both show jump well, with just one rail each. I'm annoyed that clear show jump rounds continue to elude me. There's always some excuse—Patrick's disorganized enthusiasm, Shiva's poor jumping style, my frenzy to outrun my past.

Patrick flies around the big Preliminary cross-country course, and I'm thrilled with my unflappable rogue.

Shiva doesn't want to go forward despite my kicking and clucking and humping to meet the jumps. The fifth fence is a white downhill chevron, which he approaches in retrograde, backpedaling from a hundred feet away. His engine downshifts to reverse as he gives the upside-down triangles a good stare, quits, then backs up. I hit him and he climbs over the jump.

Exhausted and fed up with my push-and-shove ride, we canter through the finish flags. I want to ride horses that are motivated to get to the other side, not fearing that a traffic cop in a cow suit is about to poke up from behind the jump and yell "moo." I've had it with Shiva and say so to Barrett, who is busy icing Patrick back in trailer parking. And Barrett is looking far more exhausted than I—snail paced, as if he'd replaced all of his blood with colored water.

It's hard to feel good with twenty jump faults as part of the day's equation. Harder still to admit that I don't want to compete my homebred anymore. On the drive home, Barrett and I make plans to send him to Kate Chadderton to be sold, as soon as he gets a little time off. With an antipodal accent and a mouthful of sharp incisors, she's a balls-to-the-wall cross-country rider, and a good horse trader.

I'm secretly glad it's the last event of the season. I'm looking forward to not having my schedule at the mercy of the next event. Time for me to figure out what's next. And next could be anything—stringing Christmas lights on the yellow tree, or finding Santa's work bench in the attic.

I MAKE AN APPOINTMENT WITH COOPER TO DO A WORKUP ON SHIVA before sending him to Kate. Cooper drags one leg behind him, the result of a near-fatal polo accident when he was a young man. Though he no longer rides, he remains passionate about the anatomy of the horse. Cooper concludes that Shiva's back and sacroiliac joints are troubling him. Ultrasound reveals bony proliferation around both left and right joints. Cooper recommends injecting them. Out comes the foot-long needle that he sticks into Shiva's rump and threads through tissue and bone all the way down to the deepest recesses. He guides the needle's progress from its image on the screen, so he can be sure of the placement of the steroids. Horse medicine is a spectacular trial for human medicine; so much is learned from experimental procedures on horses that can eventually be applied to humans. Ultrasound-guided injections for one. Shock-wave therapy for another.

Just shy of 30 degrees, winter has decided to arrive. Holding Shiva for the long procedure turns out to be a frosty endeavor. The horse stands like a drunken lamb for well over an hour, with a potent cocktail on board. I envy him that. A hot toddy would do me some good right about now. Poor Shiva won't be able to wear a blanket tonight, so as not to contaminate the injection site. He doesn't seem to mind, though, as we guide the woozy adolescent back to his stall.

"I think you just might have a new horse after this," Cooper says, encouraged to have found a reason for the horse's declining performance. Cooper is a burly, big guy with large, square jowls that make me think of Burl Ives.

"Wouldn't that be nice," I say. "Thanks for the gift."

I reserve judgment until I see some positive proof and a different sort of jump. As a four-year-old, Shiva had stifle issues. At six, he has developed SI problems. At this rate, he will be diagnosed with cancer within the year. In any event, the horse needs to figure out how to use his topline over fences in order to improve his form—and his hesitant attitude toward jumping. Maybe Cooper's injections will help. The best medicine, the best grain, the best pasture. And still, the horse must *want* to want.

The day also brings work on a poem I started a few months ago. I show Barrett the newer draft. He offers a couple of suggestions, which include curling up together after we work on it.

Psyche's Water Clock

> Shock of hair
> curtaining the view,
>> I peer through my legs
> at yours—
>> the upside-down of it,
> loving the vertigo.
>> Drawing bathwater, the vessel
> steals from its well.
>> What do the coat hook
> of my separated shoulder,
>> the spine's bumpy lane,
> sunspots littering my back—
>> the parts of me
> I can't see without mirrors—
>> look like, from your angel wing-
> to-wing view?
>> I feel the burn
> running from groin to ankles
>> as I hold myself over
> a scaffold of legs,
>> your hands steadying my hips,

thumbs of Eros.
  Hold on, I tell trembling thighs,
as you ease me down
  to the place
where you don't need
  to name what you feel.
The water clock fills—
  ten merciful bells—
and all is well.

"THERE'S HEAT COMING OFF THOSE LINES," HE SAYS, HANDING THE poem back to me after reworking the original straightforward syntax. He retreats to the couch, rests his forearm over his eyes, exhausted from the intellectual effort. It's a plausible idea, to skew syntax in a poem about sex. I make the corrections, sit back and review them, then rework the poem so it resembles the original, concluding how impossible it would be to relive this one, with my back aching the way it does today. Too bad Cooper couldn't have spared some of that juice.

Pain knows pain. "You're not feeling well, are you?" I finally say to Barrett.

"I'm ok. But my hand is killing me," he says, wincing from two different kinds of affliction. Once your hand has been reattached, it's never the same.

FROM MY OFFICE WINDOW, I WATCH GEORGIA NOSE AROUND THE backyard on her morning constitution, sun grazing the peak of the pool barn. Its hurried blessing lasts a mere sixty seconds before it moves on to the next communicant: the Japanese maple, the oval paddock, the front field and beyond. I open my mouth; nothing comes out but silence.

"I FEEL GREAT TODAY," BARRETT REASSURES.

He's lying, but I load up Calvin and his gear and head to New Jersey for a show jumping clinic. I feel like a sore thumb. Not only am I the sole eventer, but I'm also the oldest rider on the biggest horse. Everything that I've worked the hardest to correct in my position over the last twenty years is wrong in Show Jump Land. I've had a dickens of a time getting my shoulders back and sitting vertically in the tack in order to hold my 18-hand monster with my core. And now I'm instructed to perch in a two-point position before the jumps. For someone always a little ahead of herself on a strong, pulling horse, it feels like such a vulnerable position.

"Don't shove him at his fences," Anne Kursinski says. "He'll hit more rails that way."

So focused on my wide-handed bicycle grip and crotch perch, I wasn't aware that I was shoving. But maybe she has hit on something. I'm over-riding against a stop. There's got to be some reason why so many of Calvin's rails come down.

"You're always riding Redmond as if he were a stopper," Jimmy Wofford used to say to me. And stopping was not in that horse's vocabulary.

I need to stay closer to my tack. In all of my jumping photos, I notice too much air between the saddle and my body—if only I could keep my long upper body still so as not to disturb my horse's balance over fences, thereby producing a knockdown.

Stay soft, stay close to my horse, allow the fences to come to me.

Anne has the clinic participants try weird Wofford-esque exercises— tying a knot in the reins to keep low, quiet hands; using a wide bicycle grip to promote the rider's closeness to his horse; looping the reins over the head and under the neck to take a rider's overactive hands out of the equation; and riding without stirrups, both at the posting and sitting trot, and while jumping. Not accustomed to hunter hack classes, Calvin starts to piss off with me in the group flatwork sessions, inching closer and closer to the horse in front of him. With his enormous step, I feel like I have to go in reverse in order to keep the correct spacing. Calvin thinks it's great fun to be in a ring with lots of other horses to chase around. Anne is less amused.

I tell Barrett about the gimmicks, concluding that the clinic is old hat—and my excitement for the rest of the weekend wanes. Barrett's voice sounds a little croaky, and he has a faraway feeling in his telephone demeanor. Says he's ok, though. His exact words: "Never felt better."

I'm delighted to hear that the Holiday Inn in Clinton, New Jersey, has a restaurant and, more importantly, that it serves drinks. The place is decorated with white tarps and scaffolding. Tables are stacked to the ceiling.

"We're closed," a man says. "Renovations."

Food is being served in the bar, which doubles as a Joke Haus. Comedians have come from Long Island and the Bronx, all bearing hilarious chips on their shoulders and incapable of provoking so much as a smirk out of me. I keep my head down, zeroed in on my wine and shrimp diablo, as the few other survivors in the room grant the occasional strained guffaw, more polite than genuine. One comedian comes all the way from Chance's old Harlem neighborhood to tell marijuana jokes to accountants and salesmen and hockey coaches. Does she know she's not funny? Am I as mediocre in my sport as she is in hers? Maybe I should open a restaurant and call it Renovations.

BENDING LINES, ROLLBACKS, TURNING QUESTIONS. I COUNT TO MY fences, as a way of regulating my horse's stride and keeping track of where I am in a line, but apparently I can't even count right. Anne is counting backward while I'm counting forward. I get all messed up and can't find my takeoff spot any more than I can find a billy goat in the ring. Calvin stays calm and focused, jumps well, and only knocks one rail all session.

The moms and grandmoms of the other riders compliment me on how well I keep up with the younger set. That should bolster me, but it only makes me feel older. Their eyes pop when I bring out the ice tub. Calvin politely lifts one leg and then the other into the tub. The water and bags of ice go in. Everyone milling around the shed row gravitates to Calvin's stall to watch the spectacle of the big horse standing with his legs in a knee tub.

The immaculate show barn empties out by 6:00 p.m., while Calvin's front legs are still in the tub. I wrap all fours and pack his feet, feed, and blanket and top off Calvin's day with a few more Mrs. Pasture's cookies, a squeeze, and a kiss as I put my Irish favorite to bed.

Back at the hotel, it's Night Two at the Comedy Club. The same performers repeat their shticks—with the addition of a New Jersey Johnny Cash, accompanied by a zither, twisting his life of divorce, disappointment, and loneliness into pathetic comedy.

I sit at the bar, drink my Chardonnay, eat a few bites of my chicken sandwich and fries, and head upstairs with my dog bag. I open the door, surprised to be greeted by absence instead of Simon wagging his tail, eager to eat what leftovers I've brought him in my Styrofoam box. I retreat into the hallway to toss the smelly container into the waste bin by the elevator.

I PACK UP, CONCLUDING IT'S TOO RISKY JUMPING CALVIN THREE DAYS in a row. I watch the early morning session, then hit the road. I warn Barrett to kick out the dancing girls. He admits he has a fever.

BARRETT HAS BEEN BLEEDING SINCE CULPEPER. THIS MORNING, HE is shaking on the living room couch. "We're taking your temperature," I say, rummaging through kitchen and bathroom drawers until I find a thermometer that hasn't been in one of the animals' butts. It slides from Barrett's mouth, registering 104. *Can't be!* I recalibrate and shove it back in, then wait for the telltale beep: 104.5. I blink, breathe, call the doctor.

"Get him to emergency," our doctor says. "I'll call ahead."

Barrett wraps himself in a blanket and we pile into the tin can, then speed down the highway toward Baltimore, smack into rush-hour traffic. As far as the eye can see, dead in the water. He is shaking and seems in and out—aware, not aware. I turn on the flashers, veer onto the berm, and drive around all the frustrated commuters. If we get stopped, great; then we'll have a police escort to the hospital.

There is no wait in St. Joe's emergency room.

"We don't fool around with 104.5 temps," the triage nurse tells me. "What did you take for the fever?"

Barrett and I look blankly at each other. It hadn't occurred to either one of us to swallow some Tylenol on our way out the door. She hands him a couple of pills and a cup of water. Then threads the IV, hooks him up to fluids and antibiotics, encourages him to start drinking the revolting cherry fluid that will make the CT scan readable.

The scan reveals a highly infected portion of his gut—his hospital script until they can get the fever down and the infection under control.

I head back to the farm to put out any fires. One horse is milling about, having escaped his paddock. Horse caught, fence checked, I next attend to my own horses, give quick rides to Patrick and Shiva, then back to Barrett.

I call John in Los Angeles and Chance in Manhattan. I call my oldest friend, Lisa. I tell her Barrett's story, and then confide how glad I am she picked up. She is my only family besides family. I feel a little better just sharing bad news.

SOME DECADES, THE WORLD MAKES NO SENSE. BARRETT WAS DIAG-nosed with Crohn's disease in 2010. Odd, considering his age, but it was a reasonable guess, and there are always a lot more diagnoses once a "cure" is on the market. He seemed to control his illness with careful diet man-agement—no beef tenderloin, french fries, fried chicken, cheese soufflé, cream sauces, melons, cheese, spicy food, whole or uncooked vegetables or fruits, ice cream with chocolate sauce—nothing fun or worth eating. Mix a Crohn's patient with a woman who has been obsessed with thinness her whole life, and you can have a nice Cream of Wheat for dinner.

The farm is quiet late morning—an unusual phenomenon. With no one around, it's not an ideal time to work Rhapunzel—especially not for the first time since she's been back home. Yet that's what I'm determined to do, unable to check my compulsive forward motion. Because Barrett's situation is so out of my control, I doggedly attempt to control what I can.

Rhapunzel twirls mannerly in circles on the lunge, but when I ask her to stand still at the mounting block, she becomes hysterical. I can't get her within feet of the tiny monster. I coax her close, but she dances around, won't stay still the few seconds it would take me to put a foot in the stirrup. With no one to hold her, she lunges three-meter circles around the block. I give up, lengthen one of the stirrups, and hoist myself up from the ground.

She quiets once I'm on board. I walk and trot her around the indoor, changing direction frequently. We do some large circles with gentle bending and call it a gold-star day for Rhapunzel.

Midafternoon, Barrett's color is better. But the hospital staff still won't let him eat or drink.

"I can't even form words, my mouth is so dry," he manages to mumble.

My husband is anxious for me to help him take a shower and get cleaned up. We roll the IV stand he has affectionately named Charlie to the bathroom. I unhook a few wires to get his gown off, and Charlie starts objecting with histrionic beeps. A nurse comes running.

"You need a doctor's orders to take a shower," she warns us.

Barrett looks stricken.

"No worries," I say, "we'll just have an old-fashioned sponge bath."

I play Florence Nightingale, running a soapy washcloth under my husband's armpits, over his oily back and pale butt, his unusually hairless legs and large platypus feet with long yellow toenails badly in need of a trim. I scrub his hair in the sink, marveling at what a simple task this is with a man's short cut. The hospital fluorescents leave little for the imagination. The penis is a deflated and vulnerable turtlehead, the testicles wrinkled plums. My job is to wipe it clean and make it all better. I leave the butt for last, handing the washcloth to Barrett. Love is a funny thing. In so many ways, it has nothing to do with desire. I would do anything for Barrett.

The hospital gown is caught on Charlie's arm and we can't figure out how to get it off. We ring for the nurse, who temporarily detaches a couple of wires.

"These dang emergency room gowns," she mutters. "I don't understand why they can't use the button sleeves like the rest of the hospital."

She circles around this complaint for the next few minutes, repeating it every which way. Barrett is grateful for a clean gown, face, body, teeth, hair—and testicles.

"I'll just be glad when I can eat and shit again," he says.

Barrett takes a nosedive. He had a very bad night—losing a lot of blood—and now they've added steroids to the antibiotic IV mix.

I throw a few instructions around in my inadequate Spanish to Marta about the farm and horses. At the hospital, Barrett is experiencing waves of pain. He closes his eyes, opens them; tears have sprung and moistened the corners. He blinks again. I turn away.

"Oh honey," I say, "don't worry, they'll fix you up."

I run to the hospital gift shop with dim hope that they'll carry men's jockey shorts—sure enough, I find them among the puzzles and neck pillows and deodorant sticks.

I call Barrett's mother in Virginia. I am pleasantly surprised when she offers to drive up to Baltimore for the afternoon and spell me.

The nurses reassure me that it is just a matter of time before Barrett responds to the heavy-duty antibiotics and steroids. I return to the farm, nearly brain-dead with worry and exhaustion. I plan to hop on Calvin for a quick flat school. He needs to be ridden, and I also desperately need some Julia time. When I'm in the saddle, it's my whole world. I don't think about anything else, and nothing else matters.

Barrett is chatting it up with his mother when I return to the hospital, and clearly feeling much better. The steroids have begun to work their magic. In fact, if he weren't hooked up to Charlie with all the various bags hanging—iron, potassium, Flagill, etc.—you'd hardly know he had a problem. I'm relieved, but mildly skeptical, too. He hasn't had a thing by mouth today, and his body has not been asked to digest anything. The real test will be when he starts eating again.

THICK AND FUGGY, I WAKE UP WITH HOSPITAL HEAD, AND I HAVEN'T even been there yet. But this day promises to be a good one. Sudden news: Barrett is coming home.

I squeeze in a hack on Calvin before I leave for the hospital. I throw one leg over and settle into the saddle, and for the next hour the world is all mine. Off to the stream that Chance and I once nick-named Baden's stream, after Grassland Farm's manager. In reality, Piney Run is a mere trickle in comparison to the free-flowing river it was in the nineteenth century, when it powered the grinding stones of the grist mill at Trenton, as well as Millender's Saw Mill. Georgia canters on ahead; she knows exactly where we're headed.

Our new neighbors who recently bought Grassland are in the process of renovating the farm and old house, every building canary yellow. I've yet to have cocktails with the newcomers and am unsure of their hospitality to riders hacking through their land, although they are supporters of the Green Spring Valley Hunt, which relies on landowners' goodwill to keep their farmlands open. In exchange: so much land to ride over, coops in every fence line. But the neighborhood is changing. No longer do I mosey down the woods lane, lingering outside Baden and Mary's cottage, calling out to my Scottish friends as I pass their vegetable garden on our way to the big stream. We now have to skirt the buildings and come in from the backside, which necessitates retracing our steps to return home— one thing I try to avoid when hacking out, so that I feel like I've gone somewhere and completed a circuit. Even on the trail I need a sense of purpose and progress.

Calvin luxuriates in the cold water, a few brown trout jumping around us. Georgia prongs her way downstream.

I've got to get back to the farm to make sure all is ship-shape before I leave for the hospital. Calvin would rather stay put in the stream, drinking it all in.

THE SHEER EFFORT OF SHUFFLING THROUGH THE HOSPITAL TO THE car, then walking into the house has done Barrett in. He hoists himself upstairs, falls into bed, and sleeps all afternoon.

Cocktail hour for him has turned into a glass of ginger ale, spiked with a handful of ice. "I have to give up my red wine," he says. I'd felt this coming. No more magic hour, our reward for working hard all day. Eight o'clock tells the time of two sips of what used to be Barrett's first vodka tonic, then an overflowing glass of Chardonnay. Never one sip more, never any other kind of alcohol, and never, ever, at any other time of day. A control freak's rule book is strict portion control. The rest of the vodka goes in the frig. Surely some elf who craves vodka tonics will finish it during the night. Or Barrett will change his mind.

Barrett has stuck with Cabernet, and has historically drunk a lot more than I do. His excuse? He's three times my size. He's done with that chapter now; his body won't allow it. I'm selfish enough to continue my ritual. At 8:00 p.m. sharp, I make the drink that won't get drunk and pour the tumbler of Chardonnay that will, while Barrett takes his first sip of soda, which he will follow with a cup of chicken broth and strawberry Jell-O. It's a feast for him, after being on a drip for five days.

I RUN BACK AND FORTH FROM HOUSE TO BARNS, CHECKING IN hourly with Barrett while trying to have a productive ride on each horse.

Today's ride on Calvin is a gymnastic in the indoor. The Teapot sets fences while Cal and I swim through the exercise. It's a grid from Bobby Costello, published in *Practical Horseman* and meant for straightening a horse that tends to drift one way or the other in a line of fences. Made to order for Calvin, who tends to drift right, particularly when it comes time for his hocks to be injected.

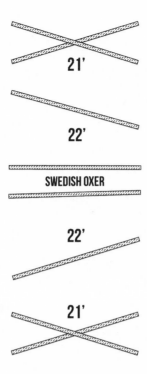

The big crossrails keep Calvin centered, the slanted verticals discourage the drift on their high sides, and the Swedish oxer has a centering effect as well.

The Teapot notes that Calvin's right hind is falling to the right. I wonder if that isn't part of the problem, making it difficult for him to push evenly over his fences. I get firmer with my right leg to motivate that weaker side.

Calvin jumps through the exercise—round and scopey—not at all interested in going near the rails. A hunter-jumper boarder compliments Calvin's jump.

"It's no wonder you feel confident going Advanced on that horse," she says. "He's got all the scope in the world."

"But he'd rather go bowling," I complain. He might have all the scope he needs, but he doesn't care enough about not hitting rails when the pressure is on. Or maybe it's the pressure that makes him careless. Perhaps further engaging the right hind will help.

It's night two of frozen tilapia and baked potato for me, while Barrett has graduated to pea soup. The pounds fall off my husband like dandruff. He has lost twenty-five in ten days.

MY INSIDE DAY STARTS OUTSIDE, IN 20 DEGREES, HELPING BARRETT with the morning feed. Here come the days when dressing to go out is an event in itself. In boots and turtle furs and mittens and ski caps, we walk slowly up our long driveway with its gentle uphill rise, Barrett huffing and puffing at my side. I match his slow hospital shuffle as we move from horse to horse, passing out grain and saying good morning to all thirty-five. Then I venture back inside to get some desk work done.

I crave inside days, but by 11:00, I'm antsy to be on a horse. Instead, I stay longer at the computer and buy winter riding clothes from Dover Saddlery, and then ponder my calendar, planning my abbreviated South Carolina trip in February, organizing it so I'll have only one horse at any event and therefore won't need extra help. Barrett doesn't know I'm still planning on Aiken this year. I won't tell him today. He's not well enough to hear my secrets.

We bundle up again for the afternoon shift and head out into a toastier 30 degrees, but with an additional twenty-mile-per-hour wind.

John calls from balmy California as I'm later warming my toes in front of the corn stove. I reassure him that Barrett is better. John and his wife Mollie have been trying to convince us to join their milder climate on the West Coast. On a day like today, it wouldn't take much convincing.

"I have a question," which John always announces before he actually asks it. He says it like a magician with a deck of cards. *Now, I will saw this question in half, make it disappear, pull a rabbit out of my hat, cut open the rabbit, and pull out the question.*

John wants to know the format of a research paper. In what order should he put end notes, appendix, and glossary? I want to tell him there are rabbits everywhere and Simon is chasing them. He has written a long, esoteric paper on the origin of sound, and he has found a publisher for it.

I scratch my head, consult my padlocked memory bank. "I think just that," I say. So nice that he even asked, with Google at his fingertips.

I remember the days of calling my father to ask some question about *Paradise Lost* or the refining of crude oil, and having to wait till I got through to him, without either getting a busy signal or no answer. My parents refused to own an answering machine. My father would rather talk "in person" on the phone. Or, better yet, write a letter—*rabbits everywhere*.

"What an awful year," I admit. "I can't even think about Simon without welling up. I'm looking forward to turning the page."

"Yeah, me too," John agrees. I'd thought things were hunky dory with my son. Or rather, that's what I always hope. I almost don't want to know what's wrong, for fear that it will break my illusion that all is right.

But now I have to ask, albeit timidly, "Oh?"

"Yeah, I didn't practice enough last year."

John gives sitar lessons—he's someone else's ghost—and plays concerts on the West Coast. And writes esoteric papers for obscure music journals. But that requires lots of internal energy and self-motivation. I know all about that.

"But I have found some pretty interesting farm lore."

"Oh?" I say again.

"Our house was originally owned by Charlotte Fowble, back in the nineteenth century."

"Goodness, you were able to go that far back?"

"Yeah, she lost her first husband in some kind of accident, but I haven't figured what it was exactly."

I imagine him peering at his computer screen, eyeglass in hand. I do wonder what it must have been like to live in this house in the nineteenth century. These old beams have seen a lot.

"Well, keep me posted," I say.

Done for the day, I pour my fill of Chardonnay, and begin to write my own esoteric essay: "The Origin of Insanity."

BARRETT PUTTERS AROUND THE HOUSE, GETTING A FEW THINGS done in his office on the couch, then totters up to the barn to check in with Marta and keep me company while I tack up Calvin. He tells me he's going to take the recycling to the drop-off center.

"Recycling? Why are you doing that?"

He has the desperate look on his face of uselessness. I go back to my rides. My doer-ism has infected even Barrett.

Calvin is good on the flat; the Myler is holding. I work on his medium trot—trying to keep him connected yet light on the forehand, while asking his hind legs to get going. To date, we have been faking our mediums. Now I want to teach him properly. I sit tall and pretend my thighs are lifting and lightening his shoulders, while encouraging his hind legs to reach and push. I have to keep my fingers active, like butterflies, or eyelashes. It is going to take some time to retrain him, but Calvin seems game to learn this new way of producing a more powerful trot, rather than the old way of letting go and crossing my fingers.

For dinner, Barrett eats a couple pieces of plain baked potato and a slice of frozen spinach soufflé, and then is up in the night more than he is sleeping. I find him on the living room couch in the morning, wrapped in a blanket.

"I was good till two," he says, as if that were something to celebrate, "and then things got really bad again." He looks ashen, and I get that terrible knot in my chest.

"Good thing you're seeing your doctor today," I say, trying to sound encouraging. "We'll work it out," I say feebly, getting up to make my pot of coffee, which I will consume by myself. I will myself to stay calm up front, and push from behind.

BARRETT'S POOR CONDITION WORSENS THROUGHOUT THE DAY. HIS bleeding is back and he's getting paler by the hour, as if he has chalk in his veins.

"Are you sure you're ok to go to the doctor by yourself?" I ask.

"I'll be fine," he insists as he sits bundled up in a blanket, still in his pajamas, his head thrown back exhaustedly against the couch.

The Ghost is coming today for his rescheduled visit. The horses, the horses, *always* the horses. Barrett calls from the road. His doctor has put him back on prednisone and changed his meds. He's in sorry shape.

"I've got blood all over me," he says into the phone. Calvin's on the other end of my reins in the driveway in the pouring freezing rain, as the Teapot chugs up in her Ford dually.

"I need you to do me a huge favor," I say to her, explaining Barrett's situation. Only another horse person would understand that having a tacked-up horse at the end of the reins and a prompt instructor is like having the president waiting to have a conference with you in the Oval Office. No matter the circumstances, you meet with the president. With nary a beat, the Teapot offers to pick up Barrett and take the prescriptions to the pharmacy. "Made your Aiken plans yet?" the Ghost says as I enter the indoor, wiping the freezing rain out of my eyes. I look at him blankly. At this rate, I'll be lucky to make it to the grocery store without a hitch.

I ride Calvin in a Myler combination bit, which has the same mouthpiece as his flatwork Myler, with the addition of noseband action like the hackamore.

"Let his nose out," the Ghost keeps repeating. I've heard this from him many times, particularly in the hackamore, which makes Calvin curl his neck. In this bit, I get a better feel for what the Ghost means. There's a place after the half halt that I'm looking for, when his nose is slightly poked out yet he's soft and carrying himself and not leaning on the bridle. If I can maintain this freer self-carrying frame to the base of the fence, his jump feels spectacular.

"I'd be inclined not to throw this one out," the Ghost says.

I've set up one of the Kursinski patterns, modified somewhat to fit our indoor. There are long lines and turning options, so we're able to focus on the two things I have most trouble with. On the tight turns, my outside leg is definitely working. So glad I found it after all those years of stalling in my turns.

I run back and forth from barn to house through the stinging needles to check on Barrett. When I'm not riding, worry engulfs me. Why can't the doctor kill the monster in my husband's stomach?

"All I want to do is ride," I confess to the one person I know will understand my yearning.

"I get it," the Ghost replies.

When I'm riding, I'm riding, and nothing else enters my brain and nothing else matters. I am in the moment and the rest of my life falls away, like so much confetti. A pastime of complete and utter self-absorption, because I'm driven to prove something to myself I can't even discern, let alone prove, but it is as much a part of my personality as the emphatic high-pitched quality of my voice.

Always the horses.

I DRIVE BARRETT TO THE HOSPITAL IN THE MORNING FOR SOME blood work, return home, get him settled on the couch with a beat-up copy of *All Quiet on the Western* Front, then head to my own battlefield. Sip of a sigh—he has perked up on the steroids.

Calvin is glad to see me, nuzzling my pockets for peppermints, resting his big old Irish head on my shoulder. He is good on the flat, just a bit of tension when we do our counter-canter work and flying changes. If only I had the next hundred years to ride him every day, maybe his body would learn to relax through the changes. Mine, too.

It's holiday grocery shopping time in the afternoon, so I prepare myself for another kind of siege and head out into a cold, wintry mix. As I play bumper cars with hundreds of shopping carts, I question why we're celebrating Thanksgiving at all—neither "kid" home, and Barrett barely able to keep down broth. Figuring it's the pretense that counts, I make three hopeless loops in the store before I break down and ask where the turkeys are.

"We're out of fresh turkeys," says the butcher.

I'm about to head on over to capons when the butcher catches me: "Here's the last frozen one. Just soak it in cold water overnight, and you'll be able to cook it tomorrow." We should probably slurp turkey noodle soup instead, but my Marlon Brando has insisted with his new muffled, scratchy voice—disappearing like the rest of him—that we go through the motions, so he can watch me enjoy my Thanksgiving meal with all of its trimmings. He'll settle for mashed potatoes.

AT 6:00 A.M., LIGHTS STILL OUT, BARRETT IS SITTING UP SLEEPING on the couch downstairs—the only way he can catch some winks. Vigorous sweats are keeping him up at night.

"We need to find you a new doctor," I say.

"Ok," Marlon mutters, head thrown back, eyes closed.

I go about the business of a usual Thanksgiving at the farm: getting my rides done early, popping in and out of the house to stuff the turkey and get it in the oven, ride a horse, make the cranberry sauce, ride another, baste. But my heart's not in it, with Barrett still sick and neither John nor Chance home.

John and Mollie are in Maui for Thanksgiving. They send a photo from the beach in which they're sporting matching sunglasses the size of small dessert plates. Squinting, I almost see the server bearing mai tais on a tray, reflected in Mollie's lenses. I glance out my office window at the farm's bleak landscape: brown on brown. On the other side of the earth, Chance calls from the New York subway as she's waiting for a train. "I can't hear anything," she says, and she probably wants it that way: her muffled subterranean voice punctuated by the whoosh and roar of the next train. She's harder to decipher than the movie star on my couch. I ask her to repeat herself, and our phones cut off. My daughter is boycotting family this Thanksgiving. I'd assumed she was having it as usual with her father on Long Island. She must be fed up with him, too, as she's chosen to share Thanksgiving with friends.

Barrett and I go through the motions of eating; I attempt to cook small, but I fail. Even with the tiniest of turkeys, the dinner turns out big. Barrett lines up along one side of the walnut rectangle of our family table the turkey and stuffing, which he has carefully carved and arranged on our holiday platter, the mashed potatoes, which are not lumpy, the green beans, a new addition—something Barrett can eat—the cranberry sauce, the butternut squash. We both spoon careful forkfuls onto pewter plates, then sit down together and look at the mountains of food, as if we were kneeling before an altar in a denomination we are skeptical of.

"I'm grateful for you," I try.

"Ditto, baby," my ashen Marlon whispers.

We begin the dainty process of selecting and chewing and swallowing. I threw this holiday meal together, and, ironically, it's delicious—the turkey cooked just right, the stuffing moist. Even the gravy has turned out ok, neither too lumpy, soupy, or starchy—it's hard to cook something well only once a year, though it's the same recipe my mother made fifty years ago and has been made in my kitchen ever since.

It takes us a long time to eat—digestible tidbit after digestible tidbit—even longer to put away the massive quantities of food we don't eat— "yummy leftovers!" I encourage, fingers crossed. The piles of uneaten food must look like little Himalayas to my dwindling husband, getting grayer by the minute. He has lost nearly forty-five pounds in a month.

"It's amazing how disease-friendly the Thanksgiving meal is," I say in a bright, strained way.

Chance calls back. The only person I can be completely honest with right now; the only person with whom I could ever think about acting like this on Thanksgiving. I fall apart, and I cry.

Chapter Three

New Ankles for Christmas

MY FRIEND KRIS WOULDN'T LEAD HER THREE-YEAR-OLD WITHOUT A lunge line, nor get on him without draw reins. Barrett did a little sleuthing at the track. Planet of Joy had dumped jockeys from New Orleans to Ohio. After he reared one too many times and refused to load onto Kris's trailer a few more, she called me. I quite liked the horse when I first met him in Aiken. I knew two people looking, so I imagined him to be a quick resale project. I asked Barrett if he knew of anyone who could drive to the Alleghenies in western Pennsylvania.

Barrett met Kris halfway at a truck stop outside Breezewood. She had spent hours coaxing Patrick onto her trailer back in the foothills of the Alleghenies for a final load. Barrett backed up our trailer to hers.

"I promise the horse won't know what hit him."

What a palm-off. It worked like a charm.

When Patrick failed his vetting because of a slight irregularity in one hock, Barrett wanted to raise his price.

"Any horse who can power that well off the ground with a bad hock is worth twice as much," he said.

He is now running around Preliminary events with ease. This one loves to get to the other side of a jump. That goes a long way in my Gospel.

The horse is not built for dressage, though. The way his neck comes out of his downhill withers, about a foot too low, makes his shadow look more like an anteater than a Thoroughbred.

Today, he does not want to play. He is obedient at the walk and trot, but we pick up the canter, and he starts boinging like a kangaroo. When I press him, he runs sideways and nearly throws himself against the indoor arena's kickboards—anything but bring his hind legs underneath his body, as he needs to do in the canter work.

I make a beeline to the local tack store.

Hope is busy shuffling papers behind the desk. She peers over her readers when I walk in.

"Do you think it's physical?" she asks.

I've got two colics, one in the house and one in the barn. I start Patrick on a course of omeprazole. If only it were so easy for Barrett, who is still on the couch, like an old dog without a wag.

Patrick's plight picks up Barrett's spirits. He shambles up to the barn in the late afternoon light, as I'm getting off Patrick for the second time.

"What if we start cooking his meals, the way we did for Goldrush Aaron? We could get the crock pot going up here."

"Cook his meals?" the Teapot asks, with a gleam in her eye. She has just arrived at the barn, her arms overloaded with sugarless treats and a spanking-new turnout blanket for Ego.

"Barley, oats, a little molasses cooked for hours in the crock pot," Barrett reminds me. I can see some color rising to the surface of his colorless face. My husband, the nurse; it just takes a sick horse to get his blood going again.

Barrett cooked Goldrush Aaron's meals for the first two years of his life, his tummy was that sensitive. We almost lost the colt to colic three times before Barrett came on this simple remedy.

There's that twinkle in my husband's gray-green eyes, as he plans to run out for barley and dig out the crock pot. Maybe he'll crank one up for himself as well. Slow-cooked crock pot meals—just what the gastroenterologist ordered.

I'M HOPEFUL THAT A QUIET TRAIL RIDE WILL EASE PATRICK'S NERVOUS stomach. Coincidentally, the Teapot and Ego are tacking up for same.

I hear shots as we thread our way between one of the splits dividing pastures. The first day of deer hunting season. Adjacent neighbors allow hunting on their properties. Lydia has permits for sixty kills based on crop damage. It's either the farm's back field or the Mekong Delta. My plan is already looking bleak.

Barrett makes it as far as the mare barn. In his lumberjack hat and oversized down coat, he looks ready for a snowstorm.

"I haven't heard a gunshot all day," he offers brightly.

The Teapot and Ego, Patrick and I head out to the back field. Patrick is devoted to his turnout buddy—in fact, Ego is the only horse on the farm Patrick will tolerate without venom oozing from his fangs. He follows Ego around their field as if they were leashed together, and nearly shares each blade of grass with him. This is just what cranky Patrick needs, walking leisurely along on the buckle. We see one of our boarders on her horse in the near distance. We wave, and I ask her to join us. Patrick loads his Kalashnikov—pinning his ears and hopping up and down, running sideways, giving the horse the evil eye, rearing and plunging—doing everything he can to intimidate.

So much for our relaxing trail ride. So much for giving Patrick's stomach a break.

Calvin has been taking it all in from his end stall, never missing an innuendo in the barn. His inquisitive head peers over his stall guard, studying the situation.

"I don't blame him," Barrett offers at cocktail hour—me with my trough of Chardonnay, Barrett with his cup of bouillon. "That boarder's horse is a mess," he adds.

"He was vying for Ego's attention," I explain. "It had nothing to do with the other horse."

THE HAZINESS IN BARRETT'S FACE IS IN HIS MIND, TOO. I REMIND him to phone his doctor to get his lab results, no doubt buried under a stack of faxes.

"White blood count normal, thyroid, cholesterol. Maybe testosterone a little low, mate," the internist chuckles.

Barrett throws his head back on the sofa in an early morning stupor, phone to ear.

"Wait a sec," the doctor stops abruptly and whistles through the mouthpiece.

Dead air. Silence. The internist reveals what Quantiferon markers mean: Barrett has tuberculosis.

Barrett turns on the speakerphone and plops his cell on the counter. The doctor begins to stammer, as if he were Googling the ancient disease—how it most commonly affects the lungs but can be present anywhere in the body, even in the gut or, like Thomas Wolfe, the brain. That it comes from cows. That it can be passed through their urine, feces, snot, and milk. It's often present among immigrants from poor countries, where not every glass of milk is pasteurized. When TB is in the gut, it is often mistaken for Crohn's.

Barrett has been sick with TB for five years without knowing it. All this time, the disease has waited patiently in his body to kill him.

Grimly, he makes an appointment with an infectious disease specialist.

I GO ON A LONG HACK WITH CALVIN AND GEORGIA PAST THE WISNERS' dairy. Georgia chases after the occasional squirrel and the frequent scared, running deer. We loop around the farthest reaches of our neighborhood, then meander home. Georgia stirs up roosting geese, watches them whoosh into the safety of endless sky when she gallops toward them. She looks back over her shoulder at me: *How come I can't do that?*

You can, I say, *follow me.*

In the past five years, the cow population in our area has increased threefold, and so has milk production. After Uncle John's death, the Wisner cousins erected a football field–sized dairy barn, installed fans for the heat of summer, and threw around old mattresses for the cows to sleep on.

I arrive back at the barn and accomplish my other rides, leaving Rhapunzel for last. The Teapot is heading out on Ego, so I ask if she'll walk through the woods with us. This is the first time I've tried to mount Rhapunzel outside the safety walls of the indoor. I place the mounting block up snug against the fence, the way I do in the indoor. She dances around it. I try again, get one foot in the stirrup, up and over. But before I have time to get my other foot tucked in, she lunges across the driveway. I sit the first buck, but she gets her head down. Without leverage in my off stirrup, I'm toast. She continues her violent broncing. I can feel the thud coming before it comes. I land on my left shoulder, the wind knocked out of me. I lie there and start counting.

Each year, it takes a little longer for Lady Lazarus to rise.

Rhapunzel bucks back across the driveway. She slips, and falls on her side. The Teapot runs around like a mad woman, shouting orders: "Marta, get the horse!" "Janet, untack Ego!" "Someone call the vet! Call Barrett!"

I push myself to sitting. *One potato. Two potatoes. A bloody truckload of potatoes.* Thank god I hit the grass and not the driveway. As my world comes back into focus, I see stiff noodles of shit from Marta's dog, who is often tied to the nearby pin oak.

"Rhapunzel has a bad cut! Rhapunzel is lame!" I hear from someplace out there. *Who cares*, I think. *Why call the vet? Whistle to one of those hunters out back. Turn her loose.*

At the ER, my nurse is a horse person, so she doesn't lecture me. She and the Teapot strike up a conversation and discover that they both owned a horse by the same sire. They giggle and laugh and share idiosyncrasies about their relations as I sit on the side of the bed, a knife gouging between my angel wings. The pain makes it hard to breathe.

When it comes time to undress, I'm stumped. "I don't think I can lift my arms," I say.

"No worries, I'll help," the kind nurse offers. It takes about as long to take off the first two layers as it did for me to stand up after the fall. When I get to the last one—my sports bra—I give up.

"Just cut it off," I say.

"Can't be more than twenty bucks," says the Teapot.

Out come the scissors, and I'm freed.

Nothing is broken—no ribs, no scapula. I've pulled my subscapularis muscle, though—that's the ER doctor's best guess. Once they've concluded that my insides are clean, they prod me to standing and hustle us out the door, though I can barely breathe for the pain shooting back and forth across the valley between my shoulder blades. We head home armed with drugs. Lots of them. At least I wheedled that much out of the attending physician.

"Why does it hurt so much?" I keep asking, to no one in particular.

Our vet, Rachel, calls. I explain to her where my problem is. "Sounds like a subscapularis tear to me. Very painful, I know from experience. The pain is as sharp as a knife." Bingo.

"What can be done about it?" I wince.

"Drugs," she replies.

I toss and turn all night, unable to get comfortable enough to sleep, despite hydrocodone and Flexeril on board. Barrett leaves the bed early in the night, drenched in TB sweats. He retreats downstairs. The only one who is happy in body and mind is Calvin, my beautiful failure.

I PULL ON THE LEFT REIN, AND DAGGERLIKE PAINS EXPLODE THROUGH my back and arm.

"I can't do it," I confess.

"Want me to get on him?" the Ghost asks.

The Ghost feels Calvin is straighter than the last time he rode him, though strong on his left side. He gets riled up when the Ghost asks for lead changes; he anticipates what's coming and bolts through the aids. The Ghost has to pulley-rein him into the wall, then do a tight circle.

"He's a bull," the Ghost pants.

We swap places and I try jumping him, though it's impossible to steer a freight train without a left arm. The Ghost gets on him again, and Calvin barges through the exercise.

"Why is he doing that?" I ask.

"He's against my hand," the Ghost replies.

Calvin becomes more compliant as the ride evolves. The Ghost softens the reins two strides out from the fences. Now Calvin doesn't touch the rails.

A light bulb goes off for both of us.

The Ghost tries again, giving early and exaggerating the let-go before the jumps. Beautiful and clean.

"Calvin isn't a stopper, so you can give the reins this much without worrying about dropping him for a stop."

I am in agony. I still have afternoon chores, tack to clean, horses to feed, blanket, and turn out. I put one foot in front of the other.

Barrett shuffles up to the barn, chats with the Ghost for a few. When he leaves, the Ghost turns to me: "Barrett looks awful," he says.

I freak out on the inside, but on the outside I say a cool, "He has TB." The Ghost slowly backs away.

I know how awful Barrett looks. Ashen and gray and sagging from having lost so much weight so quickly. All of our clocks are ticking; Barrett's happens to be Big Ben.

I SEE STARS WHEN I PICK UP A COFFEE CUP, PULL A SHIRT OVER MY head, press down on a safety cap for my next wafer of hydrocodone. I relinquish any idea of riding and hold my palms out for another hit of Jesus. *Amen.*

WHEN WE TURN INTO THE ENTRANCE WHERE THE INFECTIOUS DIS-ease specialist hangs his shingle, I realize it's the same building where my pain doctor works. This could be a fortuitous errand. I help Barrett check in, and because we still have fifteen minutes until his appointment, I hurry to the second floor. His cheery wife, Liz, tells me I'm in luck. The doctor can see me before his first scheduled appointment. Liz is too busy studying her computer screen to look me in the eye. I tell her of my recent fall and excruciating shoulder. She looks up briefly with searing blue, compassionate eyes. Returns to her screen, fingers tapping as her gaze moves across the glow.

The doctor concurs with Rachel. The culprit is the infrascapularis muscle, thin as a sheet of paper and lying just under the scapula to hold that bone in place.

"Good news is that your muscle can't be torn badly, or the scapula would be sticking up," he says brightly, as the first needle goes in under the ledge of the shoulder blade with its numbing agent and longer-acting steroid. *Jolly good news*, I think, as the juice slides in twice more.

I'm back up to the fourth floor before Barrett's name is even called. When a nurse summons him, he asks me to hang in the waiting room. "I don't want them to come to any conclusions when they see us both hob-bling in."

Not five minutes later, my husband pokes his head through the wait-ing room door, waving his hand briskly, beckoning me. "Changed my mind," he says.

The doctor's assistant, a young east Indian doctor, is first to question Barrett. He seems most interested when my husband makes mention of John's trips to India to study sitar. John's guru had an active case of TB while he was there in 2010.

"And where was that exactly?" the assistant asks.

"Headwaters of the Ganges," Barrett says, stalling, trying to remember the city's name. "Where they bury the dead. You know, that Holy City."

"Varanassi," the assistant pitches in. "There is a lot of tuberculosis in that area of India," he confides.

Dr. Haile ducks through the doorway, looking exactly like Ichabod Crane—tall and slim and gray and wise, with a sharp, long nose that adds to his scholarly air.

Dr. Haile asks Barrett to take off his shirt so that he can listen to his heart and lungs. I am struck by how much thinner my husband is. He has always lugged an extra thirty around, but this weight loss looks unhealthy, in a softly sagging way. Barrett turns his eyes away from mine—maybe if he doesn't see me, then I won't see him. Maybe that's how Liz feels behind her computer screen. We all hide behind our insecurities.

The doctors bend closer to Barrett when he relates in his muffled godfather voice what he ate yesterday, starting with a cup of Jell-O and ending with a spoonful of turkey hash on a Triscuit—his idea for leftover Thanksgiving turkey had been to throw it in the Cuisinart. They bend even closer, either out of disbelief that's all this large man ate, or unable to hear his weakening voice, which has lost a similar twenty-five pounds in volume. My husband's disappearing act.

We leave the office, armed with Ichabod's conclusions that Barrett will proceed with a nine-month regimen of TB drugs. But first the assis-tant wants to contact his colleagues in India to discuss the most effective medicines that have been used in that area of India. As for the connection of TB to Crohn's—the two diseases are frequently mistaken. American doctors aren't expecting TB in the gut, and Indian doctors aren't expecting

Crohn's. They seem as miffed as we still are, or at least unwilling to say one way or the other until Barrett has had another colonoscopy.

As we are walking to the car, I realize we forgot to tell the doctors about the immigrant workers on our farm and the possibility of Barrett having contracted TB from them.

"You've got to call Dr. Haile back today," I prod. My husband seems relieved to be able to make the India connection rather than pointing a finger at our El Salvadoran employees. Barrett has always been protective of Marta and her husband, Roberto, and for good reason—without them, we would be sunk. But it's more than that. A mainly Spanish-speaking undocumented immigrant in this country is often not treated well nor with respect, and Barrett is keyed into this bias against our workers. To him, literacy and financial independence mean nothing without com-passion. Marta and Roberto have been with us for eight years, and they underwent enormous sacrifices to arrive safely in the United States, having endured gang warfare, political corruption, and economic depression in their country in exchange for a terrifying trip overland—walking, swim-ming, riding the rails of La Bestia, skirting thieves, extortionists, and cor-rupt police officials to get here. Five years later, their ten-year-old daughter made the trip by herself to join them.

The fact that we live next to a herd of three hundred dairy cows is lost on both of us.

I offer to help Barrett with the afternoon shift. We are in trouble. Forrest has taken his front end loader down to a hydrant along the farm road to give it a bubble bath in today's unseasonably warm sun—with-out asking permission—and at feed time. The vicious dinosaur gets the horses running just as Barrett and Marta and I are leading them in. One of the horses, Uncle Sam, gets so riled up that he runs into the fence and gashes his neck open, requiring stitches. We are cold-water hosing the horse when Cooper pulls in the driveway. My phone rings.

"It's Cooper."

"Aren't you in my driveway?" I ask.

"I am. Is it all right by you if we inject Calvin's SI tonight, after I'm done stitching Sammy, rather than waiting till tomorrow?"

Sore Sacroiliac joints. They seem to be going around my barn.

"You're the only nice thing that has happened to me all day," I respond, beaming through the phone. Which isn't entirely the truth. Doctors' spontaneities in general have been kind to me today.

The day ends as it started—with needles going into backs—only this time, they are a foot long in order to reach the deep recesses of a horse's sacroiliac joint.

This page, the thickness of the muscle that holds my angel wings down.

THE FARM IS IN ITS USUAL FUROR—BOARDERS OUT, HORSES RIDDEN, loud lessons, trailers and delivery trucks stacking up in the driveway. To escape, I take Georgia for a walk along the Gunpowder River. The weather is breaking and the sun coming out, after having cold-rained all night. Georgia has her nose out the window. She smells the chatty waters of the Gunpowder before bounding out of the truck. She scoots down the trail, greeting the few walkers and runners and bikers. They look askance at my unleashed dog. We come to a more civilized part of the trail, where the path is wider and more manicured than a little farther up country, and the river is a few hundred feet down a steep incline. We find a small trail leading down to water. Georgia pounces on what sticks she can find and brings them to me. With my good shoulder—which isn't all that good—I throw them into the pewter waters gurgling downstream. Georgia is carried swiftly to the stick by the current and her own eagerness, but has to fight an upstream battle to get back to me. She doesn't care. We repeat the endless mission until her tongue is lolling and the stick has broken and re-broken. Then we clamber back up to the trail and carry on.

I blank-slate my mind. I want to erase farm business and bad luck, Barrett's health and the horses' various issues, my bum shoulder and inability to ride all week. I concentrate on the rhythm of my walking and the world around me. A horse path branches off from the Torrey Trail, and we take that for a mile or so, carving a large loop around thousands of beech saplings someone has planted in these lowlands, giving privacy and ground cover, so quiet, and so green. There is nothing else.

We wind back around to the trailhead. Something catches Georgia's eye, and she dashes into the woods. I hear scurrying and a terrified bleating.

I step through brambles and peer down over the edge into the gully, calling for my dog, who is thrashing some creature in her maws.

A fawn, already having lost her spots, twice Georgia's size, flops on her side, then lies sickeningly still. Georgia loses interest once the fight is over and the animal has gone quiet.

I grew up in the heartland of hunting. My father hated deer hunting, and each year he posted the perimeter of my family's farm. Still, gunshots were everywhere around us, and I wasn't allowed to ride out during deer season. As I waited for my mother in the car at the grocery store or bank or post office, I counted the vehicles with fresh deer kill tossed into flatbeds or strapped over car roofs and hoods, happy loud men in their hunting gear, stopping for gas and a brag. They were so omnipresent I swear I could smell the musk of deer blood as I walked down the streets of Warren.

Here, nobody cares about a deer carcass lying by the side of the road. It is merely unsightly, hardly to be mourned.

I call my dog off the carcass. I took my chances, allowed her freedom off leash. My remorse and anger rise for having wanted escape from the sadness and bad luck that have been trailing me. Hadn't I lost my spots so long ago now when something within me died? I've spent fifty years trying to bring it back to life.

Georgia returns to the trail, obsessively licking her chops, speckles of deer blood on her snout. Minutes later, she's running off again—the leash, waiting for its job back in the car—only this time, I spy up on the ridge on the other side of the river several fluorescent orange vests and rifles slung over shoulders or hanging limp at men's sides.

"Good shot," one of them yells, pulling on a leg of the barely dead doe. Another is poking the deer in her gut with the butt of his rifle, probably figuring the least messy way of dragging the carcass down through the brambles without getting deer blood all over himself. I don't even want to think about the connection between the doe and Georgia's kill, or her sideways role in this one's death.

My dog, motivated by instinct once more, charges up the hill.

"Watch out, there's a dog right behind you," a hunter farther up on the ridge calls out.

I scream for Georgia, but my voice comes out as weakly as Barrett's current tenor: my ripped shoulder muscle sits right on top of my lungs. I hack my way through treefall to get to my dog before a new volley of hot lead.

Maybe Georgia senses she's pushed me far enough. Or maybe she realizes she has met her match, up against several hunters and their black powder. Or maybe it's just no longer any fun, once she knows that their deer is lifeless, too, without the thrill of motion. For whatever reason, when she sees me punching my way through the briars, she trots docilely back downhill, with her ears pinned to her head and her sad, mournful gray eyes beseeching me.

"I can't even go for a walk with my dog without a catastrophe," I complain to Barrett, once home.

"That's all right, that fawn never should have been born this time of year."

Still, bad omens—the killing of doe and fawn, Barrett's fuck-it-all philosophy and ancient disease, a horse without a mouth, a rider without an arm.

SIX THOUSAND POTS OF COFFEE SINCE WE'VE HOOKED UP, AND Barrett still can't get it right. Over my first sips of bitter sludge, I look out the window to a foot of snow blanketing the pastures. I turn to my husband, who has a distant look on his newly lean face.

"What's wrong?" I ask.

"Just processing the day," he says, then lists what he hopes to accomplish.

"That's too much for you," I say.

"I have to go back to work," he says. "At least two hours in the morning."

"That's too much," I repeat.

"With both of us hurt, we'll lose everything if I don't," he explains. "I've got to."

I look out to the little piles of snow triangles dotting the fence posts, almost as far as my eye can see. No rest out there.

"WOULD YOU LIKE SOME MUSIC?" THE SMOCKED TECHNICIAN ASKS. Her pudgy fingers position the thin blanket around my shoulders, then reach up to adjust something in her ear.

"Yes," I say. She doesn't hear me. One of the downsides of her profession, like what happens to sound men at rock concerts. Or jackhammer guys.

"Would you like some earplugs?"

The machine inches my body along, as if I were a human toy to be assembled, car to be washed, body to be buried. "GE" is emblazoned above the mouth of my tunnel. I'm trapped inside a giant lightbulb that illuminates nothing.

I endure several minutes of pounding and hammering and knocking, followed by brief seconds of silence, before the racket resumes.

This time more insistent, like a hammer drill, chain saw, chop saw, squealing pig, combine, jet engine, air-raid siren, Flakzwilling artillery, the boiler room in the deep belly of a battleship. Ratcheting, pounding. Scritching and scratching. Is my doctor Richard Hell?

More pounding.

More.

My head starts to vibrate. The ceiling of my white coffin just inches away. Friday Fright Nights in black and white. Bela Lugosi, *Tales of Frankenstein*. I scare myself awake all night. 1965. I am being buried alive, my bum shoulder, lodged in its synthetic holster, starts to burn.

Count to one thousand. Nine hundred and ninety nine rats on the wall.

"How are you doing?" a voice from the Beyond asks.

"Ok," I croak.

"Keep your arm nice and still," the technician advises. Who is she kidding?—I am unable to move it a millimeter in its vise.

843, 842, 841. I don't need to drink to feel drunk.

Bang. Bang. Bang. Bang. Bang. Bang. Bang. Bang. Bang.

Blessed silence.

"Do you have a history of shoulder dislocation?" the voice now asks.

And still I will not talk. I will not confess my fall from an Australian horse four years ago. I was knocked out for a handful of minutes. Then woke to the panic of not knowing where I was. And to a dislocated shoulder and broken collarbone.

"Do you know who the president is?" the paramedic asked. The year was 2010. "George Bush?" I tentatively suggested. She shook her head. "Obama. But this is South Carolina. George Bush is good enough," she conceded.

"Do you have a history of shoulder dislocation?" the technician repeats impatiently, as if I were a slab of meat.

"Only in the other one," I say.

"Then we are going to continue," she says.

Ba-Boom, Ba-Boom, Ba-Boom. Che-Che, Che-Che, Che-Che, Che-Che, Che-Che. Ta-ta-ta-ta-ta-ta-ta-ta-ta. Bang, bang, bang.

Almost over, my fireworks of screaming chrysanthemums.

Once my body has been Invisible-Manned, the machine inches me out into the land of the living. The technician rolls me off the table. The pain in my back—I can barely stand up.

"You should get the results by tomorrow afternoon," she says, before disappearing down the corridors of Gitmo.

THE SNOW STARTS FALLING AGAIN, ADDING FIVE INCHES TO WHAT WE already have. My shoulder feels enough like a shoulder, so I "hop" on Patrick. He wouldn't have been my first choice after my injury, but he's the one who needs the ride the most, after his hock injections. We walk around the indoor for thirty minutes—two miles of going nowhere. His body language complains with each sour, crooked step. He swishes his tail, pins his ears, and drops off my aids. When thirty minutes are up, I walk him back to the mounting block, where I dismount slowly, kicking my left foot out of the stirrup and easing that leg down to the security of the stump.

Patrick's bad humor continues in his stall. When I blanket him, he lunges through the bars at Shiva. This one hates to be brushed, blanketed, loaded on a trailer, girthed, or ridden. I love him.

"How did it go?" Barrett calls from the couch, as I come in the door.

"He was great until I touched him."

Barrett guffaws for the first time in weeks, and my day is made.

Here's a new challenge: texting and driving in the snow.

Edwin Forrest: *Do you mind if I park my bobcat and trailer by the indoor for a couple of hours?*

Julia: *No worries.*

Another chime. I scramble for my cell on the seat, look away from the road, swipe the screen.

Barrett: *His rig is stuck at the indoor. Most people would unload the machine that does such a great job of plowing and dig himself out.*

Julia: *The bobcat's stuck? That's not the story he told me.*

One letter for each glance at the road.

"Well, it's what I'm looking at," says my husband, "and I mean stuck."

I'm on my way in the dizzying snow to get more X-rays taken: this time, of an arthritic big toe. My new podiatrist is making me orthotic inserts.

As I'm standing on the X-ray plate, my phone rings from the bowels of my bag. I ignore it; it rings again. I hear the bleating of a text, then another. I succumb, and pardon myself from the radiation.

Edwin Forrest: *Call me.*

Edwin Forrest: *Please call now.*

"How's your sense of humor today?" Forrest asks. I glance down at my red, swollen foot.

"Julia, I'm sorry. I'm so sorry to bother you, but I ran into the arena barn with the trailer."

"You did what?"

"I ran into your barn," he admits. "There's kind of a hole in the side of the barn."

"Kind of?"

"Don't worry, I will totally, totally fix it."

I drive into the farm to find a piece of plywood—ten feet high by eight feet wide, nailed to the barn.

I pick up my orthotic inserts. Along with the arthritis in my left foot, a toe on the other foot is indeed broken, thanks to Shiva's spastic shying. I've been hobbling around for over a month, and the toe is finally not crimson and scalding with pain, merely broken.

"Let me show you how to splint that toe," my sex-kitteny podiatrist with the eyeliner, mascara, and high-heeled, knee-high boots suggests—so different from the fat, dumpy foot doctor I had as a kid. I bet she doesn't have to wear orthotic inserts in those sidewalk punchers.

"Don't bother," I say. "It's starting to feel better."

Who cares if my feet become disfigured? You can hide a lot inside a riding boot. Ask St. Ignatius.

I ADD TROTTING TO MY RIDE ON PARIS, A CLIENT'S HORSE WHO NEEDS more work than his owner can give him. Running a college art department doesn't leave much room, so I've stepped in to help. I'm relieved that the posting motion doesn't aggravate the shoulder.

Barrett is better, too. "Holding at 207," he brags. We sit down together at dinner, Barrett with his squash soup, me with my chicken and potato. Gone are the days of exotic experimentation in the kitchen with dishes like orecchiette with fennel sausage and broccoli rabe, chick peas and kale with za'atar, poached eggs and nan, tofu soba noodles with ginger-miso broth. And bottomless glasses of wine.

On night check, Georgia runs into the bitter cold. Barrett returns to the house empty handed. "You gotta keep her on a leash if you can't keep her with you," I yell down from my balcony perch. I'm a fine one to talk. Memories of the fawn, and my father's similar stubbornness.

Downstairs, I call into the night. Barrett drives up and down the driveway, then out to Blackrock Road. We both have visions of Simon. I call until my throat hurts. I go back upstairs to my bed and book, then back down again twenty minutes later when she still hasn't returned. Up and down the driveway, my throat getting hoarse, the bitter air whipping around my bare ankles. No Georgia. I imagine the jingle-jingle of her collar trotting down the driveway. Nope. Nothing.

Finally, I hear her padding up the stairs.

"Where was she?" I ask.

"Just outside the door when I came back," Barrett whispers. We both let her go off leash, but at least I have a voice to call her back.

Georgia wants to hop on the bed, but we won't let her. "Under the bed," I command. "Now!" She slinks into the cave under our bed—once Simon's favorite safe spot, which Georgia tends to avoid without him. When I wake in the morning, she's spooning me.

CALVIN STANDS LIKE A SENTRY FOR HIS HOCK INJECTIONS. COOPER'S assistant twirls the twitch around his nose before the needles go in. I hardly think he needs the restraint—he is not a novice to pain. I'll start back on him tomorrow, at the walk. Nice and easy, just what my shoulder has ordered.

I Google "Who's had worse luck than me?" and get seventeen billion hits.

The farm's Goth web designer visits in the afternoon to help post a blog entry about holiday cheer. She doesn't seem at all surprised that we haven't decorated yet.

"Oh shit, I forgot to make the rum balls!"

She looks at me with a nonreactive smirk.

Barrett is more helpful. "So go to it," he says, brightly.

There were three witches in my mother's kitchen. One was named *Fattening*, one was named *Delicious*, and the last, *Easy*. If alcohol was involved, so much the better. In go the corn syrup, pecans, and vanilla wafers. A carload of sugar, and twice the called-for amount of rum; for that matter, just glug the approximate amount in and then add some more straight from the bottle. *You get more rum if they're larger* was my mother's motto.

I do a little cookie arranging on my mother's china, light a fat candle, throw a couple of ornaments around. The stuffed Santa cat acts as witness to this Christmas debauchery, his eyes perpetually wide with comical astonishment. I remember my mother's clumsy Polaroid camera, the pungent smell of the developing solution, the slimy white background on which our young faces would magically appear. I was enthralled as a kid that a photo could reproduce us so quickly, just by counting to ten.

Barrett didn't grow up with a lot of cameras. I realize there are almost no photographs of him around the house. What if something were to happen?

"Could you take one more photo?" I ask. The Goth follows Barrett's rickety motion up the stairs, where a natural light might be found to flatter his ravaged complexion—through the bedroom and into our loft encased by windows on three sides, illuminating the farm as well as my husband's face.

I CLIMB UP ON CALVIN, HAPPY TO FEEL HIS BARREL BETWEEN MY legs. There's a lot you can do at the walk. Kind of like eternal foreplay, without the pressure of a full-blown canter. Walk to halt, leg-yield, shoulder-in, haunches-in, turn on the haunches, rein-back, even half pass. There are so many different ways to kiss.

My shoulder is screaming, so my rides on Patrick and Shiva aren't as romantic. Patrick, after his own hock injections, will be ready for canter tomorrow. Ouch.

Edwin Forrest pulls up to the entrance of the indoor to look for numbers on our steel beams so the manufacturer of the barn can dig up our records. I'm pissed before he even opens his mouth.

"What year was this barn built?" he asks.

I retrieve the memory of a tractor trailer cortege arriving from Colorado in the middle of one early spring night, with the arena barn in thousands of pieces.

"Spring of 1995," I say. "I was eleven."

The builder will have to dig through old files to find our records, kept in storage at another location, somewhere in Mesa Verde. Once a week an employee drives out there to have a look around, check for trouble, and search through the company's past. Forrest is annoyed that Barrett and I have pressed him to go through the original manufacturer and not Dunsinane Wood, where he has an account. I want the job done right, with the exact color match for the siding. Because I'm allowing Forrest to fix his own mistake, I want him to do the job the hardest way possible as payback for his carelessness, or anger, or whatever his state of mind was on that snowy day. Who runs into the side of a two-hundred-foot barn, anyway?

PATRICK WARMS UP ALL RIGHT, BUT TWENTY MINUTES INTO THE ride, he runs sideways, hopping up and down, then rears. Anything but put his head down and go to work. He gets worse as he goes, which makes me think it's a pain-related response. Or fatigue. I make a note to be generous with breathers tomorrow. I wonder if he's objecting to the bit, and make a second note to ride him in his jumping bridle next time to see if that makes a difference in his willingness to work.

It starts snowing in the afternoon. Barrett and I cancel our plans to venture out to Woofie's holiday party. We're delighted to have an excuse not to go. It's pelting snow, the roads are rough, can't leave the farm in this—none of it is normally a deterrent for me. I grew up in the Snow Belt ninety miles south of Buffalo, but I'll use bad weather to my advantage when I need to. If it were a horse trial I wanted to get to, I'd slog through three feet of the white stuff without blinking.

I've never been much of a party person, but partying is impossible since Barrett has been sick and unable to partake in good food or spirits. What fun is it to go to a party to stand around sipping ice water? Instead, it's a glass of wine for me—carrot juice and chicken noodle for Barrett— and "Bastogne," episode 6 of *Band of Brothers*. We've already watched it countless times, so familiar with the plot, but this time, I notice that Captain Winters's eyes are the same hazel as my father's. We see men in snow like what we have outside our window battle for their lives, giant birches and beeches splintering and falling on top of foxholes. Nothing like that here, dressed in my fuzzy PJs, huddled beside Barrett on the couch and draped by our fleece throw. I arrange myself so that I'm not lying either on Barrett's pocked insides or my shoulder. I can't get it right: the pain shoots down my back.

A SUBSCAPULARIS MUSCLE TEAR IS HARD TO DIAGNOSE, DIFFICULT TO treat, and even trickier to see on an MRI, because it is obscured by the bone that it lies directly under. That's me in a nutshell: trauma that's hard to find or get to.

Patrick requires the most from my subscapularis. An opportunist: he senses my inadequacies and takes advantage of them. For the third day in a row, he has a fit whenever we approach the northeast corner of the ring, where ten years ago Barrett found a mummified raccoon buried in the footing. My shoulder zings when I insist he walk and trot small circles into the haunted corner. We are both mules, refusing to relent.

Barrett is at the gym, doing one-pound curls with his bionic wrist— the equivalent of two beer bottles. He is struggling to take some time for himself in his effort to get healthy, which never works when you've got a horse farm to run and a demanding wife to please.

"I'm not getting enough out of our relationship these days," I say through cyberspace.

"You mean you're not getting enough out of me," he replies.

Thick silence.

"I'm sorry I got sick," Barrett now spits his own venom. "Sorry the revolution got in the way of your horse show."

I'm glad he can't see my crimson cheeks. I'm so used to him being here all the time that I curse the two minutes he's away.

"When I had my trainer's license, you didn't come to one race." He's on a roll now. He won't let me get away with my spitefulness, daughter of pain.

I turned my back on the racetrack early on in our relationship. I said it was because I didn't like asking so much of young horses. But really it was more a matter of time and energy. I put all my focus into my event horses, when I wasn't being a mom or a farm owner or a writer. My sand had always run out when it was time to leave for Pimlico. I was either too busy or too tired.

IF YOU'RE GEORGIA, WHEN THE POOL'S CLOSED AND THE SNOW FALLS, you pad around its perimeter and gaze into the white mirror, longing for the splash of warmer days. As if waiting and longing were enough.

THIS MORNING, I WAKE WITH THE LIGHT, AND BARRETT REJOINS ME in bed. Apparently, he got up with the dark. At last, a quiet moment with my husband, who has forgiven me again. We talk about my shoulder. About dealing with pain. About growing older.

"I've been dreading the time when your body can no longer support your mind's neurotic need to be perpetually moving," he offers.

I'd rather not be forced to stop riding. I want it to be a conscious decision. My sixtieth birthday is right around the corner. It is so hard to stop, to accept the fact that I'm not going to get any better as a rider, or that the sport has become too dangerous. The only reason you don't hear about older riders getting hurt is that there are so few of us left. I'm no longer willing to get on just any horse and run around a cross-country track, for instance. And yet I beat on with my horses against the current.

Miguel decides to harrow the moment I enter the indoor on Shiva, so instead I take him for a hack in the snow. It's an unexpectedly pleasant walk, despite the cold—around the back pasture and through Lydia's cut cornfield, down to her woods and along the edge of the soybean field, through her old dairy where thirty head of cattle were stabled when her husband was alive, including a sweet Jersey calf she once named Chance, after ours—and finally up the steep hill toward home. Shiva tries to jig up the hill but surrenders when he feels the resistance of deep, crusty snow.

CHATTING ON THE PHONE WITH KITTIE WILKINS, I REVEAL MY HES-itant desire to sell Shiva.

"Why do you want to sell him?" she asks. "Isn't he the really squirrelly one?"

"Used to be," I admit. "Not anymore. He's quiet now. And his flatwork is lovely. You can do anything to him, take him anywhere. And he's about ready to move up to Prelim. As long as you don't attempt a trail ride."

"I'm not sure I can sell Shiva," I admit to Barrett. "But the Ghost wants me to buy another horse."

"Then you're going to have to sell two," my husband grumbles, as we slog our way up the icy driveway toward the afternoon feed. "We can't afford to compete more than two."

I know when to stop talking.

"This is a sport of jumping," the Ghost says, when I ask him whether I should sell the sweet, comfortable homebred or the hard-as-nails mean motherfucker with an upper level jump.

Kittie solidifies a showing for Shiva on Saturday.

The temperature soars to 50 degrees and the sun comes out. It almost feels balmy. I pause before returning to my life of perpetual motion—three horses on the flat.

I BREEZE INTO THE HOUSE AFTER A SNOWY RIDE ON SHIVA. GEORGIA runs to tell me what's wrong, who's here, what I've missed, what's unfair, and how glad she is to see me. Daisy looks up from her staunch position on the rug, feigning annoyance at the intrusion.

John's old grade-school pal Ariel is perched on the couch beside Barrett, chatting about the exotic white-and-green flowers she has brought as a gift that neither one can identify.

"Don't ask me," I say. "They're lovely, though. Thank you, Ariel." Leveling my gaze at her, I add, "You've been sent as a spy."

Ariel always felt misunderstood by her stodgy family because she was so different—her pale skin assaulted by a plague of freckles, a mop of curly red hair that she periodically shaved. While at Brandeis majoring in gender studies, she realized that she identified more as male and so became a he. I have a hard time thinking of Ariel as anything but female, and I have to keep reminding myself. She has with him a new boxer/shepherd/pit bull mix named Lucy who has just graduated from obedience school. The dog will touch my hand given the command "touch," but still growls at Georgia when she claims one of the toys that Georgia is surprisingly not trying to retrieve. Lucy is a masculine-looking dog with a feminine-sounding name, just like her owner. Ariel does everything in life to ward off cliché and expectation, except when it comes to his dog.

Georgia coaxes the thief to engage in a game of roughhouse while trying to sneak back her possession. Ariel asks pointed questions about Barrett's health and my accident, which I'm convinced John and Mollie have instructed him to ask. I sit on the edge of the chair in my chaps and spurs, between rides, my shoulder pounding, lying that I'm next to healed, that Barrett is next to healed, so relax, Maxwell Smart and the microphone hidden in your shoe.

In the middle of catching up, chatting about his master's degree, I sneeze for the first time since my fall. My body feels like it is being blown apart. Apparently, we need a whole and supple subscapularis muscle to sneeze without excruciating pain. I can't hide it any longer; I'm doubled over.

"Doctor Ruth equates sneezing with having an orgasm," Ariel offers.

Barrett exits to shed more blood, leaving Ariel in the lurch, for as long as it takes me to catch my breath and composure.

"Well, we're mostly ok," I say between gasps.

SHARKS FRENZY MY RAFT, LEAPING AND SNARLING. AND SHARK PUPS that want me to swim with them. They surround and protect me from their viciously hungry parents. Rats insinuate themselves into my nightmare, too—a fear that has plagued me since I was a kid. Rat tails are swirling all around me.

It's still dark outside. My mind spins around my winter trip to Aiken. My friend, Esther, is eager to sign on the dotted line for a shared rental. The tiger sharks of my doubt and indecision won't leave me alone, and there goes the rest of my night's sleep, as they circle in on their sinewy feast. It isn't realistic to think I could leave the farm and Barrett and Daisy, with Barrett still bleeding, Daisy peeing out her kidneys, our winter farm busting with horses and boarders. Plus, my shoulder is a stone tablet on which a Mesopotamian novelist chisels nightly paragraphs. The sky turns from black to gray. I haul myself out of bed, struggle to get partially dressed, and inch my way down the back stairs, holding tight to the rail.

I pull Shiva out of his stall to get him ready for our trip to Kittie's. Barrett appears, armed with shipping boots.

"What's with the knee?" he asks.

I look down. Shiva's got a cut above his right knee, and the leg is blowing up. On goes the hose. Out comes the cell phone. I call Rachel, explain my dilemma.

"Take a photo and send it to me," she says, thick tongued through her first cup of coffee.

In sixty seconds, she has a photo of the knee. Calls me back. "No go," she says, "the cut is right above the artery."

I am secretly delighted.

I change course and put my leg over my giant black swan, to get him ready for a jumper show.

CALVIN AND I ARE THE ONLY ONES IN THE 1.10-METER DIVISION. WE wait till the low and high hopeful jumpers finish their bipolar divisions. Calvin is rigged in the Myler combination bit and the weighted show jump boots that, at least in the eventing world, could land me in the brig. He warms up well, doesn't go near the rails. I quickly memorize the courses—the hardest part for me, memorizing multiple courses. Not exactly the equivalent of a trigonometry test, but at this point in my life, I have to debride each memory from brain plaque.

Calvin jumps a clear first round. I'm the only one in the next class. I ask the in-gate person if he would mind raising the rails a couple holes. No problem. I return to the warm-up area to jump a bigger oxer. Calvin knocks it down; I pull him up. "Come on, Cal," I growl. "You can try harder than that." But he knocks it again, and again. We're back to our old problem: once he hits one, he decides all the rails are fair game, as if the point of the sport has morphed to knocking down the rails rather than leaving them up. This is how Calvin's brain works. He makes a mistake; he knows he's made one, but he is hardwired to repeat the same error, over and over, even as he gets increasingly agitated by the fact that he is doing something wrong.

Kittie Wilkins: *My clients still want to try Shiva. Will 5:00 today work?*

I take off the boots. What the hell.

Kittie: *Can't get there till 6.*

We go back into the ring for the higher jumps, maybe at 1.15 meters now. Not terribly big, by Calvin's standards. He jumps well, but he still jumps by Braille, ticking too many of the rails, and dropping one of them. Same in the next class, only the rail that falls is mine; I don't see a distance, so we get to an awkward takeoff spot. When I'm not perfect, Calvin won't make up for my mistakes. How do I instill in him a desire to be clean over the show jumps, the same way he eagerly looks for the flags on cross-country? It seems like a psychological rather than a training issue. It's not a matter of sharpening him, but of motivating him to keep the fences up. It's impossible for anyone to be good when they don't understand how to be anything.

Kittie: *Just leaving Virginia, is 7 ok?*

Julia: *As long as it's not 9.*

I wait in the mare barn tack room with the Teapot.

"I think I'm sending the wrong horse with the Ghost," I admit.

"How so?" she asks, always eager to talk about my plans with the horses.

"I can't ride Patrick with my shoulder," I say. "It kills me. And I'm getting the clutchies about sending Cal."

I don't want to part with my failure right now. The Ghost will "sharpen him up" no doubt, then I'll get back on him and it will be the same story: we'll have our mediocre show jump rounds and I'll make a few mistakes, which will result in rails, and I'll also give some good rides, which will result in rails. I'm desperate to try something different.

"Well, there's your answer," she says. "Send Patrick instead."

Kittie: *Won't be till 8 now. Remember that you love me.*

I fret.

Julia: *I'm sorry, that's just too late. Would be happy to show him in the morning.*

I'm afraid if I send Patrick, I won't ever want to ride him again. I sure won't miss him. He's a grouchy, if not downright mean, presence in the barn, and he's a bear to ride on the flat.

The thought of having a month of psychological training with Calvin is enticing, as is the ability to sleep around a bit with Stephen and Jimmy. And go to more jumper shows.

"Maybe you shouldn't jump him so much," says the Teapot. "He needs to really want it. Maybe he's gotten bored." I don't doubt that, with the same grids over and over.

"Just make a decision and stick with it. Don't look back," my father used to say. But what do you do when things happen that modify the picture? Sometimes you have to look back; hell, I've made a whole career of it as a poet. You can't reinvent the future but you can reinvent the past. That's the beauty of it. My father couldn't do it. He was the pragmatic businessman; I'm the dreamer. He was the oilman; I am the goal chaser. My hometown literally smelled of my father's business; I guess my own backyard smells of mine, too. As a kid, I used to complain about it, holding my nose and whining when we passed the refinery. "That's the smell of your bread and butter," my mother would admonish me. I'm grateful for how hard my father worked, but I still detest the odor of oil. What do my dreams smell like, I wonder? They smell like Fair Hill.

The Black Dahlia comes to the farm to give dressage lessons. I've lined up a few takers, plus Calvin and Shiva. The Dahlia sports French nails. I am amazed that a horse person could maintain such elegant personal hygiene. I'm inclined to hide my age-spotted, grungy-fingernailed hands behind my back, or stuff them into a pair of riding gloves.

The Dahlia hasn't seen Calvin in a lesson on the flat since he was a Three-Star horse. On paper, we've come a long way since then. She offers tools for quieting Calvin in the dressage ring. Lowering his poll—top of a horse's head—is key, she advises. If I can keep his poll down in the test, then I can keep his back up and his mind and body relaxed.

A judge emails me about a horse she is putting on the market. Do I know of anyone who might be interested in buying Sleigh? He's "special," so the person would have to be "special." Without asking if I'm "special" enough, I ask whether he is one of the Canadian crew. And yes, she answers, his sire is a full brother to her Zydeco.

Sleigh is therefore related to my lost Redmond.

"Can you send me a video?" I reply.

The YouTube clip won't open at first, and when it finally does, it gives me only a twelve-second snippet—I don't see enough to get much of a feeling for the horse, other than his color, which is dark.

MY PRESENT: NEW ANKLES FOR CHRISTMAS.

Cooper injects Calvin's, and I'm off to the train station to pick up Chance. Chance has recently had sinus surgery and has been upset over the prospect that her nose might have changed. She has found "the best" ENT in NYC, whose specialty is Metropolitan Opera singers. Not quite ready for La Scala, Chance has a nice throaty quality to her voice and has spent several years in voice lessons, but she still struggles with the accuracy of her pitch. And without that inherent quality, well … she is almost so good. Just like her mother in the tack. I wonder: what inherent equestrian quality am I missing that keeps me from excellence?

I worry that Chance is spreading herself too thin. I worry that she is too much like me. I worry that Calvin is too much like all of us. I worry because, well, isn't that what I'm supposed to do? Lately, she has been writing plays. Still, she is vain about her proboscis, maybe in hopes of one day salvaging her career as an actor and singer.

I expect her to arrive in a trench coat, hat, and shades, looking something like the Elephant Man, but she exits Penn Station all Brooklyn chic and unblemished—black pants, sweater, boots, coat, plus a black wool ski cap she has carefully positioned on her mop of wild long curly black hair, as if it were part of the hair style. Probably a new mod look on the streets of Manhattan. Even at 5'2", she is a huge, dynamic presence. Gorgeous, as always.

Our first stop is the grocery store. Not exactly where anybody wants to be on Christmas Eve. We manipulate our way around hundreds of hungry shoppers with an oversized shopping cart, piling up with holiday goods. Chance is used to getting her way in crowds, and she's hardly polite about it. I man the cart while she leads, twisting and bumping and dodging her way through the horde. I try to keep up with her, but it's hard work, without bashing into other shoppers. She complains that I'm slow, that I'm shopping impulsively as I pull items not on the list off the shelf, and that I can't keep up with her.

What's impulsive about chicken stock?

I shut my mouth and do my best, because that's how I've always dealt with Chance's controlling nature, though I'm hardly a submissive sort myself. In the presence of Chance, I waffle eternally between biting a bleeding tongue in order to keep the peace, and telling my daughter the truth as I see it. Now she's barking at me to keep up, and our circus is drawing attention. I become pushy myself, to silence my daughter, who doesn't care if she cuts off other people, or pushes herself in front of those waiting at the seafood counter for shrimp apocalypse. All in a day's disaster on the streets of Old Laredo.

Once home, I get on Patrick, bump into a couple of boarders, chat it up with them, and return to the house. Chance is sitting at the kitchen counter, hugging herself and perusing something on her computer screen. She looks up as I come in the door.

"It's freezing in here. I turned the heat up a little," she says.

I check the thermostat. I had no clue there were 80s on the register.

"Chance, we keep our thermostat at 68 in the wintertime."

"I'm cold," she repeats.

"Why don't you put a sweater on?" I suggest, eyeing her short-sleeved T-shirt.

"This is all I brought," she explains.

"Would you like to borrow one of mine?"

"No. Can't we just turn up the heat?"

"I can't afford eighty-two trombones," I say.

"My feet are freezing in my boots," she responds.

"Would you like my fleece slippers?"

"What, with your big feet?" she says to her screen.

I retreat to my drafty office to cool off. Heat control is not the issue. It's the concept of control. Chance resents that my attention is busily elsewhere. I can't stop riding and getting things done—the only way I have of controlling my fate. The life of perpetual motion, my self-defense. Chance must wonder why I can't stop and spend more quiet time with her. It's too late for that now. As soon as I get hurt and my emotions become involved, that possibility done left the barn.

Mercifully, it's cocktail hour. Chance is still brooding at the kitchen counter, her mascara smudged, making her darkness more so. We drink, we eat salmon; Barrett, his mush. She returns to the counter, complains again about how cold she is. And that her twenty-year-old cat, Fuzzy, is too thin.

"Why don't you go sit on the couch?" I offer. "It's warmer over there. The throw is really cozy."

"I don't want to sit where dogs have been," she says.

That does it.

"This is a farm," I remind her. "There are dogs, cats, and plenty of horses here. If you don't want to be around animals, then you shouldn't come home."

This is the first time Chance has been home since Barrett has been sick and I got hurt. If I weren't so stubborn, I'd have asked her if she would come home to help out. Far from throwing herself into the fray, she won't even sit on my couch. Surely the city is dirtier than any of the animals. I remember that girl racing home from school to spend each day's last hours with her pony, Sunny—hanging out in the crossties while she slowly tacked him up, then hopping on and dashing up the long steep back hill at a two-minute lick. Long summers spent riding Sunny bareback with her friends over to our neighbors' pond, where they swam the eager horses. Not once did a younger Chance make a point of washing her hands after touching the animals.

Barrett reappears from the bathroom, looks Chance's way. "Hey," she says, "isn't it cold in here?"

"What happened to your nose?" he responds.

Chance glares at both of us from her counter perch, snaps her computer shut, pounds up the stairs, and slams her bedroom door. Merry Christmas. I retreat to the bedroom, take a scalding bath, then spend the night tossing and turning. Sleigh bells, where are you?

CHANCE PEEKS AROUND MY BEDROOM DOOR AS I'M FINISHING MY ablutions.

"Merry Christmas, Mom. Are you going to be nice to me today?" Nothing left to do but smile. It's Christmas morning, after all.

"Merry Christmas," I say.

Stuff the stockings, light the tree, finish the barn chores. Christmas morning, always a stressor on a horse farm. The horses have no idea what day of the year it is and expect their norm, while humans expect just the opposite. I sweat the gift-opening, hoping my husband and daughter are happy with my selections—socks and gloves, candles and PJs, earrings and rings, pants and scarves. Barrett rounds up the boxes and wrapping paper to toss in the fireplace we traditionally light on Christmas morning. John and Mollie call from their 75-degree San Fernando Valley abode. How I wish they were here.

"It was an accident with his wagon," John says.

"Huh?"

"Charlotte Fowble's husband. He was hauling a four-horse wagonload of bark to Scott's Tanyard. He fell off his horse when the wagon over-turned, and a wheel ran over his neck. He left Charlotte with three kids."

Now he has piqued my interest. I look up at the hand-hewn nine-teenth-century beams in the dining room ceiling that we didn't know were there till we punched out the drywall when renovating the house. What else did they leave behind?

Barrett hauls out the juicer and gets to work on the leftover bushel of apples he bought as gifts for the boarders' horses. He presents his tumbler of apple juice to me for a sip with a bartender's pride, as if having created the consummate Manhattan.

"Taste," he says. "Six apples in this."

What's left is a pile of peelings for the horses as a Christmas treat.

"They dove into their feed tubs and wouldn't come up for air," he explains, offering me his palms, which smell deliciously of apples and horse spit.

I'm antsy to bundle up and retreat to the barn, to be touched by noses that smell like the Tree of Knowledge.

By the time I'm able to do that guiltlessly, it's already afternoon feed time. I pull Cal out of his stall, saddle him up, slip on the hackamore, and get the hell out of my life—Georgia jogging alongside. The rest of the world falls away. I have my horse and my dog, the weather and the land. Nothing else matters. Unseasonably warm weather, replaced by a cold front, has frozen the mud into miniature craters. Calvin navigates the uneven terrain around the back field, through Lydia's soy field, and up the steep hill and home. I sure hope he doesn't slip and overturn this wagon. Georgia darts off toward the end—her usual—and returns shortly with a deer leg in her mouth. She smiles at me and canters on ahead, proud of her catch. I praise her for her find, pat my happy horse, dismount.

My Christmas, this small hour with Calvin and Georgia.

BROOKLYN IS A GREAT PLACE TO LIVE, IF YOU LIKE THE CITY, WHICH I don't. Chance lives in a twenty-foot-by-twenty-foot box stall and works a job answering telephones for restaurant reservations. Sadly, I prepared her for a lifestyle and not for life. My parents encouraged me to go to school to enrich my life, rather than to get a good job. Times are different, and I've done my intended job as a mother, having passed on to both of my children the desire to work hard at something they love, no matter how lucrative. I used to tell them I'd back them up if they decided on any professional career, as long as they did it with dedication and passion. No longer. I wish I'd better prepared them on a practical level for life as it now is.

I sit at the kitchen counter listening to Chance talk about her sinuses, her grant applications and plays she's working on, her desire to be single again. Why am I antsy? Why don't I feel more engaged?

I long to be with the horses.

Chance doesn't seem to care about connecting with me. I wish I could relate the year I've lugged around on my back like a tortoise: my fall at Jersey, my eye surgery, the sudden loss of Redmond and Simon, Barrett's illness, my fall from Rhapunzel and ruined shoulder. It has been a miserable passage of loss and failure. How I would love to spill it to Chance. Our roles are changing, though she won't acknowledge it yet. I need her. Instead, I listen to her woes as she perches at the kitchen counter to avoid the dog-haired couch, until it is late afternoon and time for her to leave for the train. An impatient beat starts up, staccato and erratic, encouraging

me to throw on my layers of fleeces and coats, muffs and gloves, and head
out into the cold.

Gift Horse

The tarp inhales
and exhales with wind.
He might be napping,

except for one stiff hoof,
hovering above pasture grass.
I peel back the plastic hide,

try to push the leg back down,
drape my body over his swelling barrel,
shoe a fly drinking from his eye.

If wind is Odysseus, then I
am destined to love
an empty horse, bound

for a flatbed truck. Oh, Redmond!
Nothing to do but wait, navigate
from house to horse,

and back, at the mercy
of my size, a fleet of one.
Midday wanes. No news

from Ithaca. I leave,
and miss the pulley,
reeling him onto

the truck bed,
the violent mechanical winching
of a dead ton.

They never said what became
of the Trojan Horse
in the peace after slaughter,

but mine lies in the paddock,
waiting for the undertow.
Who has the courage to relinquish

what could never have been hers
in the first place?
That is the trick.

To the Ghost, with Patrick in tow for a jump lesson, and to drop him off, bound for the low country. We tackle a short gymnastic in the Ghost's jump field, which involves a series of one-strides. I'm rusty jumping on terrain. Though my horse handles it well, I see nothing but long distances. Patrick harbors an impulse to burst over his fences, resulting in a sprawling, disorganized landing. In this exercise, he has to snap up his front feet as soon as he lands from each effort. It's good for both of us—for me, jumping on uneven ground, and for him, compressing his naturally long stride.

"I'd leave it there," the Ghost says.

The waters driving home are cold and sluggish—the schools of fish are congested on I-95, and it's stop and go all the way. I should have gone the back way on a Friday afternoon. Instead, I thought the fish might be feasting on holiday cookies and eggnog by their mothers' fires.

Home again, home again, jiggity jig, minus one horse.

An email from Gretchen: was I able to view the video? Yes, it was an amazing eight seconds. *May I have a sit on him on Monday?* I ask.

"Relax," I say to Barrett. "There are still only two horses in our corner of the barn."

DANIEL TALKS ME INTO A JOINT JUMP SCHOOL IN OUR INDOOR, while Barrett talks me out of my upset with the beautiful young man. Daniel is boarding at the farm for December and January to get a start on the season before he leaves for Aiken, and I don't want to miss the opportunity to pick another serious event rider's brain about Calvin.

Daniel and I set up a line of four one-stride verticals at twenty feet apart, and a simple bending line off tight turns at both sides of the arena. At first, the line of verticals is set barely more than eighteen inches, or cavalletti height. Following Houston's lead, Calvin skips on through. As the heights increase, the horses have to adjust their strides accordingly. No two verticals are set the same height after the first pass, so the horses must remain flexible.

Calvin is *on* today. The hackamore keeps him soft and waiting to his fences. He cranes his neck around to my hand as I reach down after every good effort to offer him a cookie. He knows he's done well. Houston, on the other hand, is rusty, and Daniel explains that he always is this time of year, and that it will take lots of regular jumping to raise his form.

The barn is blessedly quiet without Patrick. No lunging at the stall bars for Shiva, no swishing of tail and mock biting and kicking when being blanketed. The horses, especially Shiva, who took the brunt of Patrick's meanness, are in much better spirits now that he's gone.

I LOVE THE RAIN. IT BLINDS, WALKING FROM THE MARE BARN TO THE arena with Cal. The ground, already saturated, is begging for it to stop. But nothing can disturb my mood this morning, with the house and barn so quiet after Chance's and Patrick's departures. I work on changing Calvin's flexion in the counter-canter. He gets excited and offers a couple of spontaneous changes, but he eventually maintains the counter-canter on the circle. Lots of pats and treats, plus a moment afterward when I lean into his Brobdingnagian head and kiss the side of his muzzle.

We walk back to the barn. Woofie is waiting for me, her face crimson.

"Who wrote this?" she spits, running over to the white board and pointing at some scribble.

Without my glasses, I squint to see what's there.

Last night, Daniel couldn't find Houston's ankle boots. He wrote on the barn's white board, *Has anyone seen my Eskadrons?* Searching the barn, the Teapot found them in Woofie's daughter's groom box, then wrote on the board, *Sassie, don't take Dan's stuff.* She neglected to write *Ha ha* afterward.

Woofie raises her voice. It appears she is even mad at me. I'm still holding my horse, unable to get past her to the wash stall to untack Calvin. I hold up my hand, palm outward in a gesture of surrender, "Woofie, Woofie, Woofie," I say, with a slight warning tone as if to suggest she's mad at the wrong person.

The day goes from soothing rain to a fucking downpour.

Barrett calls. He's on a walk with Georgia.

"I think I may have found the old sawmill," he says.

I take the phone away from my ear and look at it.

"What are you talking about?" I say. "I need you here!"

His excitement isn't listening.

Barrett walks into the tack room still talking to me on his phone. He looks up.

"The old Millender Sawmill down by the bridge. They would have needed the stream for the mill. I'm sure it must have been there."

I cannot get away from it—my life, my home, my work, my husband, my daughter, my family, my farm.

IN DAMASCUS, STEPHEN HAS SET A SIMPLE OXER WITHOUT GROUND rails, plus a rail set at nine feet out on either side. We canter back and forth a few times, Stephen urging me not to place Calvin at the fence, but to let him figure out the distance on his own. Not adjusting the stride in front of the fence is harder to do than it sounds, and I wonder if that hasn't been part of my problem all along. I have to learn to do nothing. Or unlearn doing something.

"The best thing to do for a horse that isn't all that careful," Stephen says, "is to let him make his own mistakes in training. Let him figure it out."

Huh.

"Doesn't the Ghost have you do that?" he asks.

"Not really." I've been struggling to perfect my eye so that I'll make as few mistakes as possible, even in training. It is possible that I've been supporting my horses too much, making their decisions for them. I think of all those recent times cross-country that I've fiddled my way down to a fence, looking, looking, looking for that perfect distance. I think of Jimmy Wofford's adage: *there is no perfect distance.* In an effort not to run at my fences—my modus operandi for years—I've turned a 180, going overboard with placing my horses. A lightbulb moment turns into a light show.

We also tackle a canter gymnastic, three oxers set at twenty feet apart. Calvin jumps well, though he does have a couple of rails, in part due to his right drift. As the fences go up, my hands get dangerously high, and Stephen reminds me to lower them, in an effort to arrest my nerves from interfering with technique.

Stephen constructs a "V" with two poles on the middle oxer to correct Cal's drift. When we turn the corner to the gymnastic, Cal's eyes get big when he sees the poles; he starts to backpedal, crashes through the first oxer, and runs out at the second. He gets offended when I hit him a couple of times for his disobedience, and gets strong and runs through my hand. He's not used to discipline; in fact, I generally avoid it because he's so sensitive.

He nails it on the second pass, straight as an arrow.

Stephen recommends that when warming Calvin up, I only jump five or six oxers before going into the ring.

"The more you jump him, the more careless he's going to get," Stephen says.

That's a good tip on a dead crab, as Barrett would say at the track.

Shiva jumps well, and Stephen says he has improved since the last time he saw him. He recommends that I keep him connected and round when I jump him. It's a more involved ride, but I have to work to keep his back up, or he tends to lose his form. Dressage over fences is key for Shiva.

"He'll make a really nice Training horse one day," Stephen says.

In other words: *sell him.*

GRETCHEN PRAISES SLEIGH'S ATTITUDE AND GROUND MANNERS. "He's more like a dog," she says. He has a desirable uphill build. And he's narrow. Tall, with a thin chest—something I've never been too keen on, a horse built like Dover Sole.

I squint in the growing dark as Gretchen rides him. He has a lovely trot. There's only one small vertical set up outside, which she jumps a couple of times. By the time I get on him, it's darker still. I jump the small vertical, but can't tell much before the shadows swallow us. I like the feel of his jump, but the obstacle is so small, it's hard to get a sense of the horse's scope.

That night, I'm sleepless, trying to decide if I want to go back and try Sleigh again, or whether I should listen to my gut.

"THERE YOU ARE, YOU LITTLE STARTER OF THE SHIT STORM," WOOFIE greets the Teapot, who turns and walks away. Woofie follows her to Ego's stall.

"You can't just walk away from me!" she warns, her voice rising.

"This conversation is over," the Teapot states flatly, and turns her back once more.

Barrett zooms up the driveway in the tin can. Woofie is sobbing outside the barn.

"Two and a half years I've been here," she chokes, "and I've always tried my best to be a considerate, respectful boarder."

"No boot is worth a friendship," Barrett says.

This incident colors our night. It is impossible to shake either one of us out of our hooded moods. We both hate stress and upset. I get stressed and upset easily. I resent Barrett's detachment. But is it detachment?

Maybe he just doesn't want to start bleeding again. I long for the calm reserve he is able to muster in the face of barn squabbles and infuriated clients. For me, sex and desire are the same. Barrett doesn't have to be making love in order to feel desire. His detachment is the very sprezzatura that Jimmy has earmarked as the quality of a great rider.

NEW YEAR'S DAY, I'M AT MY DESK, WITH THE PELLET STOVE CHURN- ing away, the morning sky lightening to gray, the pastures covered with their pallor of frost, tree branches paused in midair.

Chapter Four

Forget About Sex

The impeded stream is the one that sings

−Wendell Berry

BARRETT'S HAND IS HELD ONTO HIS ARM BY A COUPLE OF SCREWS and broken titanium. It is coming apart inside his skin.

The surgeon holds up the X-ray of Barrett's wrist, taken with a fluoroscope. A jagged line runs across the sepia film.

"The plate broke," Dr. Widdstadt says. "And the bone is separating."

"Now what?" Barrett asks, sitting on the table.

"Well," the hand doctor says, drawing out the word like taffy, stretching one syllable into five or six, "Once the TB has cleared, we'll go back in and replace the plate. Until then, your hand will just have to stay broken."

TEN DEGREES. THE WIND TAKES IT WELL INTO THE NEGATIVE RANGE. It's the kind of cold that seizes up the lungs as I struggle to the tin can, hidden under a foot of snow. I'm too impatient to knock off the snow and ice, or free the paralyzed wipers. I stick my head out the door to navigate my way up the unplowed driveway to the mare barn. I've got an hour and a half before we leave for St. Joe's.

Calvin and Shiva are still in their stalls, windows wide open. No one has thought to close them, nor give them any hay, nor check their water, now frozen in their buckets. I'm angry before I even start to tack up Calvin, who seems confused about the order of go this morning.

We slog our way to the indoor ring. Its end doors are wide open, and piles of snow have blown in and created miniature Raniers in the footing. Miguel is going about his chores, oblivious to the blizzard happening around him. I can't remember the Spanish word for *Shut the goddamn door*, but anger is anger in any language.

Marta shows up with a ladder and sledgehammer to jimmy the unwieldy doors closed. Calvin is terrified of the white stuff in the footing. He comes off my aids each pass through it, as if the snow is going to scorch his heels. We accomplish nothing. My joints are locked up, my fingers numb, even tucked in my Sub-Zero riding gloves.

I notice one of the horses pacing her stall. I ask Miguel three times in my Spanglish before he nods understanding: *does Cello have ensalada?* Not only does she not have any salad, but there isn't a single flake in the hay stall. He slaloms the gator down the unplowed driveway to fetch more bales out of the bank barn—which should have been done yesterday before the snowfall. One of those details a healthier Barrett would have done without thinking.

I give up hopes of riding, and we toboggan our way back to the mare barn. Calvin untacked, I bark at Barrett about the small catastrophes in the barns. He mistakes my annoyance for anger at him, gets prickly and defensive, and lickety-split we're engaged in an all-out war encompassing our entire past and future: how we should never have bought Charlotte Fowble's land, nor gone into business together. He's ruined his life, giving up his best years to my delusions. What I don't admit is how enraged I become when circumstances go haywire. The tin can is about ready to burst, as though we're driving an oversized CO_2 cartridge. We can't get to the hospital fast enough.

My darkness settles in like cancer. It multiplies. My husband is ill. I must have patience. There is a way out—always a way out. I sit in the waiting room, wishing I could stay all day and shut out the world. Colonoscopies are short but definitively not sweet, and Barrett's forty-eight biopsies are done almost before I take my jacket off. The nurse calls for me and takes me to "Recovery," although when I get to his cubicle, Barrett's still fast asleep. She tries to wake him, but he rolls over on his back. I jostle his shoulder, and he barely stirs.

"Baby, you're the one," Barrett slurs through tears and leftover anesthesia.

I've seen him do this before. This is another kind of love, the one that makes us familiar with each other's responses to pain and anesthesia. *Don't worry*, I remind myself, *he always cries.*

I'm a wind-up toy running out of twist.

I THOUGHT I WANTED A WORKING FARM, BUT I PREFER BEING ALONE. I couldn't have a farm alone or event alone. I couldn't have solitude without Barrett's help. That left him by himself with our race mares and their get. But being alone in his racing passion fouled his sense of shared purpose. He didn't want to do it by himself. He was successful, but he was lonely in his success. In the forty win photos stacked on the tack room shelves, I don't appear in a single one. He eventually stopped breeding and racing altogether.

Now Barrett is sick. The pounds fall off him like maple leaves. But he is well enough to know he needs something else.

After a Night of Almost Making Love

Georgia barely raises her head
to leer at me from the hooded
corners of her eyes.

I've given up taking away her loot—
the ribcages and quarters
lazy hunters didn't cart away.

This late season, as light thins
and trees spend their leaves,
I flinch

when you pad up behind me,
tasting rut and musk on my neck,
light from the half-open blinds

slicing me.
I want to want.
Maybe that's enough

FREEZING RAIN. WE BOTH FALL DOWN TRYING TO LOAD TACK INTO the back of the trailer. My husband looks at me from his fallen state, surrender on his face. I get the horses loaded, strap myself in, put the truck in four-wheel drive.

"If you can get out our driveway, you should be all right," Barrett reassures, still sitting on the ground, a fallen snow angel.

I make the error of turning on the "Talking Girl." I slip and slide to the Keystone State, turning on ribbons for roads when she tells me to. One is closed. I veer right with her ominous silence before she tells me to turn around when possible. I continue on and make a turn of my own, which takes me on a snowmobile trailhead. I go about a mile until I realize I've gone wrong. I find a cemetery lane, pull in between rows of snowbound headstones. There are over a hundred corpses buried here who'd give anything to come back if all they had were my problems. I make the Sign of the Cross and back out onto the snow-covered road.

Esther is waiting for me at the jumper show, at the ready with her video camera to film my parking job. She also hopes to get some good footage of Shiva jumping.

Shiva twirls circles around Esther, who is delighted to pass him off to me. The horse settles and starts to focus as soon as he feels my weight. He jumps a clean, efficient round in a steady-gets-it manner.

No doubt the Swan Lake helpers are in a hurry to get home to cozy oakwood fires. I throw the weighted boots on Calvin, and follow Stephen's recommended warm-up: five or six oxers. Calvin hits the fourth when it grows to 3'9." I come again, he jumps it clean, Esther strips off the boots, and we go in the ring. I hear the buzzer and look for the first fence, but it isn't where I thought it was. I've memorized the wrong course.

"Esther, help me!"

She calls out the sequence of fences. I circle once when I think she says *right* but says *left*. I strain to hear where the next jump is. Without the head space to think things through and worry about placing my horse to his fences, I rely on him to find our distances ... and my careless horse jumps a beautiful, clean round.

Revelation Warning: I have been getting in Calvin's way. In my struggle to place my horse for his takeoffs, I have been taking away his initiative. I have been fussing, and Calvin does not like to be fussed with. As my eye has gotten better, so, too, have I become more controlling. As if the better I do something, the more aware of my aptitude I become, and then strive for perfection in every breath, every jump.

Esther is a ribbon freak. "Don't you need them to decorate your tack room?" she teases. We march back to the office to settle up and collect my ribbons from the four classes, including reserve and champion prizes— silly, as there were only two other competitors in each class besides Calvin. I need three arms to carry all the loot.

RECORD LOWS FOR MARYLAND. MINUS FIVE. I'VE FELT THIS COLD before, in the Allegheny Forest. My father, listening to early-morning transistor radio while he shaved, the airways god, Leroy Schneck, inform-ing WRRN listeners about the weather. "Bundle up," my father would say on waking me for school, closing the frosted window he insisted on opening the night before, no matter the temperature. Fresh air, according to his friend Benjamin Franklin, was good for sleeping.

"You're not opening the window," Barrett said last night, although he knew better. I always do, negative thermometer or not.

I leap to the window on rising, slam it shut. Leroy wasn't kidding: it's cold outside.

I decide not to ride, to give the horses' lungs a break.

I work at my desk all morning—opening drawers, crawling behind the corn stove—trying to find money that isn't there. I check on all the horses in the afternoon, but no one has a quarter in his ear. Up and down the driveway, I skywrite poems with my visible breath. I end my day by taking care of Huey and Surf and Miro, long pensioned in the bank barn field. They're in for the night, needing more blankets and hay and water. Huey, having just turned twenty-six, nuzzles my pocket for a treat, and I find one to offer, somewhere deep where there's still a hint of warmth.

Bone cold, we can't seem to agree on what to have for dinner. One stupid comment leads to another until we're in another shouting match. Barrett's face is as red as a boil. We are on the couch with plates of untouched shrimp salad. He's making a statement, eating what I eat because I complained earlier about our life as it now is, no fun and nothing to share, going separate paths, all that.

I'm in my PJs and Ariat jacket, my long brown hair a rumpled oily mess from days of being crammed into a helmet without a washing. Not exactly Sophia Lauren.

Barrett parks a shrimp in his jowl. I've never had less fun pretending to eat in my life. And in a household where dinner has always been sacred.

"I wouldn't eat that," I warn, after I've cooled off to room temperature. I sure don't want him to bleed.

"Fuck off," Barrett says, still mad as a hornet.

"Barrett, stop, it's the prednisone talking."

He looks at me and pauses, puzzlement on his face. "I didn't know *you* were taking prednisone," he buzzes.

BARRETT CURLS HIS NECK AROUND THE LAMP FROM THE FAMILY room, raising himself partially off the couch so he can at least see a blur of me.

"You know what the most predominate side effects of prednisone are?" he offers as his "bonjour." "Irritability, impatience, quick to anger, agitation, and truth."

I finish pouring my coffee. It's too early to have a discussion about this. I take his revised Wikipedia definition as apology, and move to my desk.

I GET A HEAD START ON BUILDING THE JUMP PATTERN—MY FIRST mistake, thinking my shoulder was ready for dragging around standards and poles. Daniel won't be here till 5:00, and I'm anxious to put my feet into stirrups.

I call Barrett for reinforcement. He agrees to help, but he's irritated: why have I attempted such heavy lifting with my bum shoulder? Both he and his drug are right. But he *has* come to help, no matter how awful he's feeling, or how awful he's feeling toward me, each pole he hefts breaking his hand a little more.

Our foursome strolls through the bridle path in the woods after our school—Daniel and Houston, Calvin and me. Even under four layers of riding costume, he's drop-dead.

"He's jumping great," Daniel compliments Calvin.

I look back and smile the best smile I can muster, bundled up in a freezing cold that stings my teeth.

"That's Calvin," I say. "Trains great, goes in the ring and knocks them all down."

"Would you call him a morning glory?" Daniel asks.

He's referring to the term trackers use for racehorses that train like lightning in their morning workouts, then lug out of the starting gate and spit the race out in the afternoon. They have no heart under pressure.

I smile again. I've thought that about Cal before, which has made me a little defeatist. I should portray my Four-Star horse more positively. I should figure how to coax him to try harder. How to give myself heart, as well. Not just another follower on this woods path, deferring to a twenty-eight-year-old Adonis. Or to the Ghost, or Barrett, or the Talking Girl, or anyone else that tries to show me the right path.

Tonight, over wine and pizza for Julia, apple juice and ground wheatgrass for Barrett, Fuzzy sits next to us on the couch, marching away, and considering where to pee next. I take the nothing that is left of her and plop her on my lap, so I can better scratch the top of her head and ears.

"Days," says Barrett.

"How do you know?" I ask.

"Just a feeling. She seems pretty out of it," he says.

Barrett should know—the cat has been at his side through his convalescence, as if she were holding on until she knew he would make it without her.

I spend the rest of the evening massaging an old cat's dwindle.

I swing Cal around the indoor a few times, the softest of figure eights, true canter to counter-canter and back, until he relaxes into the work. I focus on his straightness in the counter-canter. It has taken ten years of six days a week teaching my fifteen-hundred-pound partner to get to this point—a balanced counter-canter that I still have to handle as tactfully as I can. I can't demand anything of Calvin; I have to ask with please and thank you.

I've LOST AND REPLACED THREE MILLION SKIN CELLS SINCE I'VE LAST seen my dermatologist. The years have been kind to Dr. Margaret's face, thanks to postmodern science and an aversion to the sun, but I notice a dowager's hump developing in her back, probably from all the years of hunching over patients' turkey necks.

"Pressure," she says, sewing my face slowly from cheekbone to jaw with dozens of tiny needles. "Pressure," although it feels more like a sting and a burn. "Pressure" by the eye is torture, but "Pressure" by the time several needles go in, the lidocaine that's included in the injections lessens the pain as she goes. "Pressure," I think of all the hours Calvin has stood so patiently as needles drove into his hocks, "Pressure," the foot-long ones into his sacroiliac joint, and "Pressure," most recently the smaller ones in his ankles, "Pressure," to relieve the miles and miles of pounding they will take this year, and "Pressure," I think of my husband, and wonder if he will notice any difference in my face. Has he even looked at me closely lately? "Pressure." "Pressure." "Pressure."

"We're coming down the home stretch now," my torturer says.

Eyes glued to her computer screen, the receptionist shuffles the bill my way. I must be in worse shape than I thought. I can feel my eyebrows turning gray as I calculate madly, wondering which credit card to offer. I hand over the plastic card with a Roman Centurion on the front, dreading the months of small payments it will take to reduce the bloated balance.

I TRAILER THROUGH PEA-SOUP FOG AND FREEZING RAIN TO Destination Farm in Woodbine, Maryland, where Norwegian rider Bent Jensen comes once a month to escape the oppressive weather in the Sunshine State, and to give dressage lessons.

I like Bent's soft-spoken manner. He suggests longer reins with Calvin to encourage him to relax and keep his neck stretched out, so it doesn't get high and tense and short. He also has me ride Calvin quite forward. Calvin responds well, and stays relaxed.

Bent calls me over at the end of the lesson. "Your horse does look a little short on that right hind," he says, *sotto voce.*

On the ride home, I worry that Calvin is lame. I worry that Barrett doesn't love me anymore. I worry that Calvin is done. That even my ghosts are tired of haunting me.

APRIL SETS FENCES FOR SHIVA AND ME. SHE SOMETIMES RIDES HIM when I'm away and was recipient of his rearing antics when he first returned from the track. Shiva has come a long way in the last century, and now keeps all four feet on the ground when he isn't jumping.

I complain about Shiva's reluctance to stretch his topline over fences, and April asks if I've tried schooling him over low, wide oxers. This was an exercise I learned from Jimmy Wofford twenty years ago.

I tend to forget my tool apron when I'm in the saddle. The fact that I've stopped teaching doesn't help matters. I need to get back to gearing my jump schools toward each individual. Shiva needs to be encouraged to look down at the ground when he jumps, to stretch over his back, neck, and poll, so that he learns to use his entire body over fences, and not merely pick up his legs. Low, wide oxers with a rail set diagonally across the top ought to get his attention.

"That's a good idea," I say to her.

"Learned it from you," she counters.

UPPER MARLBORO IS A LONG WAY TO GO FOR A DRESSAGE SHOW, BUT I pack up and climb in the rig and head out to southern Maryland's tobacco country. Cal needs the practice. The horse marches like a professional onto the trailer—likely happy to be getting out of the mud. The farm looks like a four-wheeler derby has come through since the last downpour, and I stew about how we are going to tackle the mess when the weather breaks. Relax, Julia, that will be eons from now, says a whisper in my ear.

It's nice to be off the farm, nicer still that the sun is out. As we climb the show's driveway to a vista of distant hills, I take a deep breath and let go. Cal is soft and focused. Amazing what can happen in a practice test that doesn't count in the eventing world, when my horse isn't geared toward jumping big fences after drawing circles and curlicues. I shorten my reins and do several downward transitions, until I feel a solid unit underneath me and not hundreds of independently moving parts.

When I reenter the ring to ride the second test, my connection is less steady. Doesn't help that we hear musketry in the distance. I have to keep the same feel, no matter what the Redcoats are doing to the Patriots.

The judge says not to worry. She liked the trot work in the second test better. "Black powder didn't help your cause," she says. But I know better.

A second and a fourth in a class of about ten horses—a hogshead of progress.

A MESS OF CONTRACTORS TO FIX OUR MUD-CRATERED DRIVEWAY. Barrett shows up to the meeting with horse shit all over his boots and gray locks sticking straight up. He is exhausted from having put in a morning of farm work. My fear is that Barrett lost his passion for the farm when he saw me cross the bridge between the earnest and the ridiculous, from focus to tunnel vision. Now, without any track horses or broodmares, the farm offers him nothing besides obligation to me and dealing with clients who question his every decision. He has little interest in answering them, or in meeting with asphalt crooks who are trying to talk me into paying them for three days of work an amount equal to what Barrett earns in twenty-five years. His innate sense of a good stallion, his flexibility leading mares and foals—as if every strange equine consideration were familiar in his presence—and his love of a good two-dollar wage—none of that is in his pocket anymore.

In the meantime, our driveway is ruined from endless trailering, as well as the added traffic of equestrians rather than the occasional visit by trackers to visit their racing lay-ups. It isn't so much a matter of twenty years' worth of use as desperate misuse that has done the damage.

I feel like a horse cast against her stall wall, unable to get up or free myself. I need to get up. I need to get up and sell this farm and everything that goes with it. I remember a wisdom from horseman Louise Christmas: it's impossible to sell what you don't love. I compose a letter to our realtor, who has been casually listing us for two and a half years. I suggest a pay-over-time option for the sole prospective buyer that the farm has seen in over a year.

In the barn, I put my arms around Calvin's neck, bury my face, breathe in deep.

MUD AND RUTS AND WATER. NOT SO MUCH RAIN SINCE 1906. CARS come in and trucks go out, splashing and veering. People come to pelt their talk on me and ride their muddy horses. The pastures are sinking like a drowned valley.

KIM'S MOUTH DOES THE WORK OF HER HANDS, EXPLAINING HOW TO pull the rolling table away from her chair, how to tilt the chair to upright, how to wrap the shawls and blankets around her, take off her mitten and put her hat on, and position the vet-wrapped joystick around her claw. I pry open her fingers so they can grip the stick. I open the door and guide her down the ramp. Her horse runs over toward the chair from his paddock, which stops just short of the ramp.

Kim lives on one side of a renovated barn. The other half is a run-in shed for her retired Four-Star horse, Bart. Kim asks me to grab the stale bread cubes and mints in her pocket, and to place them one by one on her blanketed lap. Bart nibbles them carefully, well-accustomed to this ritual. He's had seven years to get it right: to lip but not bite, to be careful not to swing his powerful head in Kim's direction, and to nuzzle his old partner.

Kim focuses the chair with little twinges in her right hand. Up the hilly driveway we go, with me right behind her, redirecting the chair when she goes astray. We wheel by the pond and the farmhouse, the other pad-docks and grain silo. It is a brisk, sunny day, finally, so we venture to the top of the drive, where some stadium fences were once set in the hay pas-ture and now linger in various stages of windblown disrepair. We stop and stare across the hilltop at the field and woods, wherein she says lie trails. "The hunt comes through," she says proudly. That must be quite a feast for Kim, a blur of black and red, a frenzy of hooves, manes, and tails, and the singing of hounds—Kim's winter gift of speed and activity.

"That was a good walk," she concludes. "We made it to the top of the hill."

We share stories and news. Georgia becomes obsessed with Kim's caged lop-eared rabbit. She dances around and paws at the cage, then tries to climb on top of it. Kim stretches her voice and tells me about the still-ness and boredom of her life. As quick a mind as Kim has, she has been unable to engage it, now that she can no longer be in perpetual motion. For both of us, motion and mind have always been tied that closely. We have that in common. Now it's only Kim's voice that dances and sways, climbs and rides and remembers when other parts of her body could move. I wonder how my own mind would fare in her situation.

"There's nothing left," she says. "I can't even eat anymore."

"How come?" I ask.

"I've gained thirty-five pounds since I've been sitting in this chair. Five pounds a year for seven years." It's true—Kim has that swollen, shiny, pale appearance of someone who is perpetually stuck, with nothing left to do but eat and talk.

Has it really been that long?

"At first I thought, ok, so I have to sit in my chair from now on. Not so bad. But I didn't realize that nothing would be the same. I could no longer wipe my nose or go to the bathroom, drive a car or feed myself. And forget about sex. I take these power naps in the afternoon," she goes on, pausing to position her mouth around one of several joysticks, on which are balanced exactly three pills, glued on the stick with a smear of Nutella. "What's that?" I ask. "Percocet," she mumbles, lipping the nearest pill until she gets it in her mouth. "Anyway, the other day I was sleeping, and the next thing I knew, Nancy and my night nurse were standing over me, shaking me and screaming my name. They couldn't wake me up. I wouldn't wake up," she repeats.

"So what happened?" I ask.

"I woke up," she says, staring at the invisible. "I woke up," she repeats. I refrain from looking at my wristwatch. I'm anxious to know the time, hoping it's close to the hour when I plan to leave and get back to the farm to ride Shiva.

"Nancy is trying to figure out a way to strap me in the saddle so I can sit on Bart again," she tells me.

I help set up Kim's nightstand with her next hit of Percocet within mouth's reach, the joystick for her computer and TV close by. Twitching her nose and looking a little like Elizabeth Montgomery in *Bewitched*, she asks me to scratch her nose, and I scratch her nose. Maybe I should be scared, or sad, or guilt ridden. Maybe seeing Kim again should drive away all thoughts of riding and competing. Maybe I should finally listen to my non-horsey friends, eager to get me off horses for their fear of something like what happened to Kim happening to me.

"Divorce," an old friend once said, "that's the whole reason I'm never getting married."

Quadriplegia barely crosses my mind when it comes to riding. If you continue to do what you love no matter the risk or injury, then that is a gift you receive though never fully understand. Sure, you weigh the risks and try to ride safe horses safely, always wear a helmet and don't do anything too crazy, but at some point, it's all crazy.

RACHEL THREADS AN EXTRAVAGANT NEEDLE INTO CALVIN'S NECK through muscle and ligament and fat, until she hits bone, to inject a vial of sugar water. She goes in six times, at six different places on each side for the vertebrae points, four guided by ultrasound and two blind. Calvin stands obediently and accepts the injections without so much as a cc of tranquilizer. Stone sober. This prolotherapy is supposed to make him more supple, his neck more malleable, and the nuchal ligament that runs from neck to back more pliable and better able to communicate with his back, thereby increasing Calvin's connection on the flat. Results should be immediate, and so it is possible to ride him right after the procedure.

"Have you thought anymore about my chia seed idea?" she asks as the fifth needle penetrates the recesses of Calvin's neck. She is convinced that farming chia seeds is the wave of the future. I've yet to see any proposal or business plan. An entrepreneurial spirit only goes so far: at some point, even the theorists and game guessers have to get their hands dirty.

"My hands are going on me," she says, showing me her chipped nails, her callused palms, her dried and wrinkled fingers. "They're man hands," she says.

I hide my own behind my back. Rachel has seen my hands plenty, has even X-rayed the worst of my arthritic fingers, before I had finger surgery.

I hop on Calvin, hoping to feel more softness than the day before. I play around on the flat with some lateral movements and a couple of changes. But the sun is shining, and I'm itching to go out. I call Georgia. The footing's no good for much else besides walking, but it's heaven to be outside, seeking the sun and solitude with Calvin and Georgia. When I'm ninety and no longer able to ride, when Calvin and Georgia are waiting for me under the piano, I hope I will remember this expansive feeling, with the comfort of Calvin underneath and Georgia and Simon beside, venturing into what awaits.

Georgia finds a deer carcass, rips a leg off, and comes running back to our side, fresh death swinging from her mouth, tail wagging, ears flattened. She drags it back to the farm, where she spends the rest of the day ripping it to shreds and consuming every bone splinter. By 3:00, there's a mere eight-inch piece that she trots around the farm, showing it off to whoever notices.

Later, old Daisy struggles off her bed when I pour a pistol of Chardonnay. She knows that if she can make it to the kitchen, she'll get a biscuit. Her tail a-waggin', she is still delighted to eat, and to sleep, and to have me rub her ears and the top of her head.

LIKE HAVING CHILDREN, YOU DON'T CHOOSE THEM. THEY CHOOSE YOU. But unlike kids, you can decide whether they stay or not. The newest stray, Marnie, has barged into the house this winter. After cat box debacles with Fuzzy and our thyroidic one-eared stray, Earie, I made a policy of no more house cats. My resolve lasted until the next cat came begging. Marnie mainly hides in my shoes in the upstairs closet, but this morning I find her settled into Fuzzy's wet food on the counter. She startles when I put my hand on her back, as if I'm going to toss her back out. But I don't. Like kids, cats are opportunists.

We buzz out later in the day to suburban Howard County, for Barrett's first reading since he's been sick. He has finished an early draft of a story, which I've advised him is too soon to read in public. This one is so close to the bone. I endlessly rewrite, never satisfied with the last draft, until the next few strands of gray appear, or the next stray cat vanishes, whichever comes first. A two-page poem can easily turn into a ten-year project at my desk. Barrett is more the risk-taker when it comes to words, and reading a piece aloud is part of his revision process. He adlibs corrections, taking his eyes off the page. For him, literature, like eventing, is an art of constant adjustments in the moment.

After the first two readers have finished, Barrett flies back to my row of seats, where I'm sitting next to his mother, who has come up from McLean, and Mollie's mother, who has hopped over from Columbia. Barrett leans over and whispers in my ear: "I brought the wrong draft." I'm not sure what he wants me to do about it, but simply know about his mistake. He then reads the roughest of rough drafts of a story that is taking its first crying breaths, some from memory, and some of it he writes as he speaks.

The room is small, but a friend has brought an amp and a microphone to help Barrett project his weakened voice. It's not like he's reading at the Folger Shakespeare Library. It's a small art-framing store on Route 97 just north of Damascus, and the roving society of Baltimore street poets is his audience, with an open-mic session at the end of the featured readers. Several poets also read jagged drafts, so at least he's in like company.

"Don't worry about it," I say to him on the way home.

My husband is quick to blame another interruption-filled day on the farm for his mishap. He looks beyond the obvious: the fact that he doesn't file in a methodical way nor back up his work properly. He thinks his way of keeping track is fine—it just doesn't work well in the hurricane of our lives.

WE ARE SO RELIEVED WHEN DAISY MAKES IT OUT THE DOOR, WE hardly care that our deck has become a kennel. Barrett has a new idea: feed the dogs outside—which means the deck—just to get Daisy outside before bedtime. There hasn't been a night-check prowl for this old Lab in a long time—maybe three months now—so feeding her outside is Barrett's way of suspending her inevitable decline. We take to using the back door to avoid the desiccated shit and frozen pee stains piling up around the front.

SHIVA IS RESTLESS WAITING HIS TURN AT A JUMPER SHOW. WARM-UP is in one indoor, and the course is in the adjacent indoor, with no place for horse and rider to stand and watch. Nor am I able to walk the course. Once on Shiva, I don't dare get off, and I've gotten on too soon. He can't hold still. I memorize the map, but when we start our round, we have to suck our stomachs to negotiate the tight turns. There's a ninety-degree serpentine line. I jump fence 1 and make it to fence 2. Fence 3 is impossibly close. In order to make the turn, Shiva loses momentum, gets right under the fence, and comes to a dead stop. I ask him to jump from a standstill, and he leaps. Good boy. No problem, jumping thirty-nine inches from nothing. Jumping out of the pasture as a yearling has come in handy as a trained horse: his instinct is to go. I always did think he was deerlike—not only in his chestnut color, but also in the lightness on his feet and, unfortunately, in his hollow form over fences. He finishes the course cleanly. I jump one more course and call it a day for Shiva.

I enter the first class on my Irish rogue. No problem over fences 1 and 2 in that difficult serpentine line. As I jump fence 2, I call out, "I don't think we can make it!" The small crowd yells back encouragement: "Yes we can!" A clean round for Calvin! Maybe the six-fence warm-up recommendation of Stephen's, plus stripping off Calvin's boots before going in the ring, are doing the trick. It also helps that the Teapot just clipped him yesterday. He would feel the sting of those rails.

"I used the number 10 blade on his legs," she admits later, back at the barn. "Close as a man's chin."

THE YOUNG GIRL WITH THE CARROT TOP TRYING SHIVA TODAY SEEMS
enamored of the horse. At least the color combo is right: red on red. Shiva
is a bit tired from the jumper show yesterday, so he is on his best behavior,
even when the girl takes him on a brief hack around the farm. If Shiva is in
a mood to give his rider the finger, then he saves it for when he is outside.
He still has adolescent insecurities and feels safest in a ring. Both the girl
and her mother manning the phone camera want to try Shiva again in
Aiken, where they can get a feel for him over cross-country fences.

Blizzard of Nothing

It snows in feet, not inches,
the fleeting, hushing plunge of it.
It snows, all day and then some,
piling silently up
on the hilly pastures.
When I've finally had my fill,
it snows another ocean—
pelting, as if falling
wasn't enough—
a crazed Einstein,
erasing what came before
to start the lesson over—
a blizzard of wisdoms
traveling at the speed
of incomprehension.
My breath comes fitfully—
slate, chalk, merciful dusk.

THE TRACTOR WON'T START.

We slog our way up and down the driveway in a foot of white stuff to get to the barns.

Calvin is all fired up—happy, alert, and too heavy in my hands. But he is jumping well. I focus on landing on the left lead, as Stephen advised last week, to help keep him straight. I ask Barrett to raise the jumps. I keep my cool and Calvin keeps his. For the horse that loves to train, I wouldn't expect less. Only two rails come down, both off tight turns, more mine than his. I get so worried about seeing my distance off turns that I tend to lose my outside leg and coast—looking, looking—and killing the Hemi.

Barrett doesn't have much to say. He positions himself on the apex of a right-hand turn, so Calvin and I have to either go around him and not cut our turn, or run him over.

Laura, one of our boarders, shows up for my jump school on Shiva. I explain to her that the warm-up fence—ground pole, nine feet, vertical, nine feet, ground pole—is not producing the effect I'd hoped for. I had wanted the exercise to encourage more roundness in Shiva's jump, but it has shortened his canter to an eight-or nine-foot stride—so up and down and bouncy that it makes it hard to see my distance and has given me only one option: lengthen the step. It all works out in the end, and later in the school we talk about Shiva's form and his tendency to lift his head and drop his back as he approaches each fence, thereby producing a flatter jump. My gut feeling is that this horse has all the scope he needs if I can get him to better use himself.

Two successful jump schools. I finish before the temperature plummets. The snow will be sticking around for a while. Time to pull out the snowshoes, ice skates, and sleds. Almost time to head south.

The tractor coughs and grumbles awake, and Roberto spends the end of the day trolling up and down the driveway, using the bucket of the tractor as a snow blade to remove what doesn't exist in El Salvador.

TRAINS ARE EITHER LATE, CANCELED, OR SOLD OUT. I AM SCHEDULED to meet Chance at 1:30, but my 10:04 is kyboshed. A control freak's worst nightmare. Well, at least the bad weather has given me permission to be out of control. I buy a ticket for a later train and sneak onto the 9:30, which has been delayed till 10:00.

Julia: *Hope the conductor doesn't toss me into a snowdrift.*

The ticket inspector frowns at my ticket and asks if I have any other paperwork. I try to look innocent, which is a hard chore for my open-book face. I'm a good girl, always have been. He mumbles something about having to talk to the conductor, then leaves me alone for the rest of the trip.

If it's one degree it's a hundred in my coach car, and whether there's a malfunction or we're all heating up the train with our communal anxiety to get to our daughters is hard to say. I'd rather be in the GE tunnel. At least I'd be by myself.

We grind to a halt. There's a track switch failure south of Philadelphia. We start moving again, only to wait in the station another half hour while a mechanic comes aboard to adjust the heat. I'd like to suggest we just open the windows and get going, but it's unlikely the window latches work, either. Another example of our ridiculous economy, griping about no jobs and never enough, while blasting rail transportation with too much heat. The worst is coming anyway—the stores and restaurants and hotels of NYC, all set in the mid-80s when it's barely 20 degrees outside. Here comes my winter cold.

The taxi struggles in bumper-to-bumper traffic. I swoon with car sickness in the back seat.

Chance: *Are you here yet?*

Chance: *Where are you now?*

Chance: *Are you in a taxi?*

Chance: *What street sign do you see?*

I glean Chance's excitement to see me. This is our best-kept secret: no matter the antagonisms between us, we adore each other. I know how much she looks forward to my visits. And much like her mother, Chance is always impatient.

The taxi lurches to a stop at a warehouse. I tiptoe up the slushy curb onto the sidewalk and enter the grungy metal door. New York restaurants can't thrive unless they offer something distressed or un–New York— Mexican sushi, hand-frosted cupcakes, southwestern décor—cacti and palm trees—or a restaurant that from the outside looks more like it manufactures steel than kale omelets and superfood smoothies.

I like to know what's in my drink by its name alone: vodka tonic, Chardonnay. No Zombies or Fog Cutters for this one.

My twenty-eight-year-old daughter looks about fifteen in her pointy ski cap, black leggings, and pea coat. I'm glad she's drinking some exotic fruit juice concoction with wheat grass and asparagus, rather than a mimosa, which saves me from vouching for her age as she flips out her ID.

I request the lightest dish I can find on the menu—carrot and avocado salad with lentil soup—and pick at it for over an hour. Good old Chance, all 5'2", 110 pounds of her, orders an elk burger and tears into it like a dire wolf.

"That's the great thing about running," she says. "I can eat anything I want now."

Tiny Chance has always been a fitness maven, but in recent months she has taken up running with a fervor that would impress the Prophet.

"I'm trying to qualify for the New York Marathon this year," she offers between jawfuls.

I casually praise her efforts while wondering how far this recent plan will go. I know nothing about human race running, though I do know a little something about conditioning for endurance and qualifying for an event. I know about the grit it takes to set sights on a nearly impossible goal.

Off to the spa for hoof treatments, and then—checking my watch—to the hotel for some fortifying grape juice. Then back onto frigid streets to make our reservation at Loco Morandi. The maître d' presents us with some amazing gooey-cheesy thing. We dive into it.

"What do you have in the way of Chardonnay by the glass?" I ask the frantic bartender across suits and ties and bejeweled fingers. He looks at me as if I've said a dirty word. I forget his name as soon as he utters it, which I never really hear anyway over the clatter and close, noisy quarters of the busy restaurant, full of boisterous gluttons, though it is already two hours before midnight.

The waiter tries to convince us to order several dishes and to share. I overreact with a resounding guffaw, elaborating how I absolutely do not like to share. Chance and I end up ordering the same dish, a salad that has so many ingredients I've no idea what I'm eating. I think fennel and something called Baquieu—handpicked by the three remaining virgins in Sicily—and who knows what else. Then a scallop dish. I need a periscope to find the seafood in among the greens. We're stuffed, and have to find room for the two dishes of apple strudel that are brought to our table—two instead of one, I suppose, because of my earlier orneriness. Chance has no problem polishing off hers plus half of mine. Maybe I should take up running.

We hail a taxi. I ask if she'll visit Barrett while I'm in Aiken. I'm worried about leaving him so soon after his hospital stay. She hesitantly says she will, but it feels like she's agreeing to it just to agree, with no intention of actually going through with the visit. Says she's crazy busy at work, is on deadline for a couple of grant applications, and has a race coming up. She wants to qualify for the marathon outright so that she won't be at the mercy of the lottery system. Maybe she's just plain too much like me: a woman with a program that only begrudgingly includes taking care of family. If she ever had a soft heart, living in New York has hardened it. Or maybe it's just that Chance has lived too long alone. I exit the taxi at the hotel, and Chance continues to Brooklyn Heights.

Mission accomplished: I've wined and dined my daughter before my annual sojourn to Aiken. At least Chance won't starve for the next few days. It feels too much like a duty done, though, rather than a connection made. I long to get lost in conversation with my daughter, to be engrossed in a subject, rather than always being slightly on the defensive.

I'm awakened by raucous goings-on in the room across the way. Various male voices laughing and shouting, and one rich baritone breaking into the troubadour song from *Carmen*. I first think an after-show Met party, until I smell cigarette smoke wafting under my door. I call the front desk to complain about the noise and smoke. A half hour later, there's a knock on my door. "Guest Services." I question whether to open, shuffling to the door in the blue leopard-print PJs I gave myself for Christmas, rumpled hair, and puffy face belying my own opera. "A candle for you, madam," the valet says, obsequiously.

"A candle?" I mumble.

"To help with the smoke," he explains.

That's New York for you. Rather than fix what's wrong, it becomes all about how to make what's wrong be more chic.

Where is the security guard, the reprimand, the sound of suitcases rolling down the hallway, the purr of an ionizer?

"Hotels are for sleeping," the manager explains to me by way of apology.

He offers me a free night's stay. I'll take it, gladly. But not the jerky, nauseating cab ride to Penn Station, the thick, noisy traffic, nor having to hoof it the rest of the slushy way to catch my train, not the elbow-to-elbow Dead Sea of humanity as I wait for delayed and canceled trains—a piped Yo-Yo Ma's unaccompanied cello failing to soothe my restiveness, as Penn Station tries to be cultured and elitist. Ha! Nor the train I finally get on with Standing Room Only. *All aboard.*

It's 4:00 in the snowy afternoon by the time I arrive home, skating down the driveway in the tin can. I layer up and trudge out to the barn to check on Calvin and Shiva, my boots crunching on the packed surface. It's as quiet as a tomb at the farm; the snow hushes the world, and no one has ventured out—a great excuse not to ride for the farm's fair-weather equestrians who'd rather be snuggling by a fire on a bitter-cold Friday evening. In just hours, I've gone from elbow-butting city claustrophobic to dancer, waltzing around the indoor with Calvin, all by ourselves. No jumps or other horses in the ring, we swing back and forth, leg-yielding at the canter across the ring, sometimes changing, sometimes not, until Calvin relaxes into what I know and love best, riding him like the ghost I've tried my whole life to become, the Charlotte of myself.

I dread the thought of leaving Maryland. How can I leave Barrett alone with his row of scripts and TB sweats? Every day, it is harder for Daisy to heave herself to standing; every day, I can feel another rib on Fuzzy.

After I gorge on Chef Boyardee pizza, the old cat jumps up on the couch, dragging her hind end behind her, to do the "Marching to Pretoria" song on my chest. Her face is touching mine, and she vacantly stares at my nose.

"Fuzzy feels like she's gained a little weight," I say to Barrett, as I finger only four ribs of her eight total.

She'll be twenty-one this spring. Those old sharks of indecision start circling again, always made hungrier at nighttime once darkness has settled into place. I crumple my Aiken plans into a ball and toss them in the trash.

By morning, I'm rummaging through the trashcan. I acquire promises from both John and Chance to visit Barrett in my absence. I start plotting what to pack, when to pick up the prescriptions, get to the dentist for various filling replacements for my bad ivory, touch up the gray hair before Barrett notices it, get the health certificates, spring vaccinations, Julia's TB test, meet with solar rep number two, do February board bills, pick up the Pentosan along with more syringes and needles.

South Carolina is home to Andersonville Prison, where one of my greats spent a summer or two. Most states with blue laws still haven't legalized weed, so I bake half my stash into chocolate brownies, a little going a long way.

CALVIN BOPS THROUGH THE TROT GRID. I FOCUS ON LANDING ON the left lead, which works pretty well, as long as I remember which way is left.

"I've got a sinister idea," I say, folding my right stirrup over my saddle. If I take the right one away, most of my leg weight will go into my left stirrup, causing the horse to go left.

"Let's not cure chaos with chaos," my husband advises. He crouches to pick a few more stones out of the footing in between my passes through the gymnastic. I worry Barrett would rather be at his desk than helping me. His indifference, which is a natural pushback against my single-minded frenzy, makes me sad. My maximalism he meets with a kind of minimalism—a path he probably feels he must take to balance mine. Still, I want him to be as excited as I am when I have a new idea in the saddle. My equestrian self is a little lonely; I long for a riding partner.

I try the stirruplessness, despite Barrett's caution, and Calvin jumps as straight as a ruler through the canter-bounce grid.

In the afternoon, April sets fences for Shiva. She smartly suggests that the nine-foot guide rail in the trot grid be squeezed to eight feet, which encourages Shiva to get up closer to the crossrail, to take that last trot step rather than launching. I feel Shiva's try as he trots in and pushes off, negotiating the first part of the gymnastic before lifting his withers and rounding over the final oxer.

"You've made my day!" I tell her brightly.

WINTER STORM LEON BARRELS ITS WAY UP THE SOUTHEAST COAST.

Kittie Wilkins: *Are you on the road yet?*

Kittie: *Packing yet?*

Julia: *Remember, I grew up south of Buffalo. No worries, I can drive through anything.*

"Have you heard of the Weather Channel?" I call to Barrett, who's dozing on the couch in the family room in a heap of dying cats and dogs.

"Don't believe them," he mumbles. "They're just trying to make it look bad to get you to keep watching their channel."

The chief of stables at Ah-Fuck-It Farm goes back to sleep. I pack and lift and haul, until every molecule in my body is burning.

BARRETT WAKES UP ON THE COUCH IN A HOT FLASH. HE GRIMACES A pained "Morning," then hits the head to deposit a few drops of magenta. I remind myself to calm down, review with him what he ate yesterday, tell him to take it easy.

The Ghost: *Tomorrow looks dreadful.*

Julia: *Since when have they started naming winter storms?*

Endless packing. After his morning protein infusion, Barrett vomits it back up.

"Oh, God, no!" I yell from the kitchen.

"I feel better now," he lies, ashen and watery eyed.

"How do you feel?" I ask him on the half hour, as I continue packing. "Same as last time you asked," he says.

I trudge up and down the driveway with endless loads. The shaggy oldsters are huddled around a new round bale—Huey, Surf, and Miro— happy as long as they've got the next mouthful in front of them, in the form of an eight-hundred-pound flying saucer that has landed in the middle of their snowy Sea of Tranquility. This is why there are tides.

Huey and Surf take a break from their grazing to frolic, playing grabby halter with each other, Surf getting ahold of Huey's, Huey grabbing Surf's—a game they've played together ever since Surf came to us as a gangly yearling twenty years ago. Before he went off to the races. Before hard-knockin' Huey retired from racing to become an event horse, completing a Three Star with me at the age of eighteen. Before giant Surf— even taller than Calvin—completed his own Two Star, probably one of the tallest horses ever to do so. It's the small things that endure, the frissons of joy; the image of a happy shadow hovering over a crib, the unique sweet-tartness of a childhood salad dressing whose recipe is long lost, the uninhabited musty smell of the third floor in grandmother's house, a perfect playhouse for children. Two young horses galloping around their paddock, stopping and spinning, rearing, coming down, grabbing at each other's faces for joy alone.

I watch for a few seconds, or twenty, or thirty, and those seconds are a handful of stars easing the stress of sorting and packing and lifting and positioning bags and boxes, blankets and saddles, and bridles and halters all jockeying for room—hay, feed, tack, buckets, and all the other accoutrements I'll need for three horses plus Cleopatra's month away from home— everything but the cobra. I take my entire wardrobe with me—and adding two 1,200-pound creatures onto my extravagant caravan magnifies my problem by, well, by about 2,400 pounds. I don't travel, my farm does. At 8:00, I collapse on the couch, and with only a few more trunks to go, I warm up night number two of leftover Indian food while Barrett simmers a can of chicken soup—and promptly runs to the bathroom to throw it up. It's a lost cause, Ishmael's dilemma. I demand that we jump ship.

I SLEEP IN TILL 6:30. WHAT'S THE POINT OF AN EARLIER RISE, SINCE we're no longer leaving today? Downstairs, Barrett has a different headset.

"I had an egg an hour ago," he says. "If I can keep that down, I say we go."

Eventing, if nothing else, teaches a person to be flexible.

Half an hour later, Barrett is still pretending to smile, so I leave my cup of half-drunk coffee and hike upstairs to throw more things into my bottomless pits.

We inch down our icy driveway in four-wheel drive by 9:00, the herd all accounted for. At least we hope so. It's not an ideal time to start a ten-hour trip along the Eastern Seaboard, but at least we've bypassed the Baltimore and DC rush hours.

We come to an impasse ten miles from home on the Baltimore Beltway. It's safe to say that it's always rush hour on these East Coast thoroughfares.

We get moving again, only to be stopped and started several more times between DC and Richmond. At a gas station near the Stonewall Jackson shrine, Barrett heaves up some blood onto a snowbank.

"Don't worry," he says to a trucker. "It will melt."

Then it's smooth sailing to Aiken. Except that the truck thermometer never registers above 20 degrees. We arrive to a shocked, snow-covered South Carolina. These palm trees have probably never seen such haints.

"What kind of hellish weather did you bring with you?" the Ghost mock-accuses, poking his head out of his camper.

"At least it's not mud," I say.

Barrett and I wouldn't last a night in such cramped quarters, both of us accustomed to the luxury of eighty-three acres to get away from each other. It's part of what has made our marriage strong.

It's a wonder we're here at all, I think, glancing over at my husband.

THE RENTAL RANCHER IS BIGGER THAN OUR OWN HOUSE, AND Georgia runs around exploring. When she tries and fails to scooch under the bed—her favorite trick back home—she looks over her shoulder at me with disdain.

Georgia: *How could you take away my cave?*

The house has a distinct Seventies feel—a long one-story brick-and-cinderblock rancher that snakes its way from room to room, suggestive of an era when loads of space and privacy meant luxury. In the kitchen, flowerpots hanging from macramé slings, Formica countertops, an old shiny hedgehog of a Westinghouse toaster, sliding glass doors leading out to an oversized deck, a dark leathery den right off the kitchen, wall-to-wall shag carpeting running throughout the house. I scroll my iTunes library to Joan Baez and Joni Mitchell, to "Diamonds and Rust" and "California."

The house is on a "flagpole" lot, accessed by a power grid channel. Through the tall, spindly pines on one side I can see a renovated plantation off adjacent Outaways Road. Weird. Through more trees on the other side, a revival campground owned by the nearby megachurch. Here, in my 1970s, I feel equally surrounded by Big God and slavery. And then Barrett and Georgia find another house—two stories, Victorian, abandoned on the far side of the revival—the perfect place for the Blair Witch to spend her winter.

The trailer ride has joined Calvin and Shiva at the hip. When I get on Shiva to trot him around the field, the two horses scream for each other. Their old friend Patrick stands in his turnout paddock, which is about the size of a slightly overgrown box stall. The MO is function over aesthetic, safety over turnout. The Ghost theorizes that horses are less likely to hurt themselves in a smaller space. My horses are accustomed to a huge pasture with the freedom to investigate a larger world and constantly stretch their legs. For me, the risk of injury is worth the luxury of space. I'm worried about their new digs in Aiken. I knew what I was getting them into before we arrived, figuring the trade-off—my ability to get home on a minute's notice, plus the Ghost's promise of help with stalls by one of his crew—is worth the horses' cramped turnout.

Patrick feels about as stiff as he ever did on the flat, but at least he goes to work and doesn't put up a fuss. Calvin is his usual worker-bee self in his repeated trot trips around the field.

By midafternoon, most of the snow has melted. The Ghost asks if I'm ready to head over to Sandy Hills Farm for a cross-country school. I find Barrett on the other side of the barn, deep in conversation with someone who has also just arrived from the snowier North.

"Do you remember me talking about Chantal, who worked with me in Fulton?"

I scratch my memory. He waves his arm in Chantal's direction as if he's introducing her on stage. When we return to our side of the barn, Barrett excitedly reminisces about the Chantal he remembers, about a hundred pounds heavier and twenty years younger. The cowboys at the Thoroughbred breeding farm were obsessed with Chantal's sexuality—breasts, butt, smile. This is what happens to men working in a small space together. The Chantal of today is a middle-aged woman like me, with a pretty smile. After leaving the track she went into the army. She's a captain now. But she still likes to talk about racehorses. I have to peel my husband away from this phantasm of his younger days.

Shiva has not seen a cross-country jump in three months. Little does he know that, in the interim, cross-country fences have grown white moss. At nearby Sandy Hills Farm, though the snow has disappeared from the footing, it still covers most of the jumps. For a spooky horse like Shiva, this has the makings of a monstrous school, but only once do I feel that subtle stall in front of a particularly shrouded table, where he spits out the contact and puts in another stride before jumping the jump. At least he goes. The Ghost suggests that when I feel the pause, I should add more leg.

"Support him," he says, "without letting him go."

The school is typically short and the sun has started to set by the time we get back—which means that the 40 degrees this day has accumulated start plummeting. As I'm cleaning tack, my hands burn with the cold. I look at their chaffed, crooked redness. *Whose ugly hands are these?*

Esther pulls up with her empty rig to join her pony, who has, like Patrick, been in the Ghost's boot camp for a month. Hugs, hugs. Long drive and all that.

"Wait till you see the house," I say. "It's huge!" Smiley faces all around. Plans for dinner, for videoing, for Sporting Days Horse Trials, where we will both be competing this weekend, plans for a whopping good time.

ESTHER PUTS A FOOT IN THE STIRRUP. I MOUNT SHIVA AND WALK OFF. I hear a yelp and turn around in the saddle. Esther is tilting sideways. Down she goes, her horse bucking and galloping off. She pops up right away. Big sigh.

"Are you ok?" I yell at her back, as she trudges off to catch her horse.

"I think so, but am I ever pissed."

When falling from a horse, anger is usually a good sign. The horse caught, I call for Barrett to come help. Where's Barrett?

"I think I better lunge him first," Esther says smartly.

I continue my ride on Shiva, wondering where Barrett got to. Probably off with Chantal eating brownies. Minutes later, I'm surprised to see our truck speeding down the driveway, Esther in the passenger seat. Barrett gets out to talk to me. He's got a dour look about him.

"She can't remember what just happened. Or when she got to Aiken. Or much of anything, really. Though I've told her about five times over already."

"What just happened to me?" she calls from the truck.

"You fell off your horse," I say.

"How long have I been here?" she asks.

Barrett rushes her to the regional hospital. They diagnose a concussion. Esther is in the midst of "repeating syndrome."

I get several phone calls from Barrett updating me on her current condition. "She keeps asking what year it is," he says, "and whether she had her helmet on. The doctors are trying to convince her that she didn't have it on."

"That's ridiculous," I say. "I saw the whole thing. She most definitely had her helmet on!"

There are three missed calls from Esther awaiting me after a jump school on Patrick, who is enthusiastic bordering on out of control. I call her back. "My parents just got here," she says. "They're keeping me overnight in the hospital for observation. The doctors want to know whether I was wearing my helmet. Was I?"

"Of course you were wearing your helmet," I reassure her.

"That's what I thought. My parents just got here," she repeats herself. "My mother wants to talk to you. Was I wearing my helmet?" she asks again.

"Yes," I say again.

"That's what I thought. I'll tell my mother that. My parents just got here."

"Let me speak to your mother," I suggest.

"My mother wants to talk to you," she says.

Her mother's timbre is exactly like her daughter's, and though she hasn't fallen from a horse, she seems to have the same problem with an endless cycle of repeated questions.

"Was she wearing her helmet?" Esther's mother asks.

"Yes!" I say, perhaps a little too emphatically this sixth time.

"We just arrived," she explains.

"Yes, I know," I say.

"They are going to keep her overnight."

"Yes," I say.

"For observation."

"Yes."

"Could you tell me what happened?" she asks.

I relate the story again.

"Did they ever find her helmet?" she asks.

Chapter Five

A Long-Dead Raccoon Buried in the Corner of My Brain

THE PART OF THE BRAIN RESPONSIBLE FOR SENDING A TEXT IS DIFFI-
cult to concuss. Messages fly on my way to Sporting Days Farm Horse
Trials. Esther is no longer repeating herself, although she has no memory
of arriving in South Carolina. After her hospital discharge, she plans on
driving back home with her parents. Her horse will remain with the Ghost.

Not enough impulsion, the judge concludes about Shiva's dressage test.
Needs to be ridden more forward for the scores to go up.

He's good in stadium, though he does have one rail in the triple combination, kissing the third element just hard enough to bring it down.

I put on the dressage bridle for cross-country, so that the kind Nathe
bit won't interfere with his sensitive mouth. He finishes double clear, with
no jump penalties and under the time.

When I return to the barn, Calvin is eager to trot and canter around
the farm's perimeter and then do a little flatwork. Patrick, on the other
hand, does not want to put his head down and accept the bridle. He
refuses to bend. He especially doesn't want to canter left. Motion is imper-
manent, but Patrick was built by a mason. It's like trying to ride a building.

Barrett is convinced that I should scratch Patrick from Full Gallop
Horse Trials. I'm not sure how I am going to be able to canter around one
of those small dressage rings with whatever gait the horse gave me today.
But it's only Saturday. The stubborn sparrow in my heart is ever hopeful I
can soften him by Wednesday.

I DRIVE BARRETT TO THE COLUMBIA AIRPORT, THEN HOOK UP WITH
the Ghost at Sandy Hills. Patrick attacks each fence, as if he were trying to

kill it rather than jump it. He breaks his canter rhythm and surges before his fences. We both see his shadow in today's bright sunshine. Back in his training hole he goes for six more weeks of lunging.

I hop on Calvin and readjust my aids. Calvin is game without being rude to his practice cross-country jumps. Both schools last only about fifteen minutes—which the Ghost feels is all they need.

I long for my day to be done, but I need to get the horses back to the barn, cleaned up, fed, and settled for the night. When we pull into the driveway, Shiva is executing airs above the ground from his tiny paddock—he is so tickled to see the rig pull in, and hungry.

As I'm heading back to the rental, John calls, beside himself with excitement to tell me more news of Charlotte, as well as of his first movie recording.

"She remarried a man named Richard Cox Tracey in 1876," he says. "And they stayed in the house. Her father and brothers and husband all farmed the land. It remained in the Tracey family until you bought it."

After twenty years, we are still newcomers, passers-through. No family tenacity here, with John settled in California and Chance having made a beeline to the city as soon as she picked up her high school diploma.

The film is called *Basmati Blues*, about an American woman traveling to India. John and his musician colleagues provided the soundtrack for the film. I wonder if Barrett can see our son executing his own capriole through the panic of his small round Delta window.

I WARM UP CALVIN FOR A LESSON WITH JO YOUNG. JO'S FARM IS A small distance from Aiken—twenty-five miles—but these are Georgialina miles. Long, slow, and often unpaved, with a flat horizon of cotton and peanut fields, and tall pines that waver in the incalculable distance, as if an hour could hold a lifetime of doubt.

"Do you have a plan, Julia?" my FEI dressage judge asks, suspiciously.

I'm more than a little played out on the concept of goal making. Probably my best shot is to return to the nineteenth century.

"I don't really have a goal," I say slowly, pulling out the syllables as if they were bits of last night's beef stuck between my molars. "Except, maybe—you know what I'd really like to do?" I ask, as if thinking of it for the first time.

My sincerity stops her. "What, Julia, what would you like to do?"

"I'd like to improve," I say.

"That seems like a reasonable goal," she says. Jo suffers from a slight nervous tremor that causes her head to trill, like Katherine Hepburn's. This one must surely understand small, careful progress.

"I'm tired of accumulating FEI stars," I say. "I'd rather focus on something less artificial. Or maybe something more attainable. Like having some fun?"

At some point, it's not about prizes. At least not ones you can touch or publish, or prove to the world. "What does it all mean?" a literary pal used to ask, over and over, half joking, half serious, when we were drunk and in love with literature at twenty-five, then tracked in our lives at forty, and disbelieving of how long we'd lived at fifty. Approaching sixty, I imagine he is still asking himself. Some questions are not meant to be answered, only asked again and again. Why do people hate other people? Why do people keep repeating efforts when the odds aren't in their favor? Why do leaders wear fur coats and pretend the planet isn't warming?

We have a great lesson, and Jo seems pleased with the progress Calvin and I have made on the flat in the past year.

Having lunged and flatted and jumped Patrick, run to the tack store, taken Patrick over to Kittie's barn to be clipped, hacked Shiva, and driven the miles to Williston for a dressage lesson, I'm not back at the Ghost's barn until almost 7:00. I have yet to do barn chores. At 9:00, my only goal is to strain bits of cork out of a bottle of Chardonnay.

HERE YOU ARE AGAIN, OLD FRIEND. AS IF I WEIGH ONE THOUSAND pounds, I force each limb to go through the motions of riding three horses. Nothing makes sense. Nothing seems bearable. The horses used to be the best antidepressant in the world. Now, they are part of the problem. I tell myself: If I just keep moving, I'll be ok. A decades-old motto, as if checking off a to-do list could take the place of Cymbalta. Still, I am exhausted and feel detached from my surroundings, even as Calvin jumps well.

"Let's stop before we screw something up," the Ghost says. The wind picks up, someone looking over my shoulder.

The Ghost no longer seems excited about Calvin's progress. Probably the horse has disappointed him one too many times. I feel the same way, and yet I keep on. The Horse That Loves to Train is training brilliantly, but that's not to say he won't unravel under pressure. He knows what competition means. He knows when he's on stage and his performance counts—trotting down centerline, hearing the buzzer signaling the start of a show jump round, the timer counting down in the cross-country start box.

Patrick's cross-country and show jumping courses at Full Gallop look doable. I walk each course only once. I've been up since 5:00 a.m., and my hundred-pound feet won't budge another inch.

I WAKE AT 4:00 A.M. TO POURING RAIN AND DENSE FOG. GEORGIA plants her front feet on the truck seat and looks back at me imploringly: *It's too early for this.* In objection to my request to hop in, she asks for my assistance. I heave her into the truck. My back screams.

Patrick is pissed to be on the trailer alone. He starts to paw and doesn't stop. We pull into Full Gallop, and he continues to dig a hole in the trailer. He's impatient yet reluctant to do anything. A loner who wants company on the trailer but dislikes sharing a paddock. Rather than empathize with someone's problem, he'd rather solve it his way to get it over with and on to the next equation. I might as well be competing myself. Our darkness is a long-dead raccoon buried in the corner of my brain.

I lunge Patrick in a downpour, get on him in same, warm up, same. In the test, I lose some of his rideability, but all in all, things go smoothly. Halfway through the canter work, I forget the next movement. The judge whistles, signaling we've gone off course. I know what I've done wrong. I finish the corrected test and exit, kicking myself instead of the horse.

In show jumping, Patrick backs off the first fence. I start riding aggressively. I hear a number of ticks, but I will myself not to look back to see how many rails come down. I still don't know why I can't get on those scales. Where is Barrett to offer some signature remark about the difference between aggressive and assertive riding?

At the coffin jump on cross-country, Patrick launches over the double chevron, making too quick work of the ditch. He needs to put in a stride between the ditch and the single chevron out, but there's barely enough room. He bulges right to create more space in the distance. The run-out to the right is calling his name. But he has his eye on the fence, does some quick footwork, and opts to jump. My right leg hits the flag and knocks it down—but we're between the flags, and so we continue on to the next fence, and the next and the next.

"He's one hell of a cross-country horse," I admit to the Ghost back at the barn.

He agrees.

On my way to the rental, I pass one Baptist church, lights blazing and the parking lot full despite it being midweek. Same at the Cedar Creek Church right across from the rental's driveway. Ash Wednesday. When was the last time I had a cross drawn in ashes on my forehead? Probably not since I was about twelve, two years before the walk on the moon. That was a lot of ashes ago. What would I choose to give up for Lent if I were wanting to give something up? Alcohol? Eventing? A part of me wants to go inside the church and sit for a while. Just sit. That's what it would be: I would give up being in a hurry. Pressing on to the next task in order to have a feeling of accomplishment, to prove to the world that I'm worth something—and so I won't feel so sad.

IT'S PITCH DARK AND THE BALL WON'T GO IN THE SOCKET. I NEED octopus arms to get the job done, but there's only me with my two, and black ink for camouflage. I finally manage to jimmy the hitch and get the ball secured, and off I go, with my only friend the Talking Girl, and my dog sound asleep in the back seat. It would appear the Talking Girl has never been to this part of Georgia: she tells me I've reached my destination as I'm looking at a field of cows. Brooklyn Baby style, I pull off the road and hail the next cab. The Georgian gent drawls so thick I have to bend toward the truck window and ask him to repeat the directions. Maybe he thought I said "elections."

"Who is that?" he says, hearing the Talking Girl.

"I'm with her," I say.

I turn the rig around in the middle of the road, follow the drawl's lead, and arrive at the event.

Disorientation is my game for separating myself from fate. If I can't get there, then it won't happen. The flip side of being a control freak and only wanting what I can have my own way is a fetish for out-of-control scenarios that will take me out of the game altogether. At Pine Top Farm, I've made so many errors over the years. I've twice left the farm in an ambulance, been eliminated, gotten lost on cross-country and in show jumping, and embarrassed myself in the dressage ring multiple times. Eventing is a sport that goes everywhere, without you having to leave anything behind. I have everything to prove to myself and everything to lose. I can't help myself. I am an eventing junkie. That dirty needle gives me so much release.

Calvin spooks in the turn off centerline in his dressage test. I settle him, except for a few tense moments in the simple change work. It's an improvement because I'm able to canter him in the ring without feeling like he's bolting. Such show nerves my poor Cal gets. I can hear it in his big gulps of air, and in his new habit of hyperventilating when I cinch his girth.

I try my new show jumping warm-up strategy—just five or six jumps in preparation, and then I ask the Ghost to strip off the weighted boots before going into the ring. It's always a challenging show jumping course at Pine Top, situated in a low, sloping bowl on turf. As soon as I feel the power and scope of Calvin's first jump, I know I have a horse today. Calvin is determined not to touch a rail and gives me a clean trip. Before I even leave the ring, I'm giggling out loud. Everyone in McDuffie County knows how I feel about my Intermediate round.

Calvin is one of the last horses of the day to go cross-country. He gallops out of the start box a bit too briskly, and remains strong around the course. I allow him a little speed because he's jumping well; I trust him, and I'm able to get him back enough so he can negotiate the combinations. When he doesn't hesitate at the first water complex, I know I have him.

"You must be thrilled," the Ghost says.

"I am," I say, beaming.

The course designer is tacking up a horse in one of the little turnout paddocks. I wave from the trailer and head over to say hi. He's getting on Redmond's cousin, a young horse that he called me about last summer. He has Redmond's signature bushy forelock and huge tail. That's about the only resemblance, except, perhaps, for a similar look of eagles in his eye. He trots and canters around the field, and I scrunch up my face and raise my eyebrows, trying to indicate *well, maybe not brilliant, but good enough*, referring to the quality of his gaits. I coax him to bring the horse back in two weeks for the next Pine Top event, where Calvin will be running Advanced. I'd like to see this one jump.

I ACHE FROM STEM TO STERN, AS MY MOTHER USED TO SAY, WHO relished imbuing her pain with naval jargon. Patrick's left hind leg has taken on water. I spend my morning icing and wrapping and bute-ing, calling Barrett for the correct antibiotic dosages, and then scrounging up the drugs and syringes and needles. I'm supposed to show both Patrick and Shiva to clients of Kate Chadderton on Tuesday. Between the swollen leg and the rain rot crud he's got all over his body from southern living, things aren't looking good for Patrick's potential sale. He's sound nonetheless, so I lunge him and ride him lightly, and the leg seems better for the motion. Something I learned from Barrett: if a horse is injured in a small space, often the remedy is a larger one, and vice versa.

Calvin's legs are cool and tight, indicating he came out of Pine Top well.

I call Barrett to discuss whether I should enter Shiva at the next Pine Top, along with Cal. Why doesn't he fly down for that weekend? Then we can drive home together a few days early, in time for him to rest up for his trip to Seattle the following weekend.

"We just had shrimp for breakfast," he tells me.

"We?" I say.

"Chance and I," he says.

Chance has gone home to check up on Barrett.

"She wolfed down an entire plate of shrimp benedict, and then ate half of mine at Woodberry Kitchen. And her play was hysterical," he adds.

"Her play?"

"Remember the one-minute play festival? One of her plays was picked."

I enter the bank, fill out a withdrawal slip: Phew, the money's there. Chance would never go to Baltimore just to go home; there's always got to be another reason. Even so, thank you, Chance, for being there in my stead.

"Oh, yeah," I remember casually. "Wasn't that the one about the two knees talking?"

"No, it takes place in a beauty parlor."

He reminds me of a reading he has in Philly on the 15th, then of the conference he is obligated to attend during Pine Top weekend. He's being paid to speak about the poetry of anger.

I'm frustrated flying solo, I'm tired, and I want to go home. Instead, I hang up on Barrett and refuse to pick up when he calls back. The least my husband could do is give me a commission, or split his poetry of anger paycheck with me. I feel like rancid meat, even after a nearly perfect run on Calvin.

I know what I need: a hack. I load Shiva in the rig and drag Georgia into the truck.

Because I'm concerned about getting lost in Hitchcock Woods' two thousand acres, we go straight in one direction for a while before turning around and retracing our steps. Shiva is a good boy, until we turn toward home and his nickel runs out. He jigs his way back to the rig, my clacking molars getting a workout. When I half halt, he shortens the jig—a decent passage is just another whistle away.

Riding in Hitchcock Woods

Bending my head
over Cal's bony withers,
I fan the map
with its cobweb of trails,
lacing together this green inferno.

If I'm lucky, hoofbeats,
and someone pointing our way.
If I'm lucky,
slackening the reins will work.

Good horse, Cal chooses the path
bedded with chestnut needles,
and sentried by longleaf pines
sighing over us.

I glance over my shoulder,
but there's only the past
trying to catch up,
and failing.

I'm desperate for my horses in their thumbnail turnout pens. Prevented from socializing by their isolation, the horses, all twenty-five of them, just stand around sizing each other up, eating hay and shitting in their sandy coops. Orchard grass is only a dream.

I'm reminded of Henry Walter's Laurel stable, how so many of his runners came from our farm, where his clients kept their mares and layups along with ours. Because they knew each other, had leaned against each other, had burst into field gallops together, had known all of nights and stars and suns rising, there was a sense of calm and camaraderie you didn't find in other racing stables. No ulcers, no weaving or cribbing, because the horse next door was likely their pasture mate. They shared the same ghost and were comforted by that in their working life at the track.

"How much do you love me?"

"I wouldn't throw you out of bed," I say to Kittie Wilkins, to get on with the conversation.

"I know of a horse who flunked his $60,000 vetting as a Two-Star horse with a couple Intermediates under his belt. Has an old slab fracture in the knee. Now the owner just wants a good home for the horse," she says. "I proposed a $15,000 lease per year for three years, with an option to buy—after three years, he's yours, if you want him."

Are we talking cars or horses? In a couple of phrases, a giveaway to a good home turns into an expensive prospect. Even so, I agree to look at the hotrod Lincoln.

Minutes before the horse is due to arrive, a text comes in from Kittie's husband, who is battling a blizzard in southeastern Pennsylvania.

She just fell off trying to mount. Hit her head, lost consciousness. She won't be able to make the showing.

A charity case, now a $45,000 official "showing."

I don't want a horse brought this far along. My idiosyncratic style won't permit it. Too much of other people in his training.

"Usually, the better the rider, the worse the management," my husband says from snowy Baltimore, heading to a poetry reading in Hampden. "Good jocks can get by without knowing which end of a horse shits and which end bites. That's why in racing the trainer is not the jockey. There is only one exception," he says, "or was, anyway. That was John and Ellen Williams. They set the standard for boutique horse operations." Barrett loves anything small. In his mind, the problem with education is that schools have hallways—they should be just one large room with a fireplace at one end and a flagpole in the yard.

This horse is indeed beautiful on the hoof as he emerges from the trailer, all 17.3 buff hands of him. His young owner vaults onto the horse from the ground. My jaw drops. But as soon as the horse picks up a trot, I notice a hitch behind. Is the old fracture a red herring? Draw attention to the knee to overlook unsoundness behind? His owner rides him, the Ghost rides him, and then I get on. He's a nice horse, despite his lameness. The body wears out quicker when you're an almost 18-hand creature, or a 5'10" woman, as I am. Ask Calvin, he'll tell you. That's a lot of spine and leg and bone to hold together on a diet of oats and protein bars.

TREES GROAN FROM THEIR BURDEN OF WATER TURNED TO ICE. Cracking, splintering, falling in enormous whooshes of white. Last night, I drove the truck into the rental's long, woodsy driveway, bushwhacking my belligerent way through limbs and branches already torn from their trees. I hoped the worst of the storm was over. The ostrich meets the bull. Georgia wakes me in the night with restless whining. Trees shatter all around us. I fret and pace and peer out the windows. Every few seconds, the crack and whoosh of another tree. I go back to bed, pull the covers close for protection. Georgia keeps whining and shifting her body against mine. I pick up the phone, call Barrett. It's 2:00 a.m.

"What should I do?" I ask.

"There's nothing you can do," he mumbles through a mouthful of cotton. "Go back to sheep."

"Oh, shut up," I snap, before hanging up on Truman Capote.

The alarm clock goes dark, and the inside temperature creeps south. I move closer to Georgia.

I peek out the door in the morning. A dozen trees have fallen across the drive, including most of the power lines. I call the Ghost. He offers to meet me at the end of the driveway, if I can walk to him without getting electrocuted. It takes him an hour to drive five miles.

We slalom our way around trucks and branches and downed wires, plus small Tetons of windblown snow. South Carolina owns exactly one snowplow, parked in Greenville.

The Ghost doesn't have power at his barn either, so I suggest we put water buckets under the eaves to collect snow melt. Everyone at the barn looks at me like I've got three heads.

Once we've gotten the horses settled in their new Ice Age, I borrow an abandoned truck and raid Home Depot for blankets and candles and flashlights. Georgia and I hunker down in our dark rental, the second night much colder than the first, as the last of internal heat escapes through the walls. In the middle of the night, I root around the house for

145

more blankets. No luck. In an accordion-door closet, I spy a row of kaftans, like what George Harrison and Cat Stevens wore. I pick an orange and brown-striped fandango and yank it over my head. Georgia presses up tight against me when I return to bed. In the morning, I wake to us both shivering.

WE CHECK INTO THE CLARION HOTEL—DOG-FRIENDLY AND WARM. After a day of chipping ice, hauling water, dragging a twenty-meter circle in the Ghost's field so he can get his horses ridden, we go to the rental and pack up, with my new miner's headlamp as guide. I left my home with its indoor arena, its backup generator, its assurance of hot water and light, not to mention the comfort of my Barrett.

Why did I ever?

WHEN I ARRIVE AT THE BARN, THE AISLE IS LINED WITH A REGIMENT of thirsty buckets.

Unlike most everywhere else in Aiken County, Paradise Farm has power.

Patrick rewards my stubbornness by putting in a decent dressage test. I'm worried about show jumping, though, which is on rolling turf. He starts by jumping well, until we get to the triple combination. He cuts the turn, and I neglect to hold him out. Out of sync with my horse, I get ahead of him and climb up his neck. Rails tumble. I exit the ring, shame pressing my tail between my legs.

WRONG WAY WENDELL DOES IT AGAIN. I GET LOST ON THE CHALlenging cross-country course at Paradise. I can't find an innocuous rolltop, one portable fence among a hundred others dotting the open field. Patrick and I lose ten or fifty seconds or so, circling around and retracing our steps, until we find what we're looking for. Not that it matters much—we're not in the running for a ribbon. I'm just glad to have finally found my way. Patrick remains unfazed by both the difficult course and his navigator.

Happy Valentine's Day! I text Chance.

Shame is a form of narcissism, she says, toward the end of our conversation.

STILL NO POWER BACK AT MY DIGS. STILL IN THE CRUMMY HOTEL room with half my stuff lost in the 1970s. I'm driven by order and routine, and without a semblance of either, I'd rather crawl back under the covers—if I had my own covers to crawl under. My body is sore from the relentless pressure I've put on it. My mind feels stagnant. The physical is all that matters.

One foot, one word in front of the other. See what explodes.

After Patrick runs around such a testing track, proving he's almost ready to move up to Intermediate, I reconsider keeping him.

"Give it the twenty-four-hour rule," Barrett advises from afar. Barrett. Barrett and his rules. Always wanting to sleep on it and wake up in the next century. Patrick is not one of his favorites, though he appreciates his gameness.

Already my focus is on next weekend—Cal's Advanced run at Pine Top. And then getting home.

I've talked Barrett into canceling his conference and returning to Aiken on Thursday to see me through Pine Top, and to rescue me from the pits of my current hell. I'm dwindling. It's Julia I'm worried about now. Barrett's poetry of anger will just have to go fuck itself.

GETTING READY TO LEAVE FOR A LATE AFTERNOON DRESSAGE LESSON, I ask the barn guy if he would mind feeding my other two, switching the horses' blankets, and flipping them out.

"No problem with the feeding," he says, "but we have a policy of not changing blankets for the living."

I think of charging rhinoceroses, black-spotted hornet heads, threatened nursing mares. Maybe I should be teaching Barrett's class.

"Whatever," I say, and turn away.

"If we did it for one person, we'd have to do it for everyone, and before we know it, we're spending another couple of hours switching blankets," he says to my back.

He keeps talking. I'm too far away to hear what he's saying. I don't even care about my rudeness.

MY TALKING GIRL IS SILENT AND CONFUSED, AS SICK OF THIS TRIP AS I am. This jaunt to Nowhere on dirt roads is a challenge, even for her, though we've both been here before.

Jo works Calvin and me with precise, demanding dressage exercises that involve ten-meter circles on the centerline and quarterlines, shoulder-in, shoulder-out, and renvers. Always forward, forward, forward. It's an energetic ride, difficult to maintain on Calvin without revving him up too much. I feel on the verge of chaos when I ride with Jo. Calvin can so easily be tipped over the edge into unrideability. It's a tricky balance to discover your inner sense of peace when your horse is discovering his inner freight train.

I tell Jo that I'm going back to Maryland on Sunday.

"Oh, I'm so disappointed," she says. "I'd hoped to have another time or two with you." I suggest I send her videos of my riding to critique, and she gladly agrees. We talk briefly about what happened to me at Jersey Fresh and my fall in the water there.

"That was such an unfortunate incident," she says. "You were riding brilliantly up till then. You should have gone the long way at the water," she goes on. "Nobody rode it well, and particularly after the near-misses that had already come through. You didn't get good advice on that one."

The Ghost never said a word about the option. Nor did I consider it myself.

"Well, it was ridiculous, because I had only one eye to see out of at the time," I explain. Jo looks aghast. At the time, she hadn't known about the eye, only about the uncontrollable nature of my mount. I tell her about my vitrectomy last summer, when the retinal specialist removed all of the jelly from my eyeball and replaced it with ginger ale, or whatever.

"I talked to my colleagues about whether to let you go, after your dressage ride. I encouraged them to allow it, saying that you had qualified, so you should be able to ride. As you were going around the course, Brian Ross turned to me and said, 'She's riding it better than anyone.'"

My neck spasms from sleepless nights on soft mattresses. I can't turn my head while driving or riding. Try backing up a Dodge dually with a neck that won't swivel. Georgia remains disgusted. In order to get her in the truck, I have to put her on a leash and drag her in. She won't budge otherwise. She has also become a stress eater, scavenging morsels of garbage or grain. I know where to find her when I can't find her—in the manure pit. Though I remind her in Dogg's Hamlet several times a day that we will soon be going home, she continues to gorge and gain. She's having about as much fun as I am, without so much as a puddle on the property to wallow in.

We march out to the training field. Calvin is on his toes, but he doesn't know what I know. I have made a pact with Calvin's future: this jump school has to go well for us to continue with our plan.

The Ghost noted something in my riding at Paradise: both Patrick and Calvin drift right when they jump, plus I have been cutting my turns to fences.

I want to say, *That has been going on for centuries.* But what I actually say is, "That's exactly what happened at the triple last weekend."

Like Stephen, he advises holding out on turns. I'm worried I'll overcorrect and start stalling if I do that. Instead, I take a feel of the outside rein, and slightly counter-bend through the turns. I try to meet the Ghost halfway without giving up my resolve.

Cal jumps well, and we keep the twenty-minute school to ten minutes. This session *needs* to be short today, as a sharpener for Pine Top—what trackers would call "a little blow."

Tonight at the Clarion: boisterous revelry. Tree guys congregate from all over the country to take advantage of the disaster that has dropped from the sky in the Aiken area. It will take a chainsaw symphony to clean up Mother Nature's vengeance. In the Clarion's parking lot, barbecues rage on the tailgates of pick-ups, men in plaid shirts and overalls smoke cigarettes and swill Budweiser—it feels like I'm on the *Andrea Gail*, and the enormous school of swordfish has been found and fished, packed away in ice, the men celebrating as they wait for the rest of their lives to unfold. The thrill of working men being blessed with plenty and lonely for wives.

"I like your wolf," one man says, handlebar mustache looking like it came off a bicycle.

I shoo Georgia in the door before I can think to smile and warn him, "She eats men."

I WAKE UP MISSING BROWN DOG, AND I GO TO SLEEP MISSING BROWN Dog. Georgia's recent nervous breakdown reminds me of sweet, paranoid Simon, always the good dog, afraid of doing the wrong thing. I wouldn't say the latter is true of Georgia, but she sure seems worried and stressed lately—and permanently starving. Each time I pry her out of the truck at the hotel, she puts her nose to the parking lot, like a metal detector scavenging for anything that will stick to her ribs.

I get word from the realtor that the power is finally back on at the rental—just in time for my imminent departure. After barn work, a lesson on the flat with the Ghost and Cal, and a late-afternoon cross-country jump school at Paradise Farm on Shiva, I decide to crash at the hotel one more night. Barrett can help me move my things back over to the rental after he arrives.

The Ghost stresses the value of riding slightly off the track in dressage, in order to give the horses more room for correction, especially the big ones, like Cal. Horses are shaped like a piece of pie, with their front ends narrower than their hind ends. Riding too close to the rail, their wedge shape forces them to travel in a crooked haunches-in. Riding the horses' shoulders slightly to the inside of the track straightens them out.

I like being taken to a fence. A horse that has to be kicked along and convinced to jump the jump is not my idea of a fun ride. Usually Shiva clicks along to his fences, unless he sees something he is afraid of—today, it's brush fences set in combination with other fences.

Cross-country schooling at Paradise, he stops at both brush fences. The Ghost admonishes me for being too fast. The younger and/or more insecure the horse, the more time he needs to understand a complicated fence.

The Ghost wants me to ride to the fence, without taking the unnecessary risk of overriding.

"Don't be a hero," the Ghost says. "Don't be a fool with your life. The worst thing that can happen is not a stop."

BARRETT ARRIVES. WE MOVE OUT OF THE CLARION. I GET READY FOR Pine Top.

I lose Calvin for an instant in the second change, but I get through the dressage test with a fairly rideable horse. It doesn't score well—a 46—but still qualifying, if we were trying to qualify for anything. This test was several tics under par, in part because I sacrifice quality for obedience.

I'm not accustomed to having an Advanced horse trial take place all on one day, and to be jumping so quickly after dressage. I get Calvin turned around and head over to show jumping. I start to warm up with Barrett's help. I jump two fences and the Ghost shows up.

"How long have you been down here?" he asks, remotely accusatory. He thinks I start warm-ups too soon and jump too many jumps before I go in the ring.

"Just got here," I lie, then add, more truthfully, "Have only jumped two oxers." He asks me to come to a four-foot oxer, and Cal knocks the back rail. The Ghost tells me to sit up straighter in the tack.

In the ring, Cal's first couple of jumps are ok, but he knocks the third in the line from fence 2 to 3, then knocks one in the combination at 4. One rail I lose track of, and when we approach the triple, he gets there on a good stride but ends up to the right of each element. We have one rail down in the triple and then the last fence at 12, a hangover from his lack of effort at the combination.

"You need to be more vertical with your body," the Ghost corrects. "You can get away with a forward tilt at Intermediate, but at Advanced, you have to use your body as leverage."

I stew whether to go cross-country. I decide that our show jumping performance doesn't warrant it. I ask Barrett to scratch me. I talk to Stephen about it, when I know the Ghost is out of earshot.

"That sounds right," Stephen says, with reserve in his voice, "unless you just want to run around for the mileage." The inference being that any mileage at the Advanced level is good mileage for the amateur rider.

"Ok," the Ghost says, a little later. He's sitting on an overturned bucket, protective vest on, head down, not looking me in the eye. I can tell he wants me to run. I bet he thinks I'm losing my grit. I bet he thinks I need to keep my eye up with another Advanced run.

I spend my time fretting about what I'm going to do or not do, rather than re-walking the course, which is what I should be doing. Barrett seems a little too eager for me to pack up and call it quits. For the first time I understand that my husband would rather I stop with the sport. Or at least with Calvin. No one likes to see their mate fail over and over; no one likes to see the person they love make bad decisions that lead to being unprepared in a dangerous sport.

"Georgia and I are going for a walk," he announces. "Call me in twenty and let me know what you decide."

I call him in ten. "I'm running," I say.

The Ghost buzzes up on his scooter just as I'm walking over to the start box.

"Ride for six strides at the combination at 7," he advises. "Kim Severson got six, and the angled brush fences come up much better."

We gallop out of the box. I lose track of the strides. Calvin is surprised by the angled brush fences and slips out at 7. I look around for my best re-approach and notice Big Brother's blue truck parked there, David O'Connor watching my debacle unfold with bloodshot eyes. If our country is becoming a surveillance state, at least I will have had some experience.

Calvin pops through the combination on the second attempt, takes the individual fences boldly and at speed, plus the first water combination, and finishes the rest of the course.

A RUN-OUT IS NEVER AN INGREDIENT IN MY RECIPE FOR SUCCESS. But when you reach and reach, always a little at the edge of your ability, that's what happens. You have to be willing to fail in order to succeed. That's why they call it dreaming.

On the way back to Aiken, the truck starts heaving every time Barrett uses a turn signal.

"I think there's a short in the electrical system," he warns, getting crankier with each turn. As if none of this would have happened if I'd scratched.

I've asked him to cancel his paying gig to help me fail at Pine Top and get us home. Of course he is not going to be happy. Of course I am disgruntled with a 46 in dressage, five rails, and a run-out. Two negatives make a positive, but what do three negatives make?

A sign on I-20 advertises the Laurel and Hardy Museum. Maybe we should pull off. Seems like an apt comparison; the Fat One and the Skinny One, the Thick and Thin, Whole and Half, Stout and Worrywart—Calvin and me.

Our primary focus now is to find a mechanic in Aiken—holding his hands up and cascading his fingers—willing to work on a Saturday. Ha.

CHANCE SENDS REQUESTS TO EVERYONE IN THE FAMILY THAT WE NO longer text her. She is overwhelmed by the mental static caused by frequent conversational messages. She wants us to call instead. Better yet, write a letter. I hate talking on the telephone, and lord knows in what dark recess my stationary is hiding. Barrett is the only one in her good graces since he doesn't even know how to text. He still uses a flip phone, for Christ's sake. Her cheeky, condescending tone causes quite a stir among the family.

Nothing wrong with her indicator lights.

There's got to be something darker going on. A bad boyfriend. Writer's block. An abscess. Five rails in show jumping. Maybe she is jealous of John's and Mollie's and my easy texting banter, which tries to include Chance but has the opposite effect. I can't seem to get it right.

I STUDY THE VIDEO OF CALVIN'S SHOW JUMP ROUND AT PINE TOP while Barrett drives. He settles in behind a stock trailer hauling pigs. Calvin has the most trouble with related distances. It looks like he's running out of room in the lines, causing him to hit rails. I rarely get his canter right, which screws up the distances. Calvin's canter isn't Mozart, it's Sid Vicious. A noisy, erratic rhythm results in rails. If rhythm is time related and distance is space related, then an inconsistent canter rhythm produces a space-time conundrum. Upset the one, and the other goes crashing.

"Don't you want to get around this guy?" I say to Barrett, still following the pigs, now in Virginia.

I write down the Pine Top show jumping pattern and make plans to replicate it for all three horses later in the week. I'll try no ground rails, and I'll play with compressing and lengthening Calvin's step. And we'll try once again not to hit the rails. Then again, maybe I should send Calvin a letter.

SICK WITH A HEAD COLD, I SLOG MY WAY THROUGH LAUNDRY, PAPERS, and tack, honking my nose as I go. I'm glad to be home, even with piles of snow and snot, and boarders' complaints.

We turn out my three boys together behind the mare barn for their first real turnout in weeks, and they race around like colts, slipping and sliding over the mud and ice. The Ghost would likely be appalled. Freedom can be so treacherous, yet essential. They are happy to be home, having escaped their Gulag. They gallop back and forth across the field until something catches their attention in the next field over—two new mares on the adjacent beach, eyeing up my hot surfer dudes. Even pleasure horses know athletes when they see them. My horses will get the day off, while I nurse my cold and tackle the rest of my life.

From my office, I watch Georgia on her morning constitution in the backyard. She lingers at the edge of the pool, then tiptoes across the snowy cover, nose to the tarp, sniffing for a way in. She makes it across the tiny rink, looking woefully back over her shoulder.

Just a few more weeks, Georgia Cakes, I promise.

Nothing but snow and ice for footing. Then it starts snowing again. I head to the indoor to trot Calvin for a spell, practice a couple of changes, then venture outside. We trudge up and down our back hills—the good fitness of hill work. Calvin slips behind, becoming more mindful of where he is placing his feet so he won't take a tumble. It's a challenge working him in this muck, but I'm happy to be home. So are my steeds—they have relaxed into themselves. Shiva no longer screams every time Calvin is out of sight, and even Patrick seems less grumpy. Calvin is his flexible good-natured self, but there's a new spring in his step now that he is home. The horses spend hours pawing through the snow in their paddock in search of a few nibbles of grass, in the same way they tease hay out of the netted mangers in their stalls, snipping away at a few strands here, a few strands there. Busy loves busy.

And literature never sleeps. The alarm blares at 3:00 a.m. The man beside me in bed pulls himself up on his elbows. He has to make a 5:30 flight to Seattle for a week of poetry. Instead of joining him when he asked if I'd like to go, I told him to take the Goth. *If I can just keep Calvin soft and more collected in his show jump lines, he ought to make the distances, and not get rammy to his fences.* My mantra, as I try to catch a few more winks.

I call Chance first thing and feebly sing "Happy Birthday" through my respiratory junk. She's alone in her apartment in Brooklyn, weeping.

A text from Esther chimes through. I can't help but peek.

Esther: *I'm so excited to get my horse tomorrow. I finally had 5 spare minutes to watch Cal's show jumping videos, which turned into watching all the Cal video clips I have.* ☺

"What's going on, Birthday Girl?" I ask, cringing to know the answer. It's like this every year. "What are your plans for the day?"

My fingers start working.

Julia: *I bet you're excited! I'm excited for you to have him back. So what do you think the difference is in Cal's videos?*

"Nothing," Chance sniffles. "I got in a big fight with Dad last night. He was supposed to take me out to dinner for my birthday, and now we're not doing anything."

Esther: *Honestly, I think his first Advanced show jumping round is one of his all-time best.*

Julia: *I agree. But why? I have my own theory, but I don't want to bias you.*

I soothe Chance as best I can from my long-distance vantage point. What I'd like to suggest is for her to get out of New York. Her plans of making it as an actress and playwright aren't panning out. At some point she's got to rebalance her canter. Otherwise, her crummy day job answering telephones will become of greater significance, because it will be all that she has. She would probably like to give me similar advice. As with Calvin: if it's broke, and I can't figure a way to fix it, then I need to do something else, right? Because if I keep trying in the face of nothing but failure, then my stubbornness and determination will eventually turn into masochism. Why not stop now?

Esther: *His shape stayed consistent as did his pace—you were able to sit quietly and stay out of his way. His canter at Fair Hill was different.*

Julia: *I think he show jumps best when he is ridden in a slow, collected canter. Cal has always been afraid of his own speed. The faster I went with Redmond, the better he jumped. It's just the opposite with Mr. C.*

"Don't worry, Silas took me out for lunch, and he's coming back again for dinner."

Although he just broke up with her, Silas is not taking Chance's birthday away from her.

"So back to the slower, more collected canter we go."

"What?" Chance says.

SIMON'S EYELIDS, UNDERNEATH THAT TARP, SO VELVETY IN THEIR permanent sleep. Trashcan eyes we used to call them. The bottom lids drooped like an old man's. The eyes that would collect a million bits of sadness. His niece Georgia has a wolf's gray eyes that are not so sad. I stroke her ears on waking. It's single digits outside. Without Simon or Barrett beside us, Georgia and I squeeze together under the tarp for another hour of hibernation.

Jumping Calvin, I use a slow, hobby-horse canter. Calvin is on the muscle and not interested in listening to me at the end of the hackamore. His drift right has become drastic and nearly impossible to correct. April reminds me to relax my elbows.

"He's one tough nut," I say to April.

"That he is," she says, from the corners of her eyes. "He's a solid Intermediate horse," she says, now leaning against the barn door, "but he's kind of like my horse—Advanced is putting him at the edge of his ability, where everything has to go perfectly and you have to give him a perfect ride."

It's funny how your problem horse can become everyone else's metaphor.

IN TODAY'S DRESSAGE CLINIC, BENT JENSEN CRUCIFIES MY POSITION, tells me to sit farther back, and to lean back, while encouraging Calvin to put his head and neck lower. When I finally lengthen my reins, Calvin drops his neck and stretches into the bit.

"I would ride him down there eighty percent of the time," Bent says through multiple layers, turtle fur, and ski cap, so that only his sapphire eyes are visible.

When Calvin stretches, I feel him relax and become better balanced. Bent wants me to be "playful" with the bit, so Cal doesn't tense up or lock on.

"He looks like a dressage horse!" Bent compliments toward the end of the lesson. "So much more relaxed over his topline. And the quality of the trot is much better."

Calvin seems happy enough to try the new maneuvers. Whereas before he appeared stuck in his head and neck, now he is soft and reaching. I never would have guessed that I could ride Calvin on a longer rein with soft, active fingers, but here we are.

If Barrett were here, I'd ask him if he thought there were a correlation between Calvin's tight neck and carelessness over stadium fences. I

imagine him taking my own stiff spine chimney in his arms, and his saying, *Let's find out.*

Chapter Six

Melting Snow Holds a Scent for Days

MARTA BRINGS SHIVA IN FROM THE FIELD. A TRICKLE OF BLOOD runs down his left front. I clean a small cut on his knee, about the size of a staple, and put him in his stall. Later, serum is seeping from his knee.

Rachel pulls into the driveway, steps into her scrubs. When she sticks a needle in to flush Shiva's joint, the saline solution spurts out the wound. The joint has been infiltrated.

"It's in his best interest to get to New Bolton tonight," Rachel says.

I wilt.

"I just don't know if I can leave the farm," I say. "Barrett is in Seattle lecturing."

Rachel wraps the knee, unrolling, rolling. "What lecture?"

"The meaning of a plot without meaning in some guy's novel."

Rachel injects Gentocin into Shiva's vein and penicillin in his muscle to cover him against negative and positive bacteria.

"What guy?"

"Alain Robbe-Grillet."

I pack Shiva and Georgia on the rig and barrel my way up the oldest road in America to the horse hospital, where the knee can be flushed in a sterile environment. I feel a welling sense of claustrophobia in Route 1 traffic.

"Do you have any interest in getting on the red eye tomorrow night?" I ask Barrett. Maybe he'll think I'm half teasing. The last day of his conference is tomorrow, and this is a valuable time for him to make connections for his magazine, and for his own writing.

"I'll see what I can do," he says. Here I go again, asking Barrett to give up his life for me.

I check Shiva into the hospital, and an attendant comes to the trailer to collect him. My boy walks through the lit alleyways outside New Bolton Center alongside the stranger, ears pricked and sound despite his swollen knee.

I'm called to the surgical suite a couple hours later. There are no complications. Shiva's left front leg is camouflaged by a Robert Jones bandage. He seems bright and happy to see me, bends his chestnut head with the crooked blaze into my shoulder, rests his muzzle in my palm. *Sorry, Shiva, you'll have to stay in hospital for a few days.*

On the way home, the New Bolton surgeon calls to remind me that I neglected to leave the culture Rachel took from Shiva's knee, and to say that they will be swiping a $1,500 deposit from my credit card account. *Deposit?*

I turn my anger on Barrett. The barn is so crowded there's only one paddock left for my horses. Barrett packs up prematurely and hops on the night plane from Seattle, bound for my ire. I gather up our household calendars and hide them in a drawer, so that he won't be tempted to flip the pages and ask, "When would be a convenient time for me to have a life?"

BARRETT STAGGERS IN AFTER HIS OVERNIGHT PLANE TRIP.

"Good thing I changed my flight," he says wearily. "They've already canceled the one I was supposed to be on tonight."

My guilt vanishes.

Another storm is on its way that will affect the entire nation, jamming frequencies, making us afraid of the day-to-day, and complacent about what should outrage us.

While I'm on my exercise wheel inhaling my daily hit of endorphins, I pick up Phillip Dutton's new book, *Modern Eventing*—an odd title, sort of like *Modern Glassblowing*—and flip open to the section on *Problems*, specifically "Jumping a Viscous Horse." My eye gravitates to "Drifting." He first encourages ruling out unsoundness. "Horses with lameness up front tend to drift away from the lameness; if the lameness is behind, then they drift in the same direction."

The answer is clear: my lameness is behind.

WICKED COLD.

THE PANTRY, CHANCE'S ROOM, UNDER OUR BED—I'M TRYING TO find Fuzzy's newest toilet. I've strategically placed cat boxes all over the house. We've put off her euthanasia several times, but when I find her droppings and spittings in the larder, and then on the kitchen floor, I'm ready to call it quits for Fuzz. Whoever has heard of a twenty-year-old cat, anyway? I feel an odd pressure, almost like a gust of wind, coming from upstairs and entering the kitchen.

I move one of the cat boxes into the kitchen.

"You've got to be kidding," says Barrett.

"That's exactly what I said to myself," I reply.

There's an outfit called Peaceful Passage that makes house calls.

"What are we going to tell Chance?" I ask.

"Tell her the truth," my husband says.

"I'll tell her she died in her sleep. Which will be kind of the truth. They say that truth is dead, anyway."

"Suit yourself, Miss Pants on Fire," he says. He knows what an awful liar I am.

I'm an open book. Maybe with a few torn and dog-eared yellow pages, but it's all right there for everyone to read. Especially my kids. Chance's motto is brutal honesty at all costs, just like her father. I won't be able to get away with a lie. Or the truth.

"Oh, I'll tell her what I tell her," I say. "I'll jump off that bridge when I have to."

Only I know how deep and untamed those waters are.

A NOTE TO CHANCE BEFORE HOPPING IN MY RIG:
As usual, you have a deeply instinctual way of being right. I think Fuzzy and Daisy are trying to go together. Last night, Fuzzy peed all over the counter. Just wanted to warn you.

"When old students come back to me, it is for one reason and one reason only," Jimmy Wofford says. "Things aren't going well."

"Calvin trains well, but then goes in the ring and knocks down all the rails," I explain.

"I saw your round at Pine Top. The two of you weren't on the same page," he says.

That's what Barrett said, that the two of us were out of sync. I didn't want to hear it then. I don't want to hear it now.

"Steinkraus always said that when a rider is in a slump, she needs to go back to basics."

He has me trot a cross rail multiple times, critiquing my upright position, which allows Calvin to squirt out the front door and get ahead of me. He also thinks that I'm not doing enough on landing to retrieve the canter I just lost from the jump. According to Jimmy, I'm a nostalgic rider, more worried about yesterday's vertical than tomorrow's oxer.

"Confine nostalgia to the poems, Julia," he reminds me. "You're a thinking rider, but sometimes you think too much and stop feeling what's going on underneath you. That's why you usually come to the right decision only after exploring every other possibility."

Echoing Winston Churchill, he gives me the only compliment of the day.

"I've got the precious cargo," Barrett says from the interstate. "I really love that horse."

I've missed Shiva's presence in the barn these past few days.

"He's been a disappointment to us both," my husband goes on. "It's almost a relief that he's been as much a disappointment for you as he was for me."

I'm not sure I understand.

"I remember each second of his races. I was so nervous, not about whether he'd win or not—" I finish for him: "But whether he'd stay on the track, right?"

Tigger comes bouncing down the shed row with a big, bright bandage to show off to his buddies. He has an eager step and a smile, if ever a horse could smile. He twirls around his stall a few times, says hello to Calvin next door, then dives into his relaxation, plucking strands of hay with his front teeth, three by three from his hay net, as if he were eating an ear of corn.

I'M FRIED BY THE TIME I LEAVE THE FARM FOR THE SWAN LAKE Jumper Show. Barrett has gone to an editorial meeting in Annapolis, making it harder for me to disappear. I ask one boarder not to park in front of my trailer, and she spits back that there's nowhere else to park. My head is spinning by the time I bump down our mangled driveway, rutted and potholed from the endless traffic of speeding rigs and bad weather. I let my frustration get the better of me. I call Barrett. I accuse him of not having his head in the game.

"I can't do it anymore," I yell into my phone, surprising even myself with my own venom.

I hang up on him, and his phone is turned off when I try to call back.

His coeditors are veterans. One was in Korea. Another, Bay of Pigs. Another, Vietnam. And Barrett? I'm his war.

In the 1.10-meter class, I keep Calvin collected and soft, and he jumps clean but slow. They blow the whistle before we can finish the course because of our time faults. In the 1.20-meter class, I let him out a little and he has a rail.

He's either too choked up or too ahead of me, and it doesn't show up till the jumps go up. After ten years, I still can't get it—the endlessness of endlessness. What is it all about, anyway? The satisfaction of a personal best effort? The drive to prove the unprovable? The search for faith in a faithless world? And what about Barrett, whom I punish for trying to make a life outside the farm, after insisting he do so. I panic, and my claws come out—as if meanness could convince anyone of anything.

I FEEL IT BEFORE I KNOW IT.

"I'm getting depressed," I say to Barrett, just before cocktail hour.

"I know," he replies. "I put it on the trip south."

He always wants to pin it on something, though that is a futile exercise in the land of the depressed. My life circumstances have nothing to do with the way the synapses are firing in my brain. Or not firing. Breakthrough episodes, one therapist of years ago called them. I feel the way I always do when it comes on: exhausted no matter how much sleep I get, and panicky. And depressed that I'm depressed, to give it a double whammy.

"Which is closer, Church Hill or Union Bridge?" I ask, to change the subject.

"Union Bridge by far," he says, "or rather, by near. How come?"

"I'm thinking of going to a dressage show next weekend to get ready for Southern Pines."

From his pained silence, I can tell he has forgotten about the trip.

"Is Esther going with you to Southern Pines?" he asks.

"I haven't heard, so I'm assuming no," I say.

More silence.

"And then there's The Fork two weeks later," I remind him. "I've got to run both if I want to do a Four Star with Calvin."

"Well, it's your sport, you better find out," he says bitterly. And then: "Can Esther go with you to The Fork?"

"I'm not sure," I say, my fingers already texting Esther the question.

My cell phone dings. "Nope," I say, "she's got some pony club gig she has committed herself to on the 6th—cross-country day at The Fork." I'm secretly delighted by her response. I can't do it on my own, and I don't want anyone else to go with me besides Barrett. Particularly when I'm spiraling into the raccoon. I have put my husband in an impossible situation.

RACHEL ARRIVES TO CHANGE THE BANDAGE ON SHIVA'S LEG. HIS knee looks terrific—just a tiny wound healing well, with no discernible swelling. She's a little concerned about a pressure sore behind the knee from the bandage wound too tight in the hospital. She has hopes it will resolve itself with a looser wrap.

"That'll learn us," my astute husband says. "I didn't call you out on a Sunday because the bandage had stayed up so well, but I should have called you because the bandage stayed up so well."

The sun is shining and the temperature has skyrocketed to 45. Filthy boulders of old snow still decorate the driveway, and the pastures remain partially covered, the footing slick and treacherous. Even so, Calvin and Georgia and I are determined to find a trail. We trudge up the hill through the split between pastures, over the back field, down the farm road that separates Lydia's soybeans from corn, and we're out of sight. I take a deep breath and let go, all my chores and obligations, depressions, complaints, and bitternesses left briefly behind. Cal quickens his step despite the iffy footing; it's the first time off the farm for him in weeks. Georgia dashes on ahead, nose to the messy ground. Melting snow can hold a scent for days. We pass through old nineteenth-century plots of land—Stoddard's Delight, Amos's Venture, Wilmot's Retirement—back when boundaries were marked by oak trees and rivulets, and pieces of land were named— like boats—for what you hoped to accomplish on them.

It's a quick one—figure-eighting the Fenwicks' big field where they've put trails of old straw down to help the horses' purchase, down Lydia's cornfield and into the woods, across the stream still studded with ice, picking our way through old snow, and up the steep back hill that in better weather we love to gallop. Toward the end, Georgia runs off as she usually does, toward a scent of deer. I call and call, my voice echoing and muffling off the hard and soft ground until it sounds as if someone else is screaming, too. Georgia knows the ground. She'll find her way.

A SHEET OF BLUE FILM ARRIVES IN THE MAIL FROM SOUTH CAROLINA with tiny script on it that I must squint to read.

FATAL ACCIDENT IN THE COUNTY—A few days since Mr. Stephen M. Fowble, of the fifth district of Baltimore county met with an accident which resulted in his instant death. He was haul-ing a four-horse wagon load of bark to Scott's tan-yard, and while descending a deep cut hill fell from his horse, and before he could recover the wheels of his wagon passed over his neck, killing him instantly. He is represented as having been a worthy man, and leaves a widow with three children.

SHEALAGH COSTELLO ASSURES ME THAT MY FOUR-STAR QUALIFICAtions are still current, with the exception of one qualifying Advanced horse trial needed within twelve months of the upcoming event. My Four-Star completions at Bromont and Fair Hill in 2012 will suffice. That's a long way from needing to return to the Three-Star level for a couple of trips. I text the Ghost my good news.

The Ghost: *Show jumping is after cross-country at Southern Pines for the Advanced division.*

The Ghost thinks Calvin tends to hit more rails after the surge and excitement of cross-country. Barrett thinks it's the other way around; that he knocks them down when he's too fresh. I don't know what to think anymore.

I page through the Omnibus.

Julia: *You're right about the order, but I still want to do the Advanced division. Show jumping was before cross-country at Pine Top and it did me no favors.*

I don't hear back, which usually means he either disagrees or has disappeared. I stew the rest of the day wondering what I should do. I am handcuffed by the Ghost's silence. By wanting to please him, yet wanting to do what's best for Calvin. By cocktail hour, I'm back behind bars, the old, internal fifty-nine-year-old mess. I still don't hear back from my gray one.

I PACK UP CALVIN AND PATRICK AND HEAD DOWN TO WEST VIRGINIA for more moonlighting. Calvin is in a group lesson with three polished Advanced horses. The sum of the riders' ages probably adds up to mine. They are better riders, too—certainly more nimble and inherently gifted than I am. Always a humbling experience, to learn from millennials.

Calvin's in the Myler combination bit, reins attached to the second ring. I can always put the reins down on the third ring to make the bit stronger if I feel I don't have enough leverage. Soon after entering the arena, Jimmy gives me his first lecture of the day. He prefers that his students' horses school in snaffles. I could get into trouble with too much hand on such a sharp bit, he advises. He scowls at me as if I should know better. I bite my tongue so I won't try to educate my teacher on the softness of the Myler mouthpiece, whose function is often misunderstood. Needless to say, readjusting the reins to the stronger third ring will not be an option. I hope Calvin doesn't start dragging me to the fences.

Jimmy is the sort of teacher who focuses on the rider rather than the horse, so everything that happens is the result of the rider. Anything that goes wrong is rarely the horse's fault. When Calvin gets strong with me, I am causing the problem—I am either pulling back or getting too far forward, or goosing him with my electric seat or spurs. I try to stay soft and still, but Calvin remains too strong without the added leverage of the bit's third ring. I make a mental note to change the bit after today's ride.

Patrick is more settled and jumps well, after Jimmy confiscates my spurs. He reminds me that I don't need any heel on this jackrabbit, and that I should underride him as much as possible—which is his assessment of my riding on pretty much any horse. I am always too aggressive to my fences for Jimmy's liking. Bringing a gun to a knife fight works better at the racetrack.

Jimmy refers to one horse dealer's scale for judging horses, where 0 is a dangerous rogue, 10 a bombproof kick-a-long. Horses in the 2-3 spectrum are ones that only the likes of Beezie Madden can ride.

"You're about a 3 or 4 with these two," Jimmy says, "I'd like to see your next horse be a 7 or 8."

I'm feeling a little hangdog by the time I've taken care of the horses, packed up, and left. I drive the two hours home, crossing the Shenandoah once and the Potomac twice. I get the horses settled, fed, hayed, watered, double blanketed. It has turned cold again, accentuated by a biting wind and a prediction of 0 degrees overnight. The first day of spring is only a week away.

While cleaning tack, I chat with the Teapot.

"I remember the slow, soft, collected feel of Calvin's jump when I first started running Advanced. It's nowhere near that now. I used to be able to soften my hands a couple strides out and he would stay underneath me. He has gotten all tense and rammy to his fences."

I'd recently sent her two videos, one of Calvin's first Advanced run at the spring Fair Hill Horse Trials three years ago, when he jumped clean in stadium, and the other from his most recent go at Pine Top, when he had five rails.

"What bridle were you using at Fair Hill?" she asks.

"The hackamore."

I drifted away from the hackamore last year, trying all kinds of bits, primarily for cross-country, in an effort to find one that wouldn't rip Calvin's mouth. Somehow, in all that experimentation, I stopped using the hackamore in stadium, only coming back to it when other bits failed. In the meantime, I also played around with different chin straps for the hackamore at different lengths. It occurs to me that the hackamore chain used to be adjusted a lot tighter. I would routinely gob salve under Calvin's chin where the tight strap dug into his flesh. But it did the trick. It held him off the jumps and kept him soft. How did that detail elude me?

Slow the canter, sit in the tack. Make whatever adjustments in order to get Calvin all the way back between fences. Keep a slow, quiet rhythm. Tell yourself that you know what you're doing. Lie to yourself if you have to.

The wind blows shingles right and left off the mare barn roof. I duck my way to the trailer tack room to rummage around in search of the hackamore's original chin chain.

THE EFFOL BALM WILL HAVE ANOTHER SORE TO HEAL. I CRANK THE chain on Calvin's hackamore until I guesstimate it's as tight as it used to be. I need to find the line between too much and not enough. I used to count the holes on the chin strap and write it down so I'd get it precisely tight enough for the next ride. One hole could make the difference between control or chaos. And yet something tells me that if I'm so dependent on properly adjusted equipment, then the horse's training must be out of whack. He needs to want to keep the rails up. He needs to want to be a good horse.

Calvin is feather light in the reins. During twenty minutes of trotting, I alternate between going forward and collecting, to see if I can maintain his softness. At the canter, I add in some poles. He lengthens slightly and leans against my hand. I halt on the other side to make my point. It's a successful school, and Calvin feels much more like he used to in the bridle, with his jaw in a vice. He has barely broken a sweat but is keen on searching my pocket for a reward for today's efforts. That's my Irish monster in a nutshell: sensitive as a lop-ear, yet hard as a truckload of nails.

I wake in the night to a raging neck ache. Barrett stirs on the other side of Georgia, who sleeps between us every night, like a kid afraid of the dark.

"You wouldn't get me some Advil, would you?" I ask, from the Land of Pain.

My good husband swims up from deep sleep, pads downstairs, climbs the back stairs slowly.

"How many?" he mumbles.

He shakes the bottle like a maraca, an Advil flamenco.

I TOSS AND TURN ALL NIGHT WITH A SEARING PAIN IN MY NECK AND wake to more. Barrett mans the coffee pot. I wait till its welcoming aroma wafts upstairs to hoist myself out of bed, fumble for the banister, and inch my way downstairs. Fuzzy has missed the cat box and peed on the kitchen floor. Barrett is cleaning it up with coffee filters—the only absorbent he can find.

"It's way past Fuzzy's time," Barrett says.

I study the puddle next to the stove, seeping into the cracks of Charlotte's old wooden floor.

WE TRUNDLE OUR WAY TO AN UNRECOGNIZED DRESSAGE SHOW IN Union Bridge. Calvin is relaxed in warm-up, even through the counter-canter work and the changes. He is starting to soften in his canter as I've become more subtle with my aids. He has also learned to wait for the signal from my seat and legs before changing, and is willing to counter-bend in his counter-canter in preparation for the change without having a spaz attack.

Calvin keeps his relaxation throughout the new Advanced Test B. It's easy here, though. So quiet, only a couple of trailers in the parking lot as riders come and go for their tests, no jumping, no pressure, no hoopla. The judge compliments our test and my horse, says *how lovely* and *what is he?* She praises our lateral work, and adds that he needs to be quicker behind with more jump in his canter, which will help our changes. She reminds me not to let his canter lengthen across the diagonal before asking for the change. What we need is short, quick, active. I'm just delighted we stayed in the ring. It has taken three years to get this far in the work with Calvin's flying changes. Calvin's not stupid—quite the contrary—but his mind veers toward hysteria. It takes the patience of Job—or the determination of a rat that bloodies its head on its tunnel walls—to teach Calvin something new.

Barrett raises his brow when he sees the blue ribbon. "Relax," I admit, "we were the only ones in the class." A flicker of disappointment crosses his face. Barrett is competitive, and Barrett likes to see results. If I cared about either of those, I wouldn't be doing what I'm doing. And certainly not with Calvin.

WE'RE WEARING WHITE TODAY INSTEAD OF GREEN: IT'S SNOWING again, has been all night. Five more inches on the ground, with more to come. St. Patrick will need sleighs to drive out my copperheads.

"This has got to be it," I say to Barrett. Weathermen are boasting that this is the worst winter since 1896. Not only is there new snow, but it's also 22 degrees. We won't be burying any potato eyes today.

I crank down Calvin's hackamore, then kick up his disappointing medium trot. I canter some poles on the ground, trying to keep his canter exactly the same before, during, and after the rails. We head out into the snow to walk some hills. Up and down the splits between the steep paddock and the alfalfa field, trudging our way, six times up, six times down, my snow-covered Abominable Calvin starting to breathe and work, adding to the fitness he has already attained, putting the finishing touches on his readiness for the Advanced track at Southern Pines.

Calvin's masseuse comes, pronounces him sore where the saddle goes, and resistant to touch. She suggests that a saddle fitter look again at the way his saddles are fitting, now that he is so much sleeker and trimmer.

"He's sore even after the shock wave?" Barrett asks, disgustedly. Barrett's not much of a fan of equine gadgets, thinks they are more lucrative for the vets than helpful for the horses. Like commoditizing horsemanship instead of relying on spirit and grit.

The Teapot arrives.

"I think the cheek pieces can go up some," she says, assessing the hackamore. "Maybe they've stretched."

"Or maybe not," I say. "I've fiddled around so much with this thing over the last couple of years, I've completely lost track of the original settings."

In trying to produce the larger canter so I wouldn't have as many time faults, I didn't process that the horse was running through my hands. If he is too much ahead of my aids, he is going to knock rails.

This is the way I learn best: by allowing myself the space to figure things out, rather than doing what someone else tells me to do. That requires a self-confidence I've always been short on. I learned as a much younger woman to stop taking writing workshops and just write the poems; now I have to learn to stop taking lessons and just ride the horse. Which means I need to let go of my ghosts. Even if the horse is not just a horse. Even if the horse is a metaphor for the worst thing that can happen to anyone.

MY HACKAMORE READJUSTED—TWO TIGHT CHAINS AROUND THE chin—I work to get the soft canter that Calvin and I used to have in stadium. It's surprisingly easy to reproduce. I've set up the same pattern I jumped last week at the Wofford clinic. I start by trotting a cross rail. I want to establish the quiet, waiting ride, right from the get-go. April places rails in a gymnastic, and then I jump single fences in a bending line.

The fences are at 3'6", no ground lines, no fill or decorations, and Calvin cleanly negotiates the exercise, even when I put the fences together in the bending line. The fences go up to 3'9"—same. April builds the gymnastic.

The situation is reminiscent of all the lessons with me on the ground and April in the tack, back when she was in high school.

April has a few things to correct in my position. She's at first shy about critiquing me, but after I encourage her, she goes for it.

"I'd like to think I had a little something to do with your focus on the rider's position," I tease.

"I still remember you telling me to land with the weight in my stirrups. It was such a foreign concept to me," she says.

When the fences go up to 4'3", I see the move-up distance; Calvin becomes a bull and hits the rails. I must not override. I must establish the balloony canter and keep it to the base of the jump. Even if it feels like we're crawling out of a trench.

THE LITTER BOX ON THE KITCHEN FLOOR RORSCHACHED WITH PEE, though I mucked it less than an hour ago. Plus a puddle on the floor.

Barrett is definite. I am not, though I realize the absurdity of stationing a cat box in the kitchen, especially with someone in the house suffering from TB.

I call Peaceful Passage.

"Be there in a half hour."

Dr. Rabinowitz arrives at the farm in a mid-length skirt, dark tights, black flats, and pillbox hat. Her gaze settles on Daisy, who doesn't budge when the stranger comes into the dog's space. Did she get the animals mixed up? "One day soon she won't be able to get up," the Death Panel says about my love.

Quick, light footsteps upstairs, and a whine that sounds like a child's.

The skeleton cat camped out on the couch catches her eye.

"I'll sedate her first. The needle prick will be the worst part. She'll get drowsy, then just go to sleep. I'll administer the other and she'll sleep right through it."

Barrett is on the couch next to Fuzzy. The two of them have spent so much time together this fall and winter, through Barrett's illness and, more recently, through many of his hours writing book reviews. His belief: just because he can't create is no reason not to react to creation. Fuzzy has been his constant companion, her world having dwindled to the distance between the couch and the kitchen floor. Because Barrett's world has shrunk, too, he's the one who knows it's Fuzzy's time to go.

When Fuzzy gets pricked, she screams and leaps out of Barrett's arms and into the kitchen—the fastest I've seen her move in months.

"That's the worst part, I promise," Dr. Rabinowitz reassures us.

Yah, except you're about to take her life, I think.

"I'm heading up to the barn," I say, after Barrett has collected Fuzzy. She's on his lap, starting to get quiet and drowsy. The vet draws up the poison.

I walk up to the mare barn tack room through the pissing rain, sit down on a trunk, and wait ten or fifteen potatoes' worth of minutes. The hearse pulls out, and I text Chance. *She's gone, Honey. She just went to sleep.*

I sit still a while longer to give my heart a break, then get up to pack for Southern Pines.

I DON'T ANTICIPATE DAISY'S REACTION TO FUZZY'S DEATH. THE TWO have been inseparable, camped out together at their watering hole—two aluminum bowls that need refilling multiple times a day for their parched kidneys. Daisy seems, if not unsettled, then slightly depressed in Fuzzy's absence. She is a little slower to respond to our voices, and won't pick her head up when I come in the door.

I toss Marnie back outside into the rain. I want no part of the younger cat.

I wake at 2:30 a.m., a half hour before the alarm, panicked about leaving Daisy for the weekend, though Marta and Roberto and their daughter, Carolina, will be housesitting. When I leave the house to head to the barn,

Marnie is perched on the boot bench right outside the door, wanting back in. Conflicted and relieved, I snag her and toss her back inside.

"If anything happens to Daisy, I will kill you eight times," I say.

NERVOUS HORSES AND RIDERS HEAD-ON, BEHIND, CUTTING US OFF, amid loudspeakers and flags blowing and bleachers stuffed with spectators. Calvin's brain disintegrates. I take a deep breath and stay in the moment, coaxing my horse to stay with me, with longer reins, deeper poll, stronger half halts, upper body, and outside rein. The Ghost unexpectedly appears in warm-up.

"Shorten your reins," he commands.

I do what I'm told. I shorten the reins.

It's a congenital disease, this need to be loved and admired. To be the good student, at all cost. The good daughter. The friend of all the ghosts.

"Leg-yield him all the way across the diagonal, if he feels tight to you."

There is no diagonal to leg-yield across. With so many riders and horses clogging the arena, I would have to run someone over to make a clear pass.

"I don't think I've ever seen him look so tight in his back," he adds.

Just what I needed to hear.

The Ghost leaves before my test to get on his next horse, but I don't have enough time to salvage Calvin's relaxation. It's hard to admit that my Ghost is wrong. Harder still to make my own way.

I enter the ring. Calvin's gaits are mediocre and tense. The test will score toward the bottom of the competitive pack. The only difference is that I keep my cool in the midst of Calvin's firepower.

WE ARE STAYING AT THE DAYS INN IN RAEFORD, CLOSER TO THE horse park and farther from dining culture in Southern Pines. Exhausted, we settle into our room. I wipe down the drawers and unpack every panty and sock. Barrett is doing his own version of unwinding with a Styrofoam cup of rotgut Cabernet he picked up at the Chevron gas station. It's well past 8:00 by the time we leave for dinner. There are no restaurants in town except for one dimly marked Mexican café.

"Go in and see if they serve tequila," I say.

Families are piling out of the restaurant with their baby rockers and preschoolers in tow. Barrett takes one peek and returns to the truck, shaking his head. By the time we find another restaurant that serves margaritas, it's so late that every bite tastes like cardboard.

"Authentic," I say, hedgingly, smearing gray beans around on my plate, vaguely the color of baby shit.

Barrett drops me off at the motel before returning to the horse park for night check. Small huddles of men mingle outside their rooms, beers in hand, smoking lamps ablaze. We are obviously ducks out of water, me still in my dirty britches, Barrett's gray mop of untamed hair sticking out in every direction.

I putter around the room, then take a shower. The water is lukewarm, the drain is clogged, the tea-towel-sized bath towels translucent. I position myself carefully on top of the bedspread and sink into the spongy mattress. The party outside my door seeps through the paper-thin walls, cigarette smoke wafting under the door. I lie on my back on top of the bedspread, afraid to put my body between those sheets, twirling my thumbs and seething, waiting for Barrett.

"Just so you know," I say as he's unlocking the door, allowing the blast of noise, smoke, and cold air to hit me in the face, "I'm not staying one more night in this shit hole." I draw an imaginary blade across my throat. Barrett's face wilts, knowing how much time he'll have to spend tomorrow finding us another room. Time he could better use recovering from the long drive down and preparing for the trip home.

SHOW JUMPING AT SOUTHERN PINES IS HUGE. AS I WORRY OVER THE height of the jumps, I realize that the course is set for Intermediate, not yet Advanced. I've got some recalibrating to do.

I organize my time, memorize the course. I even remember to take a photo of the Advanced course map posted at the in-gate before I walk it. I get on my horse and arrive in warm-up well in advance of the official course walk for my division. The Ghost and Kittie Wilkins are leaning against the fence, waiting for the tractor to harrow the ring before we're allowed to walk.

"What time do you go?" the Ghost asks a little suspiciously. There's no one else in warm-up and competitors are anxiously waiting to walk the course. I'm sure he suspects I've already jumped about fifty fences in anxious preparation.

"Thought I'd get on and warm him up on the flat a bit before I walk," I say. I'm trying to give myself as much time as possible, knowing how long it takes me to feel comfortable enough with a new course to be able to ride it well.

"Don't leave your ride in warm-up," he warns.

I've calculated that we'll have only a morsel of time to walk before we have to warm up and go, so I'm trying to be efficient. I can't wing anything with Calvin, or he'll eat up the distances and punch out rails. I have to have a plan. Who am I kidding—I can't wing anything with myself either.

The Ghost joins us in warm-up with his own horse. "How many jumps have you jumped?" he barks at me.

"None," I say, defensively.

We start off slowly and start jumping.

"You need more canter," the Ghost warns.

I go on with my ride.

"More canter, Julia," he insists.

I turn him off and ride my way. I enter the ring at a trot. I halt. I take my time, circling the ring. Fences 1, 2, and 3 are lovely. We come around the tight turn under par to fence 4, a 4'3" Liverpool. I see the long distance but Calvin puts in another stride, gets under the jump, and stops. The whistle blows.

I used to be undone by failure. Now we are such good pals. Failure can finish all the sentences I begin. We poke each other in the ribs, swap stories, complain about husbands and horses. We know each other's bra sizes and hip measurements. And, at least today, we are not afraid of each other. I keep my cool, get the canter, and Calvin and I come again. We jump the Liverpool, which he knocks with a hind toe, and it comes down. I think ahead, counting my strides. There goes fence 5, the line at 6 and 7, 8, and then 9, which is a skinny that he taps, and it falls. He jumps the line through 10A-B and 11 and the line at 12A-B cleanly, and we've finished. We've had mostly good jumps, one stop, two rails, and thirty time penalties. It doesn't matter. Because I stuck to my guns, I don't even care about the stop. I rode my plan. I experimented, and I won. I rode so softly that I dared the stop. But the overall round was better.

Even the Ghost admits it was good.

I receive a text from a 540 area code.

Much better. I saw your troubles at fence 5. But the rest of it was good. You're on the right track.

I didn't know Jimmy had my number.

CROSS-COUNTRY DAY I GO BACK OUT TO WALK THE ADVANCED course for the fourth time, by myself. I'm troubled by two combinations—one is at fences 7 and 8, two skinny cabins up a rolling hill in eight strides, then down four or five strides to either a right- or left-hand corner. When I first walked the course on Thursday, my eye was drawn to the left-hand side of the corner. With Calvin's tendency to drift right, jumping a left-hand corner might be prudent. When I walked the course with the Ghost, however, he felt that the right side was better, and encouraged me to go that way.

Calvin's warm-up is frayed, and we are out of sync over our first few jumps. His big body is several steps ahead of his mind. There's a hold on course for a fallen rider, which puts me off further. I never develop a rhythm in the warm-up, and I'm too distracted by what's going on around me rather than focused inward, where I need to be.

Calvin jumps the first several fences on course well, before galloping uphill to the corner combination. I get him back for the first cabin, which he jumps a little too big. I half halt, and he puts in an extra stride, which makes the effort at the second cabin awkward. He launches down the hill toward the corner and bounces off it. I circle and come again; he pops over it, and we're back on our way. The rest of the course unfolds according to plan, even the tough combination with two extremely offset oxers. The second water, a few more jumps, another combination, and through the finish flags toward a qualifying round. Not perfect, but good enough.

We cool Calvin out, ice him, wrap him, pack up the truck and trailer, and head the eight hours toward home.

Barrett and I spend the drive discussing his desire to find a life outside the farm and what that might require. I voice my own needs: to keep at this game a while longer, see where Calvin and I end up. How can our two disparate paths mesh? Barrett is considering a Plan B. It's not so much about making a new life, but repairing the one he already has. Before we know it, we're pulling down our potholed driveway, punchy and laughing our heads off at the jarring mess.

THE FIRST HORSE INSPECTION AT THE JERSEY FRESH FOUR-STAR IS forty-two days away.

IT IS SNOWING AT 7:00, AT 10:30, AND STILL AT 2:00. NOTHING TO worry about, I tell myself. It has got to be the last dump. Too wet. It will never stick.

At 3:00, people show up, dressed for a biathlon, to open the pool.

After the first sloppy inches, I tack up Cal and head out on a hack with Georgia. *Can't be that bad*, I think optimistically. Cal perks up, his walk forward and bouncy, like any good jock's. He's Irish; he loves the muck and snow. Foul weather is sunshine to an Irish horse. We head out to the back field, into the third and fourth inches.

The course designer calls. He offers to swing by with Zurich on his way north. Will we be home?

"Actually, we'll be at The Fork that weekend," I tell him.

He is anxious for me to try Zurich and wants to leave him with me for a spell.

Barrett agrees to the caper, even says he'll haul Zurich to Upstate New York if he doesn't pan out for me. After cocktail hour and a dinner of left-over crab, he takes a different view, however. Must have been the backfin lumps that soured him.

"A fourth horse would bury us," he says, "at least it would bury me. You'd have to figure out something else for one of the others. Let Shiva down, sell Patrick. Something."

He knows not to say anything about Calvin, though there's nothing my husband would like more than for me to back off my competition frenzy with the Irish One. I sense he's right. But it seems impossible to let go of the dream of getting Calvin back to Fair Hill International. Nor can I pass up the opportunity to try one of Redmond's kin.

SWELLING IN CALVIN'S RIGHT HIND ANKLE BUYS ME A TICKET ON THE Worry Train. First come the endless staring and running my hand up and down the leg, checking for heat. I compare it to his other hind with the chronic fat timber ankle, making it impossible to judge the new problem against the old. But he's sound, so I trot him for a twenty-minute set in the indoor. Deep sigh: he is his old game, forward self. He must have either knocked the ankle or it's the fungus I've been battling on his legs since Aiken. Either way, it's a minor event.

Right?

I poultice the leg and wrap it for the night. The train whistle blows long and steady. My dreams thread in and out to Allentown.

ON MY WAY TO ANOTHER BENT JENSEN DRESSAGE CLINIC, THE RADIO takes me back to grade school, college, and beyond, my early life condensed to a few pop songs—"Your Song," "Here Comes the Sun," "Knockin' on Heaven's Door," and "Margaritaville"—memories I quickly sketch on stray diesel receipts I find on the floor of the truck as I drive to Woodbine. Texting and driving? What about writing poetry and driving? Surely it's grounds for some sort of expensive punishment.

Cal shines today in spite of the broken ankle. Again, Bent emphasizes the importance of working him in a deep frame on a longer rein. In Bent's system, lengthening the reins eases Calvin's tension and promotes the lofty step I'm able to draw from him today. A tense, anxious horse is never going to score well in the dressage ring.

"I'm really impressed," Bent concludes, "he looks like an entirely different horse."

Wow. I haven't received a compliment like that in a while.

"How old is he?" Bent asks, under his Charlie Chaplin moustache.

"He's eight, and I just turned thirty."

Your Song

For Calvin, on our anniversary

In a few brief measures
I've gone all the way from grade school
to college.
I'm waiting for the sun
along with Ringo and John,
my father singing along
with his transistor as he shaves
before rousing me for school:
*Up and at 'em, hit the deck, rise
and shine!*

Then I'm knockin' on heaven's door
at a corner booth in Ithaca,
my unsteady hand on Howie's steady knee,
as he rims a merengue beat
using table as tambora,
composing a future
that does not include me.

When was it that Jimmy Buffett
visited Margaritaville?

Had I given birth
to John and Chance yet?
Or had I already left their father
for a more sober town
of horses and hard work,
and you?

It's more than the throat
can bear, as I drive through a double-blurred
rain, choking on my 58th year.
I send out what signals I may—
S.O.S., *Help me,*
I think I'm falling
too fast.

RAINING SIDEWAYS. I WAKE AT 4:00 TO LEAVE WITH PATRICK FOR Morven Park Spring Horse Trials. The trees start swaying.

"Forty- to fifty-mile-per-hour winds predicted for today," the Teapot tells me.

"Why didn't you say something about that before we left?" I say, slightly annoyed.

She shrugs at the wheel, while following the parking attendant's directions. "Knew you'd want to come anyway," she explains.

It's truly awful: rain, wind, and way south of 40 degrees. We go to the secretary's office to pick up my packet. The technical delegate has canceled cross-country and refashioned the day into a combined test. That would mean cooling our heels in the rain till midday, to ride a dressage test and a stadium round without cross-country. I bag the day, feeling guilty as I do.

"Good decision," the Teapot counters. I guessed she'd feel that way.

"Don't you want another chance to get Patrick back in the ring?" my tenacious Ghost advises.

I talk myself into a decision I've already made.

We get home, the wind picks up again, and the rain stays constant all afternoon, teetering on monsoon-like. The horses are whack jobs from the crazy weather. Barrett brings them all in at noon.

I condition Calvin in the indoor—twenty minutes of trotting followed by three sets of six-minute slow canters. Dead fit, he barely breaks a sweat during the eight-mile effort.

I'm back in the barn, trying to get my chores done. Everyone wants a piece of me. One boarder seeks me out as I'm wrapping Calvin's legs—usually a quiet, serious time to focus on my horse.

"Would you like a five-minute culinary adventure?" he asks.

One of the barn doors is lifted by a gust and slaps back against the building, as if it were speaking for me. I don't have the heart to say no.

He tells me the step-by-step of a slow-cooked tomato sauce, followed by a fancy frittata. It's agony trying to be polite and listen with half an ear while my attention is being drawn away from a patch of fungus on my horse's left front. I'm nearly choking with claustrophobia. Barrett returns to the barn for the afternoon shift, and I wiggle my pointer at him.

"I can't take it anymore," I confess to him from Calvin's stall.

The rain turns to sleet, then a stinging hail, and finally morphs into a blizzard that continues into the evening, reinforcing my worry that spring, in fact, will never arrive.

Chapter Seven

Doesn't Everyone Love a Deviation?

"I HAVE A REQUEST," I GASP, AFTER I JUMP THE FIRST OXER.

The Ghost screws up his face, tilts it sideways.

"What's the matter?"

"I must have pulled something," I wince, before blurting, "I want to go back to the slow canter."

"Well, the risk is that—"

"I know, a stop," I interrupt, squirming in the tack to get more comfortable.

"No, I was going to say time faults. By the way, did Barrett tell you that eight of your time faults at Southern Pines happened before you even crossed the start flags?"

"No, really?" I perk up, trying to keep my composure.

Daggers through my ass for the remainder of the ride.

I pick up a bag of ice at the nearest convenience store to sit on for the trip home.

I'm anxious to finish my barn chores so I can whip up a cheese soufflé for Barrett's birthday. The Teapot shows up to ride Ego. She heads out to fetch her pony from the pasture, and I get a phone call a few minutes later.

"I need you here right now," she says.

I grab a shank and some horse cookies and hobble down to the front field to find Patrick herding Ego. Pasture dynamics: Patrick doesn't want the Teapot to take his friend away, and the Teapot hasn't thought of the easy answer—catch the instigator first. I call Patrick in my shrill, horsey voice, and he canters over to me and stops, drops his head, waits for his treat like a lamb.

Both horses are panting and drenched. The Teapot is silently pissed, I'm guessing because Barrett turned out Ego with Patrick before her arrival at the farm. She strips off her pony's blanket on the way to the barn and walks him for a good half hour as I throw some water at my renegade, then toss him in his stall to stew. When I leave the barn, the Teapot is finishing a call to Rachel.

"Is Ego ok?" I ask.

"I'm worried about his left hind," she says.

"Have you jogged him?" I ask.

"No, but you can see it at the walk."

"At the *walk*?"

"Well, he's not exactly lame," she says, "but there's a delay," she further explains.

"A *delay*?"

She leads him, and he walks out fine.

"He's tracking up," I say. "In fact, he's over-tracking. If there were a delay, his left hind wouldn't be reaching forward that well. Let me see him jog."

"I think he's run around enough for one day," she bites.

"We need to assess his soundness. How do you know his left hind isn't right if you don't know whether he's sound or not?"

She jogs him, and he looks sound enough to my eye.

"What did Rachel say?" I ask.

"She said to cold water hose him, give him some Bute and Banamine, and wrap him for the night."

I call Barrett. "Please come up here," I plead. "I've got to get going on dinner. Someone should be in the barn with all this going on." Big mistake, but making a cheese soufflé is not exactly like making a ham sandwich.

Up the driveway trudges my birthday boy.

It's after 8:30 when he returns to the house, the soufflé long deflated.

We don't talk about what went on in the barn. It *is* Barrett's birthday, after all. But from the steely look in my husband's eye, I bet there's one less rabbit in this world.

I WAKE IN A HOLE AND STAY THERE—THROUGH CALVIN'S LAST FLAT session before we leave for The Fork, and Patrick's jump school, in which he jumps about as politely as he ever has, and Shiva's shenanigans on his first hack since the puncture fiasco. Shiva starts out quietly but returns to the farm in a lather. I hose him from ear tip to tail dock. He noses my pocket for a treat, but he has another think coming if he thinks he earned one. He must sense the blackness in me.

The Teapot scurries around the barn, getting her pony and trailer ready to leave.

"I'm taking Ego to a quiet farm in Monkton for a few days, so the vets can get to him. Given the state of your driveway, I was afraid they wouldn't have access."

This is the last I'll ever see of the Teapot or her pony.

I TAKE MY HEAD OFF, SHAKE IT UP, PUT IT BACK ON. THIS TAKES ME the entire eight-hour trip to Norwood, North Carolina. I'm relieved to be in another mind zone, where pork rinds replace the basic pretzel. I'd just as soon never see the farm again. As for the Teapot? I already miss her. She kept my loneliness at bay.

We're stabled a couple barns away from the Ghost and Kittie Wilkins, and across from Olympian Becky Holder. It's nice having only one horse at the show—it gives me time to focus on Calvin and all the minutiae—polishing my boots till I can count the wrinkles in my face, brushing an entire cat's worth of hair off my shadbelly, rubbing baby oil on Calvin's nose, carving diamond shapes into his pumpkin ass. My funny jack-o-lantern.

The atmosphere buzzes with horses and riders competing this weekend, prepping for Rolex or Jersey Fresh. I tack up Calvin to settle his mind. He maintains a relative calm in the melee of horses and loudspeakers blaring and international flags waving in the brisk wind.

SOMETIMES YOU NEED A GIRL SCOUT, SOMETIMES A CROOK. THE FEI is doing random drug tests of the athletes this weekend.

"I'd be fucked," I say to Barrett, thinking of the residual marijuana roiling around in my system.

Barrett is unfazed. "You should ask Chance for a pee sample," he suggests.

"Huh?"

"All you'd have to do is freeze it, then put it in the cooler when you go to FEI events."

"You're a genius." I pause to speculate. "She'd never do it," I conclude. "Why Chance?"

"Well, you'd need a woman's pee. And Chance is such a goody two shoes about not taking drugs. She'd be perfect. Plus, surely your two pees have something in common."

I can hardly wait to have that conversation with my daughter.

In Best Western's lobby, we run into another Olympian.

"Nice shirt," Barrett says, nodding his head at Bobby Costello's green-striped wrinkle-free Oxford number. Barrett is his typical disheveled self—a long day's worth of horse shit from head to toe.

"Oh, well," Bobby explains, "I have my daytime shirts and my night-time shirts. How about you, Barrett? Do you have any nighttime shirts?"

"All of my daytime shirts are the same as my nighttime shirts," my frowsy husband says.

CALVIN GETS AWAY FROM ME IN THE DRESSAGE TEST, BUT WE COM-plete our half passes and flying changes, our extended canter and half circles to a centerline halt. I cover my ears and start humming, so I won't hear the announcer reveal our score. Knowing a good score makes me feel too much pressure to jump well. A bad one makes me want to pack up and go home.

Awareness inevitably brings disappointment. I refuse to get on scales when I go to the doctor—in fact, I haven't been on scales since I was preg-nant with Chance. I won't look at the number of calories on the back of any food container, either. I'd rather not know and hope for the best—or least—rather than being assured of the worst before the enjoyment of eat-ing. It's a great way to resolve—or at least avoid—a lifelong problem with anorexia; not so good for improving your riding. I'd rather not know the score, which makes me one of the worst competitors in the world.

Barrett comes back to our tack room with a bounce in his step, waving the test in his hand.

"Did you hear it?" he asks, with a smile in his voice. "Do you want to know?"

"Only if it's good news," I say.

"You nailed it." He brightens, "You got a 39!"

He's got me there: any score under 40 is something to celebrate in my book.

The Fork itself is a thousand acres of rolling green stuff. Sporting clay shooting and duck and quail hunting are the other sports practiced on this ground. I hack Calvin. Trails diverge, aptly named for what you'll find on them. There's the Stable Trail, the Silo Trail, the Duck Trail, which winds along the marshes, the Pond Trail on which—you guessed it—is a pond plopped in the middle of the woods, the Elm and Maple Trails, and the Sunken Road Trail, which is basically a trough gouging through the woods. Calvin is happy to have an opportunity to be a trail horse in the midst of the competition hubbub. I'm relaxed and happy, too, deep in the woods, tucked out of sight. I just hope nobody mistakes us for clay pigeons.

This is what I'm missing. When I was a kid, bombing around the woods in western Pennsylvania was all there was or was ever needed. My real and imagined world of horses and cattle drives, saddle bags packed and fires built, sleeping out under the stars, the horses picketed nearby. Their restless chomping as they polished off their small circles of grass. Waking to the smell of wet leaves and a fine mist covering our sleeping bags, my pal Darlene sleeping next to me. We opened our eyes to every possibility. Nothing is ever real till it's imagined.

Barrett finds a crummy townie roadhouse called Al's in old-town Albemarle. As we enter, several couples and families with packs of kids are stuffing themselves with hamburgers, mounds of spaghetti and meatballs, fried pickles, and hush puppies. A sound man with reversed ball cap and long hair in need of a good scrub is busy adjusting dials twenty feet away from us. He must be new at it because every couple of minutes an excruciating squeal emanates from one of the gorilla amps perched on the table in the middle of the dining room.

We wolf down our calzones and sketti and Bud Lights, just as the Butt Rock Band starts screeching. We get our timing right and extend our canter out the door.

COMPETITORS' FACES GET A LITTLE PALER ON SHOW JUMPING DAY. Warm-up is a den of nerves, and I'm sizzling away, too. I walk the course first thing in the morning for the second time, then the Ghost and Kittie Wilkins join me. I file away his tip about holding out on the turn to one of the combinations. That's about it for the Ghost; he can barely get a word in edgewise with Kittie consuming so much of the talking space around us with her nervous chatter.

Coach Silvio Mazzoni is requiring of US team riders a different sort of show jump warm-up than they are used to—over low, wide oxers. Down Under is catch-riding a couple of horses for his broken comrades, who stand anxiously on the sidelines in various braces or leaning on crutches. Nervous horses and riders are whizzing past. Down Under begins his warm-up on one of his horses just as I start jumping Cal. I'm hoping Silvio is as good a coach as he is good looking—dark, smoky, sexy—so I brazenly follow Down Under and do what Silvio says, as if Calvin and I belonged under his elite command.

Calvin is jumping well today, and I have him in hand in his slow, show-hunter canter. I focus as I enter the ring. Calvin balloons fences 1, 2, and 3. I feel his try and desire not to touch the rails—a rarity. I miss the inside turn to 4, and I momentarily panic, but recalibrate and continue. Calvin doesn't go near a rail until the last part of the triple. That's only one rail, but sixteen time faults. This tortoise is striving toward careful and clean, not fast and careless. Still, that inside turn eats at me.

I seek out Wofford. The first combination on cross-country at 4A-B—a wide table bending downhill to a right-hand corner—is a similar configuration to the corner combination we missed at Southern Pines. He tells me not to worry, but to bow the line in six strides. It's a completely different can of soup than the Southern Pines series. I'm not so sure. With

Cal's right drift and jumping downhill, he can too easily get away from me. I will have to jump the oxer as quietly as possible if I'm going to make the turn to the corner.

I KEEP MY JITTERS UNDER CONTROL AS I TACK UP AND HEAD OUT, walking the mile and a half from stabling to the cross-country track.

When we start to warm up, Calvin feels heavy in the bridle. The chain needs to be tightened, although it is already one hole snugger than it was at Southern Pines. I opt to leave it where it is, mainly because Barrett isn't in warm-up yet to help me.

Calvin launches out of the box like an Irish car bomb and over-jumps fences 1, 2, and 3. I struggle to get him back as we approach the fourth fence and the first combination. Despite my tugs, he jumps too big over the first element. I attempt to bow the line as Jimmy had advised, but we get to the corner on a half stride, and he skips out to the right. I groan as we circle and re-approach; he jumps it and we go on.

I let him run to the next fence. And the next. And the one after that. As we approach the keyhole jump combination, I stand up in my stirrups and water ski, my legs jammed forward in the stirrups, leaning way back, nearly lying down on my horse's back. I feel a rip and a tear in my left hamstring. Pain shoots up my thigh. I somehow get the combination done and finish the last few fences.

Three Advanced horse trials this spring, each with a run-out. It's no longer an anomaly, but a pattern. If I'd been able to get Calvin all the way back, I know I could have gotten the turn done to that corner.

I couldn't, and I didn't. I put so much bit in his mouth and clamp his mouth shut in order to be able to rate him, and then I can't turn him. The more forward leverage, the less steering ability.

Calvin's mouth changes so much from event to event, it's almost like figuring what container could best hold the sky.

AFTER EIGHT HOURS OF OVERBITTED TRAFFIC, WE START TO FEEL THE gravitational pull of DC and Baltimore.

"He's bigger than I remember," I say to Barrett, who's scooping Calvin's mash in his feed tub. I run my hands over Zurich's glossy blood-bay coat as he noses my pockets for a treat.

"He's got a nice eye," I note, "and a luscious tail." I remember the tail from when he trotted across the field at Pine Top.

"Let's see if he can jump," Barrett says cautiously.

I TAKE A DEEP BREATH AND TACKLE THE MAIL THAT HAS ACCUMU-lated in our absence, as well as the over one hundred emails selling Viagra and life insurance that have plopped themselves into my inbox. I'd rather be playing with Zurich.

He seems restless in his stall and glad to have company when I knock on his door to say hi. His ears are pricked.

I throw a leg over his back. Five feet, ten inches of me don't feel like too many on him, even though he stands at only 16.1 hands. His large barrel takes up my leg nicely. He has a big shoulder and a long neck, too, so I feel there's enough out in front of me. Even Barrett concludes he's a nice horse.

I'D RATHER NOT CHANGE THE BIT SO LATE IN THE SEASON, BUT MAYBE a heftier noseband would increase the effectiveness of my aids. Instead of riding Calvin, I search the Internet for a stronger cross-country noseband. Some show-hunter sites have nosebands with chains and tacks sewn into them. Hmm. Our country satellite connection cuts me off before I can find one with razor blades attached. I call Hope.

When she arrives at the barn, I adjust Calvin's cross-country bridle exactly as I'd had it at The Fork. Cal stubbornly takes a couple seconds too long to open his mouth for the bit. *Didn't we just do this?*

Hope looks at the get-up, purses her lips, and frowns.

"You've got the curb chain way too tight," she says. "When it's that tight, the bit can't rotate. And when the bit can't rotate, it becomes fixed and loses its effectiveness."

She demonstrates by loosening the chain and pulling on the reins, which cause Calvin to throw his head up and start backing up in his stall. Then she tightens it again, exerting the same pressure on the reins, and the horse doesn't budge.

"That answers that," I conclude.

"What else?" she asks, as if we were just getting started.

"LET'S SEE WHAT HAPPENS NEXT TIME HE GALLOPS OUT OF THE BOX," the Ghost says. "I'm going to give you the lecture I give to the living," he goes on. "Don't pay for your own training."

He wasn't wild about Zurich at Pine Top, and he's not wild about him now. Or rather, he's not wild about his price tag. He'd have to have either a spectacular trot or jump, and preferably both. He has a smooth and comfortable trot and an enthusiastic yet uneducated jump. I get the feeling that the Ghost had already decided he wasn't going to give him his thumbs-up before he even pulled in the driveway. Zurich's little devil ears flick back and forth as he "listens" to his new rider, trying to decide whether he likes her or not. But horses don't get to choose.

IN LIEU OF CAMOUFLAGE, I GO THE BACK WAY THROUGH HAMPSTEAD and Finksburg to get to Waredaca Farm.

Jimmy says he doesn't plan on doing much with Cal after his efforts at The Fork.

He has an exercise set up of three-, four-, five-, and six-stride lines, and talks about measuring strides within a line so that they are equal in length. Just what the doctor ordered: practicing varying lines over small fences. When we get to the bending three-stride line to the left, our ride is less smooth, and Jimmy tells me to put my right hand on Cal's withers to block his right shoulder from pushing out. Interestingly, it's the same configuration as the table-to-corner combination where we had a run-out at The Fork.

"Cavendish needs to go see Dr. Green tomorrow," Jimmy concludes.

I look at him quizzically. "Right," I say, "Dr. Green. I need to let him be a horse for a couple of days." Jimmy smiles his incomparable Cheshire smile.

He identifies Shiva, whom he is just meeting, as the sensitive Thoroughbred type who doesn't like to have his face touched. He suggests I ride him on a loopy rein, until over time and with increased confidence he will take a hold of the bit. Then I'll be able to ride him to his fences in a more connected way. Shiva's unwillingness to take the bridle is directly related to the weakness under the saddle. Jimmy suggests that I sit on him a little more lightly and closer to the pommel to relieve his back.

I run into Gretchen as I'm cooling out the horses and wrapping their legs. She compliments my ride at The Fork.

"Oh thanks," I say. "Yeah, we've been making some progress, I think."

"It was good to see," she says, with a slightly judgmental tone.

I'm anxious to get home to Zurich. My body thinks otherwise. Between the whopping pings in my hamstring and neck, and the usual lower back annoyance, I should be tapering my work, not beefing it up. But I can't help myself: there's a new horse in the barn.

I BREAK OFF THE SHOWER KNOB. WATER GEYSERS ALL OVER THE bathroom. Barrett galumphs into the depths of our creepy dirt-floor cellar, steps over the bodies gathering there, and turns off the main water valve. I wake in the night after inadvertently sleeping on my raging hamstring. If I position myself so it lessens the pain, I aggravate my neck.

I PULL MYSELF OUT OF BED IN STAGES WHEN THE SHADES START TO lighten. Right, no water in the house. Doubt creeps in with the light. How am I going to manage four horses? I'm crazy to consider it. My days are too pressed already. Yet Zurich is such a nice horse, the sort of boy you'd be happy to bring home to your mother.

My aching body says, "Slow down."
My father's soul says, "It's all about balance."
My smoldering heart says, "Buy him."

TENSION BUILDING AT THE IN-GATE AT PLANTATION FIELD HORSE Trials. I hate the pressure when people are watching. I get distracted from my inner focus. I canter into the ring to start our round, Patrick trying hard and jumping well. Until the last line—a four-stride to an in-and-out. I see a move-up distance, and Patrick crashes through the first oxer, then the vertical, almost getting a pole tangled in his legs. Jesus. Walking down the long, steep hill to the trailer, I keep my chin tucked tight to my chest.

I get sleepy while driving home and have to pull into a shopping center off I-95. I'm in Snooze Land as soon as the key turns. Georgia is conked out in the back seat. Even Patrick is too tired to paw when the engine stops. I wake up after a quick twenty, then get stalled in rush-hour traffic.

I'M UP AT THE CRACK. PATRICK DOESN'T WANT TO GET BACK ON THE trailer for cross-country day, and I have to smack him till he relents, my fury rising with the sun. Confucius says: A horse refusing to load on competition day does not bode well. Barrett insists on coming with me after yesterday's highway hypnosis. Misery loves company.

Plantation Field is not my favorite venue. Parking, show jumping, and dressage are at the bottom of a steep hill, all the way around the backside of the cross-country field. If it weren't for the excellent cross-country course, I wouldn't come here: too much hiking to get anywhere.

Despite my superstition, Patrick runs around the cross-country course easily. We accumulate nine time faults. We scooted along, but I slowed for the combinations. Still, we finish in sixth place. I'm relatively happy. Happy with Patrick, that is.

I want to curl into myself after the long day at Plantation. Every night I want to back off, scratch the next event or farm project. Every morning, I wake a little creakier, but nonetheless gung ho to start the day of horses and more horses. Until I'm too exhausted for much else besides my glass of relaxation … and the cycles of perpetual motion and perpetual indecision continue, an endless spoked wheel starting with work and ending with self-doubt, and starting all over again with the next day of work.

I CRACK A MOLAR CHEWING SOME LETTUCE. I SCHEDULE ANOTHER trip to the dentist.

The Ghost: *I'm worried about the lessons you've missed. Something I need to know?*

A breeze rustles the maple leaves in the front yard. The rope swing in the tree jostles. I cancel my dental appointment so I can get Calvin to the Ghost. That seems to satisfy my specter for now. He has probably gotten wind of my West Virginia trips, or maybe he's able to be in two places at once.

I stew for the rest of the day. My change in plans means I won't be able to take Calvin to the Stephen Bradley clinic this week—back-to-back jumping, too much for his legs. I go deeper into my funk—the blackout shade is pulled way down. Between my cranky hamstring and crankier mood, I plod around the farm as if I weighed three hundred pounds, eating protein bars on one side of my mouth, crying on the other. The tooth will just have to wait.

RAIN. THE LAST THING I WANT TO DO IS HEAD UP TO THE GHOST'S to jump outside in this weather—I consider fibbing. I text Esther for advice. She suggests a flat tire, wink, wink.

Julia: *But what would you do?*

Esther: *I'd sure think about it, but I'd probably end up going.*

I pop an extra Wellbutrin, go on with my plans.

When I get to the barn, Barrett has already studded Calvin for sand.

"No way was I going to put mudders in," he says, a decision that will limit my jumping to the Ghost's ring. Good choice. It won't be possible to show jump in his washed-out field today.

My tooth aches all the way to Sleepy Hollow.

The Ghost is chipper and inquisitive about the jumper show our farm is hosting this upcoming weekend for two of Maryland's Rolex hopefuls—where is everyone going to park, and do I know how many people are coming, etc., etc. Not one query about my recent whereabouts, as if he were covering his reprimand. He's all smiles, despite the blinding rain. He even asks where I'd prefer to jump—in the ring or in his field, and when I choose the ring, he quickly agrees. The Ghost is not all that different than I am when it comes to confrontation. We'd rather not have it. Not only does it require a lot of thinking outside the crypt, but it is so interruptive to a doer's compulsions. It's hard to get anything done when you're bitching about it.

We begin our jump school with the usual figure-eight over a plank vertical, proceeding on to the habitual grid.

Calvin jumps the exercises with a lot of try. I make two mistakes, off a left-lead canter when I bypass a better distance and Calvin has to chip in. The Ghost thinks I need more canter. I think I need more horse.

"I picked up a tip from a vet I'd like to share with you," the Ghost says at the end of the lesson. "Rather than joint injections, which can become less effective as the horse gets older, this vet recommends giving six doses of Adequan two times a year for older competition horses, plus a shot of Legend two days prior to a competition. I'm on my sixth shot with my stallion, and he feels like a million bucks."

Everyone has a slightly different recipe for the hard and soft parts to mend. As a tracker, Barrett has tried many of them. Once hurt badly himself, he empathizes with sore horses. As for myself, I know all too well how painful life can be. Best to just keep moving. To get things done.

I fight rain and traffic, arriving back at the farm at 1:30—in time for Calvin's massage, and for the rest of my day to begin.

Rachel coincidentally follows me into the farm. She is here for a pre-purchase exam of a horse April is selling.

"I was tailgating you the whole way," she says when we both pull up, "because I'm afraid of storms," she admits.

Too busy scribbling notes on my truck's center console, I hadn't noticed the dark skies brewing, nor the wind whipping up. Nor Rachel's white truck snuggling up to my taillights.

I pull my sweatshirt around me as the temperature starts dropping.

"Then you must have seen me swerving," I say.

"No kidding," she replies.

There's a law in the Free State forbidding texting and driving, also no hand-held devices, no vibrators. As far as I know, no one has outlawed cursive while driving—yet.

I pull out the horses' medium blankets from the laundry stack; apparently, we're not done with them yet.

As I turn the horses out, it starts sleeting, the pins and needles blowing sideways kind of sleet. The horses turn their backs to it in order to avoid its sting.

My accountant calls. "No," I reiterate, "we did not make a profit last year."

I MAKE MY COACH HAPPY, AND MY OWN DARKNESS LIFTS. I CAN attack the big fences, but I can't stand up to my Ghost.

Patrick balks when I try to load him. I grab my dressage whip, then decide not to force the issue, opting for the lead horse trick. Zurich marches up onto the trailer ramp as if he's been loading on my rig every day of his five years. The company is good enough for Patrick: he decides to go for a ride, after all. If it's Wednesday, it must be a Stephen Bradley day.

Patrick takes Cal's spot in the Intermediate/Advanced group. No worries—he rises to the occasion.

I arrive home to fifty trailers parked in our eastern hay field, a hundred horses and ponies milling about, and triple that number of people. Grills going, wine flowing, ponies zooming around the indoor. Daniel holds forth as judge for the jumper show we are hosting for his and Kate Chadderton's benefit before they head to the Rolex Three-Day Event in Kentucky next week. Barrett is having a ball, chatting it up with neighbors and admiring how many have come to our doorstep to school their horses and ponies and help two up-and-coming riders fulfill their dreams.

"Are you going to Rolex this year?" someone asks my husband.

"Not going to Rolex unless I hook up a trailer," he responds.

"Right," I say, ironically. Deep down, I am envious of Daniel and Kate, and all the other riders who have a chance to attack that Five-Star dream. I'd hoped to get there with Redmond, but he got hurt and had to be retired. And then he died. Calvin is not mentally sound enough to attempt it. If I work hard enough and am very lucky, my hope is to take Calvin around the Four-Star track at Fair Hill.

"It's a lot more fun if you don't have a horse with you," Daniel admits. He has had a bit of a shaky season in dressage and show jumping, and even got wet cross-country once, falling in the soylent green water at Pine Top. Still, I suspect that he will repeat last year's stellar performance in Kentucky. Daniel is mounted on a cross-country dream machine. Plus he's got the self-assurance needed to survive a Five-Star track.

Georgia introduces herself to the little girls and their ponies, leans against the mothers and fathers, begs for a scratch, stares at the hamburgers and hot dogs everyone is chowing down on, sniffs around the overflowing trashcans. When we retreat to the house to begin the end of our day, she sneaks out and returns to the party and won't come when called. Barrett trudges up to the barns to retrieve our party girl.

ONE OF THOSE SPRING DAYS THAT SMELLS AS THOUGH IT SHOULD BE eaten. Dogwood, forsythia, azaleas in bloom, the air heavy and moist, birds going nuts from their fencepost vantage points. I shove Calvin's mediocre dressage test under my saddle, and we tunnel under Gallaher Road to the Advanced cross-country course at Fair Hill Horse Trials. Calvin flies out of the box like a homesick angel, jumps the first three fences well. He's a little bull headed, but I get him back for the brush table and corner combination. He jumps the table big, and I get jarred behind the motion of my horse, causing the reins to slip on landing. Not enough time to regroup before the corner, I steer on a long rein and try to get my horse to the out of the combination. Calvin feels the soft escape on my right side and takes it. I swing around to re-present him to the B element, and he runs out again. I announce to the jump judge my intent to retire. But, like Calvin, she doesn't listen to me. Pen and clipboard in hand, she looks at me blankly.

"I retire!" I scream. "I retire! I retire! I retire!"

Two things built Rome: dreams and architects. The Ghost helps me with the dream of the sport. Jimmy and Stephen help me with the blueprints. I need both. A dream without technique is nothing, as is a technical plan without a dream.

I shouldn't put the blame on anyone else besides myself. It's ultimately my responsibility to be best prepared for the events. Still, sports training can be so psychological. I've become dependent on my ghosts for so much more than technique or self-confidence. It is a nebulous and necessary attachment, bordering on superstitious, like carrying a rabbit's foot.

The Ghost sends me an email: *What happened? You ok?* I don't answer until long after the sun has set, and I've lifted my head out of the morass of bad feeling. *Something's going on and I don't know what it is*, I say.

I don't want to ride, and I sure don't want to ride Calvin. He pokes his head out of his stall, looking for me.

I take Patrick on a long hack, I work on some basic dressage on Zurich, and then I take Shiva into the back field to work on his fear of open spaces. Calvin looks longingly at me as I walk up and down the shed row, busy with everyone else.

"What if you take me to Morven and run me around at Intermediate?" Calvin says. "What if we shoot for the Four Star at Jersey, or even the Three Star, and head to Bromont in June? I promise to be good."

I can't help my fantasies of a rearranged future with Calvin. Unless I want to bag the rest of his season, I better get his conditioning work done.

Calvin lets out a big belly breath as I enter his stall to pick his feet.

I keep Calvin on a longer rein and low in the poll for his medium trot work. Long and low, where he will stay relaxed. When I pick up the reins and ask for more, he tenses. What Calvin fears most is a loss of balance, and a change in speed changes the balance. So does shortening the reins. This is the first place he must learn to trust: change does not necessarily mean chaos.

His loss of confidence started at least two years ago, probably at Plantation, when he fell at the ditch and bank and we both went down—his nightmare loss of balance. He was never quite the same at Advanced after that. Certainly not at the Fair Hill International Four-Star Event, when he clambered over the third open oxer, then stopped at the water. He was excellent a year ago at Fair Hill Horse Trials, but then we had our fall at Jersey when I rode half blind. Part of a horse's ability to take a joke is the rider's ability to tell a good one, and Jersey was definitely a gag.

THE GHOST CALLS ME AT 8:00 A.M. ON THE BUTTON. HE'S IN Kentucky, prepping for his weekend at Rolex on his Five-Star stallion.

"So what happened?" he asks.

I explain Calvin's boldness out of the box, his enormous jump over the brush oxer, my loss of rein, my inability to get his balance between the two elements, his skid past the corner. Too big, too bold got us nowhere.

"GRC got the run-out," I say, having just studied the sequence of mistakes in the online gallery from the event photographer. "It's pretty clear what happened," I admit.

"Well, I wouldn't let it change your plans all that much," he says.

I interrupt his train of thought. "I don't think so either. Calvin needs a confidence run, so I was planning on Loudoun this weekend."

"That's a great idea," he says.

"I have to play it by ear from here on out," I go on. "In a way, he's going better than ever," I explain, thinking of his recent efforts in dressage and show jumping.

"I would agree," he says.

He suggests an exercise involving a maximum-height oxer set in my ring, four bending strides left to a corner, four bending strides right to a skinny. It's a deviation from his standard gymnastic exercise. It's what I've been waiting for.

Rachel enters Zurich's stall to begin his pre-purchase exam. She glances down at his front legs.

"He's crooked!" she exclaims.

"You'll have that," I say, having noticed his offset knees but not thought too much about it. Plenty of good horses have crooked legs. Hang out in the winner's circle at Pimlico, and you see all sorts of conformational defects trotting up for the win photo.

Rachel is a terrier about vetting—she won't let go. She investigates further. His crookedness has already affected his suspensory ligaments, which are both enlarged. One is reactive on palpation, and the other is active on ultrasound. She also has a lot to say about the faulty conformation of his hooves. She hauls out the X-ray machine, but stops after taking the first of thirty-two views. There's a small displaced chip in one of his fetlocks.

She wants to like him—who wouldn't like this adorable nice guy?— but she wrinkles her nose one too many times and finally tells me straight out, "I'd pass on this one, Julia."

I thank her for her honesty. I feel a wave of disappointment mixed with a curious sort of relief. How could I have managed four horses without any help except from Barrett—who seems to be auditioning for a role in *The Walking Dead*—his days strung taut from sunup to way past sundown? Like him, I am exhausted, with no time for anything else in my life besides deskwork and horsework. I can't even seem to buy a horse successfully these days. This is the second kin of Redmond's I've passed up this year. What does that say about my drive to get to the other side?

Barrett sets up the oxer-corner-skinny exercise, and Calvin jumps it perfectly, first time through. I suspect the lack of grade in my ring makes the exercise too easy for both of us. Next time, I'm going to set something similar on my hillside. Barrett tells me he's worried about running Calvin at Loudoun, the same track where he became unrideable after gaining too much confidence at the Two Star.

"The horse is making mistakes," he says. "Do you want to teach him to make mistakes bravely, or teach him not to make mistakes?"

"What the hell does that mean?" I say, although I'm pretty sure he is referring to the temptation for Calvin to be bad if he is not challenged enough on course. Bravery is only an asset if it's used for the greater good.

Esther arrives at sundown with storm clouds brewing, to get my help cross-country schooling her horse.

"There's no way you could have gotten that corner done, considering the way he landed off the table," she says. Though she struggles at the lower levels of eventing, Esther has made a careful study of the sport and has developed a good eye.

"Too big, too bold, too off balance. I need to get him all the way back for the combinations," I say.

"Easier said than done at the front of the course," she says. She knows what a brute Calvin can be out of the start box.

"Our issues *have* all been at the first combinations," I say. Next time, I'm going to trot that brush table if I have to. I hear Jim Wofford's voice booming from an approaching cloud: *These Advanced fences are a joke to Cavendish.*

"WOW," THE COURSE DESIGNER SAYS. "TALK ABOUT LEFT FIELD."

He needs a day or two to consider what he is going to do about Zurich.

In a perfect world, imperfections are the wonder. But this is not a perfect world—this world of eventing. It won't tolerate Zurich's imperfections. It isn't ready for his wonder.

I CALL CHANCE.

The fight that started with her father back in March is ongoing in April, the breakup with her boyfriend, same. Her unrewarding job of eight years still has its health-benefit hold on her.

I suggest she consider leaving New York, going somewhere where theater isn't so competitive.

"What, like Bawlty-more?" she asks, drawing out the syllables in her birth city's name, as if it were a dirty word.

"Well, maybe," I reply tentatively. It's true, I did notice that the local dinner theater is putting on a production of *Joseph and the Amazing Technicolor Dreamcoat.*

"The theater in Baltimore sucks," she says.

"Well, at least it would be something," I say.

In her mind, coming home is the equivalent of failure. Isn't that true for nearly everyone?

"She doesn't want advice," says Barrett. "You have to learn to diffuse her anger, not incite it. And suggesting she make a change is only going to make her mad."

"But if she's so unhappy, why wouldn't she want to change?" I say.

"She must get that from her mother," my husband says.

CALVIN DRAGS ME OUT OF THE BOX AT LOUDOUN HORSE TRIALS. IF Advanced fences are a joke to him, then Intermediate fences are a comedy show. I have zero brakes for the first three downhill fences. I'm pulling with all my might to the first combination—offset houses set three strides apart in a tree line. Calvin plunges in despite my yanking and sails out of the combination in two strides, gallops across the field, and takes off like a scud missile over the single fences. He Supermans the water, leaving me reinless. I should pull up, but I have just enough stupidity left in me to get the job done. I'm still pulling on the course's backside to the ditch and brush and rolltop offset three strides away. I neglect to ride forward, worried that Calvin is going to leave out another stride. I half halt too close in, and the horse ducks out.

I cannot believe it. Calvin has run out at the Intermediate level. He begins to sing his favorite song, "If You See Kay, Tell Her to Come on Home."

Our stadium round is just as noisy. In a severe bending line to an in-and-out combination, I see seven steps, and Calvin sees eight. I ask him to leave the ground too soon. Now Calvin says, *Va te faire foutre*, and stops at the one-stride. I re-present, he jumps it, and we go on.

JOINING THE OLD FARMHOUSE WITH THE MILK PARLOR, RENOVATING the bank and barracks barns, planting saplings that would flourish into trees, carving paddocks and pastures from cropland, designing the mare barn in the shape of a cross, figuring where the indoor should go, how many stalls, what size ring. The delicious fun of conceiving how to mold and fill an empty space. Like riding by feel, with no end in sight, but only the next tree, stream, woods path. This is how we built the farm.

I come home after a solid Preliminary run on Patrick to find the new frame for the mare barn apartment addition. I stand in the wash stall and look from its door past the mare barn field and rising hillock of alfalfa, to the last twinging green on this late spring day. I expect I'll miss the view once the addition is complete, where I've stood for twenty years, looking out, always in wonder—no matter the turmoil in my life—at just how beautiful fields can be. Horses grazing the new spring grass, the light so brilliant and clear, as if giving life to what it illuminates, like a Renoir.

You build, add on, and you take something away, too. As with Calvin. I train and I train, I take away a little of this or that, and add something else. As soon as I have a clue, it slips away. I try a new bit, a different training technique or instructor, a new medical procedure, but I am unable to mold my concepts into a workable form. The building has always got some crack or malfunction. Try as I might, it falls apart.

Six hundred miles away, the Ghost has run around double-clear on cross-country at Rolex, but he has a somewhat disappointing show jump round. I text him to congratulate, and he calls to talk about our respective weekends.

"I think you need to consider that Hope was wrong," he says.

GEORGIA THINKS WE'RE HEADING OUT ON A TRAIL RIDE, BUT WE'RE only circling the hay field. We return to the barn several times for a wardrobe change. As usual, I'm in search of a bit that will hold Calvin. Georgia gets fed up and retreats to the house.

I try a hackabit, which has a rubber nose and hackamore action, plus a rubber bit with a long shank for leverage. I add a tack noseband to see if Calvin will tolerate the little pin pricks digging into his nose. He seems to respect the bit because of the added pressure. I already know I'll like the Mikmar swoop, but I also know it will tear up his mouth. I settle on my old standby: the three-ring Waterford with a chain attached, plus the tack noseband. Ah, that's the feel I've been searching for: lightness in my hands.

I have a quiet night with the dogs. Barrett's off to New York to visit Chance. I follow my usual routine as if he were here, but allow each thought to hover and have that one-on-one with myself that is impossible when he's home.

Barrett has said for years that the Maryland Combined Training Association's horse trial would be perfect for Calvin. I hate running there. I feel like such a fish under glass at a venue so close to home. It is impossible to concentrate. Every time I turn around, I have to have a conversation with someone I haven't seen in a while. Ogre-ish recluse that I am, talking inwardly all the time, or on the page, but—God forbid!—not to anyone else.

BARRETT AND CHANCE HAVE PLANS TO GO TO AN *ELECTRIC LITERATURE* gig in New York and to scout for venues for his magazine to host. And, of course, plans to eat. This trip has special importance, as Barrett is the only member of the family still in Chance's good graces. She needs to talk to someone who will listen to her troubles, share her side-eye at life, and help her laugh. She needs an advocate.

I plan my day around the Ghost's appearance in the afternoon. Calvin, as usual, is first on my list. The Ghost shows up in my tack room with a new Professional's Choice western bit. He successfully used a lesser version of the rig on a couple of his stronger horses. He thinks this longer-shanked model will hold Calvin, who, he admits, is stronger than any of his. The mouthpiece is very thin, and I'm worried it will damage his mouth. Even so, it's more important that I be able to hold him than save his mouth, this close to the Four Star.

Calvin feels feather-light in the new bit and nearly jumps me out of the tack over the first fences. I'm slightly intimidated by the brakes, fearing I'll make a mistake while using the bit. But I have hopes that it will hold Calvin. Once I get a feel for it, I swap back to the hackamore mid-lesson. I don't want to dull his mouth.

The Ghost is happy about his successful run at Rolex, though a little disappointed, too, in both his dressage score and show jump round.

"That horse is not the hardiest of creatures," he reminds me, referring to his Five-Star stallion. "And it's a little harder for him now at fifteen," he continues. I wince, thinking of Calvin's same age.

"We are both running out of time," I whine.

"But I don't think you should stop on Calvin," he says. "I just think you have a control issue. How does that saying go? Why stop five minutes before the miracle happens?"

The only bit that holds Calvin hurts Calvin. And then he has to repair from the hurt, which takes time. I'm a stubborn woman, bent on repeating the unrepeatable, controlling the uncontrollable—Calvin's bid at the first combinations, Chance's unhappiness, Barrett's sickness.

My eyes sting. I turn away from my Ghost.

Barrett returns home as I'm making dinner. He waves his prize in front of my nose: a small Tupperware container, whose contents are the color of the heirloom yellow tomatoes I'm using for pesto. He puts Chance's drug-free urine in the freezer. I hope no one mistakes it for Limoncello.

BARRETT CALLS ME FROM THE BARN—"BENTLEY'S SICK."

Bentley was April's first pony, and he's one of Barrett's favorites.

"Have you called the vet?" I inquire.

"I'm here with Rachel now," he says.

Bentley's colon is displaced, making it a potential surgical colic. Bentley is twenty, and April and her mother have decided he will not be a surgical candidate at his age.

The vet comes and goes all day. The rain keeps at it, with long bursts of heavy downpours. Rachel shows up again at 11:00 to fill out a health certificate for Zurich, who is leaving with Brook Ledge Horse Transport for Florida, and to evaluate Rhapunzel's questionable hind-end soundness. She then returns to Bentley. It does not look hopeful, though the pony is stubbornly hanging in there. Rachel hangs bag after bag of fluids and injects enough painkillers to keep him comfortable. April and her mother walk and lunge him, even take Bentley on a short trailer ride to try to jostle the colon back into place. Nothing works, and his heart rate continues to climb. Around 5:00, once the heart rate reaches 85, Rachel says it's time.

They lead him out under the apple tree, struggling to keep its blooms in the cold wet rain.

"What am I going to do without him?" April's mother, Fleur, asks. Fleur inherited Bentley from her daughter. "He is everything to me. This farm is the place where I leave the rest of my life behind and feel peace."

"You'll have that again," I say. "It'll be ok," though I have no idea if it will be or not.

"Would you like to take a piece of his forelock?" I ask. "Barrett, why don't you go get a tarp," I suggest. I turn back to my husband to see him in tears. Rachel, too.

"Would you like to bury him here?" I ask. Fleur and April look somewhat startled by the question, and confused about having to make more decisions.

"Could we do that?" Fleur asks. "Would that be ok with you?"

"Of course," I say, and Barrett pipes up, "He'll go next to Charm and Old Mare." "And Show-Show," I add. "And Charred Angel and Little Tommy," he goes on, beginning to list all the horses we've buried on top of the hill over the last twenty years. I'm surprised by how few of them there actually are.

Kevin Powers arrives with his backhoe less than an hour later, and Barrett helps him load up the body and then, in the relentless rain, accompanies him to the top of the hill. I watch from the mare barn wash stall the distant dinosaur reach again and again into the sopping earth, as if digging for eggs.

Chapter Eight

The Impeded Stream Is the One That Sings

A WEAK SUN STRUGGLES AS INTERMITTENT CLOUDS SPIT ON ME. Shealagh Costello at the USEF reports that I'm not qualified for the Four Star at Jersey Fresh. I need a clean Advanced run within the last year.

"I thought I could have a twenty," I say, meaning twenty jump penalties cross-country, the equivalence of a run-out or a stop.

"No, it has to be clean," she corrects.

This will mean a long road trip to Quebec in June. I reroute the training chart to Bromont, an old Cajun word meaning "expensive disease when you've run out of options at the foot of the mountain."

I'd hoped for Jersey and an early end to Calvin's season. Now I'll have to keep the Gaelic torch burning for another month, thirty days past his present peak.

Black clouds. Troubles. The sky's piano has only sharps and flats today.

SOME CANADIAN EVENTERS SHOW UP FOR THE WEEKEND. THEIR horses will stay at our farm. Over hamburgers and ears of corn, Kelly raises her finger to pause the conversation, runs out to her truck, and returns with a canvas she jimmies through the front door. She places it across from me: Frida Kahlo in red, with her dark caterpillar unibrow, hand patting the neck of Calvin's exact likeness.

"I don't do people very well," Kelly apologizes for her colorful impressionism. "I painted it from a photo I took at the Bromont jog two years ago."

"No one has ever painted me before," I say, trying to find the right words for my appreciation.

We prop up the painting against the piano in the Ancestors' Room. A photograph of my parents descending the stairs at their wedding reception hall in 1943 fills one wall. My father, in his Navy dress blues, has his head turned toward his new wife. My mother looks demurely down, probably to avoid tripping over her train. A large oil of an eighteenth-century man and wife, distant great-greats, fills another wall. The eighteenth-century groom turns his head and grasps the plump, white hand of his beloved. And now this: Calvin cocks his head toward me. The eighteenth century and I gaze out toward a future audience, sipping beers and Chardonnay and wondering what kind of run we'll have tomorrow.

CALVIN'S DRESSAGE TEST IS DECENT. HE LOSES ONLY ONE RAIL IN show jumping on the uneven wet potato field next to the busy entrance. I have a gulp moment cross-country when he jumps a big table and has to bend to a left-hand corner. He hesitates—likely considering a left run-out, made easier by the narrow side of the corner. I put my left leg on and keep that rein snug against his neck to prevent the mistake.

"Told ya so," Barrett says at the finish flags. Barrett has been saying for years that Shawan Downs would be an ideal Advanced track for Calvin, because of the short ship and yielding turf. In reality, Barrett prefers venues like Seneca, Middleburg, Fair Hill, and Shawan Downs, which all incorporate a race track into their design.

It's possibly the best run I've had with Calvin. I could send him, turn him, rate him, and he was, most importantly, happy to jump the jumps. What I don't admit is that, two years ago, I would not have felt his momentary deviation at the corner. Two years ago, I did not have to ride Calvin defensively. He still trusted me then.

There's our Jersey Fresh qualifier, a week late. Too much for his legs to run again next weekend, three weekends in a row. I opt to eat the entry fee and brush up on my *passé composé* instead.

The Ghost is sitting on his mounting block, dressed for cross-country, resting a moment between runs. I ask him what he would recommend for Patrick's conditioning schedule in preparation for the Two Star.

"Two trips up your back hill at the trot, then one trip at the canter. Work up to three trips over the next few weeks," he throws out.

Patrick could have done that in his sleep six months ago, I'm thinking. It would not have occurred to me to ask someone who's licensed in four states to train racehorses—my husband. I amend the schedule according to Patrick's present readiness—trot for fifteen, then three trips up the back hill—with a mental note to check Down Under's conditioning charts for readying a Two-Star horse. And to discuss my plan with Barrett at magic hour.

Esther marches up to my trailer waving a green ribbon and red halter—Calvin's prizes for the day. I rattle on about the western bit, and how well he turned in the combinations.

"Well, those barrel racers in a bull pen sure need to turn!" she quips.

One combination still gives me trouble—a call from my ex. I take such a hearty sip of my Chardonnay that my hair gets wet. Jack is still on the outs with Chance and isn't accustomed to that position. Usually I'm the bad cop he saves her from. No longer. Chance, like her father, is quick to react and to anger, and must always have the last word, which makes for long arguments.

I remind Jack that Chance needs to figure out her life for herself. I encourage him to try to distance himself from her for a while.

My son would rather cut off his hand than encounter conflict. He is capable of understanding and coming to terms with just about anything. When one of his best friends in high school committed suicide, it was Chance who went to pieces. He remained stalwart through the ordeal of mourning, of understanding how something that horrible could happen to one of his friends. When a second friend killed herself two years later, he was again calm and reasonable, a soothing helper to his sister and friends who were in anguished shock. How do you find ways to be happy when you're wired to be otherwise, and when the world around you is mirroring your own despair? Like mother, like daughter: as I have continued to test the limits of my own unhappiness by pushing and pushing, what else could I have expected from my daughter? It involves a lifetime of searching and compromise and discovering ways to balance a life always on the verge—that nebulous frightening unknown space right before anything could happen, between the saddling and the running of a race.

It has taken me twenty-five years to realize that my kids' personalities spring from the same essence. Subjected as small children to violent arguments, their opposite reactions to stress have manifested in two radically different ways of dealing with life's problems: John calmly retreats, while Chance gets in everyone's face.

FOR THE LAST COUPLE OF DAYS, WE'VE HAD TO HELP DAISY UP THE three steps at both front and back doors. She is hardly able to hobble from the kitchen to the family room. Still, she perks up for treats and is always bright eyed to see us. Managing Daisy has become nearly a full-time job, impossible if one of us isn't on the farm during the day. Impossible to manage, yet impossible not to manage. This is my agony.

Julia: *I just don't think we're quite ready.*

Peaceful Passage: *Ok, you'll know when it's time.*

An adage I don't trust. So much of my caring for Daisy and reading her feelings is guesswork. I don't believe I have that kind of power to know.

Julia: *When would be the next day you have available?*

I have already canceled three previous appointments.

Dog Zodiac

1.
I don't like outliving my dog.
Or even the next pup, if I'm lucky.

In fact, I wish I *were* my dog,
living his whole life with the one and only

me, who, yes, grows older,
but how

slowly! *Meanwhile,*

2.

my fatty tumors

multiply,
until I feel

her disgust
when she grooms me,

or massages an ear,
after her first, languorous glass,

during the one they call the lonely hour,
the only one in her day,

where she'll take the time
to learn the ways

I am inexorably changing.
And preparing to leave.

DAISY CAN'T GET UP WHEN I FEED THE DOGS BREAKFAST, AND WHEN I hoist her up in her harness, she lets loose all over me and the kitchen floor. She can't stay standing and plops back down like a rag doll. As I begin to clean up the mess, she shits where she lies and then looks up at me yearningly.

The dog struggles peg legged to her favorite place on the living room carpet.

It's a brilliant, sun-shiny day. Calvin and I walk across Mt. Zion Road and up a steep climb through a stand of maples and ash, back down again and across the road, crossing Baden's stream. The grade tumbles fourteen feet from the Old Trenton Mill to the saw mill downriver, making the current swift and sure, to once mill a thousand bushels of wheat, or cut enough planks to build a church in one day. Or take the sting out of sore ankles. We climb up a steep woods path, galloping across the hilltop to the long walk through the last set of woods, the last rugged uphill and down, across the treacherously banked smaller stream that skirts Stoddard's Delight and runs adjacent to our steep paddock. I spy what looks to be a cornerstone from an old building.

"I think I may have found Charlotte's schoolhouse," I say to Barrett through my cell. In my mind, I've already built the building and lit the fireplace, and the schoolkids are jockeying for a close seat to the fire on a cold winter's day. Anything to escape my present moment. Barrett is too preoccupied with our old dog to care much about what might have been.

Calvin is still puffing when we return to the barn, and my mind has settled into that almost peaceful state that happens when I escape my immediate worries on a long hack with my horse. When Daisy was a younger dog, she'd be right beside us.

Barrett and I spend the rest of the morning in the house with Daisy, waiting for Dr. Rabinowitz. I lie down next to my old dog and hug her while she sleeps. When the vet comes to the door, Daisy doesn't lift her head, nor flinch when the vet administers the sedative. I whisper something in the dog's ear I will never admit to anyone, before Georgia and I return to the barns, and before the second fatal shot. Barrett stays with our dog for her last moments.

DOWNSTAIRS IS VAST AND EMPTY WITHOUT HER. GEORGIA MOPES around, won't get out of the big bed and come downstairs when she hears my pourings—she knows there's nothing in store for her. No Daisy to greet. She may as well catch a few more dreams.

I'm up and at 'em in my sorrow. Grief is a luxury. Or is it? I simply know no other way than to keep moving, get the horses ridden, office and barn chores done, the list checked off and added to, even as I accomplish the last task of the day and the light leaves me, Daisy now gone, we are all leaving, gray lumps of ash accumulating underneath the grand piano.

WE GET TO PLANTATION FIELD IN UNIONVILLE BY 6:00, WALK THE course until 7:30, in the tack by 8:00—all so Patrick can decide he doesn't want to play the dressage game. He is slow to react off my leg for the first medium trot, picks up the wrong lead, won't go forward, then breaks into the canter when he is supposed to be trotting at test's end.

After my second course walk, I come back to the trailer to find Barrett taking a thermometer out of Patrick's ass while the horse is peeing in the crossties.

"That's the second time he's done that and the trailer is a mess," Barrett says. "I think he may have a problem."

"What sort of a problem?" I ask.

"You know, like what you get," Barrett says, sounding almost embarrassed, "a UTI."

"You've got to be kidding," I say.

Even Barrett is succumbing to the way of all failing event riders, desperate for a medical excuse for poor performance. He wants me to succeed so badly.

"Geldings get them all the time." He goes on, "They spend so much time lying on their penises in the dirt."

I didn't wake up at three this morning for dressage. "Let's see how he show jumps, then decide whether or not to run him cross-country."

In show jumping, Patrick knocks fence 2, then jumps extravagantly over fence 3. I nearly eat Heaven. Patrick jumping like a jack-a-lope means he feels well enough to tackle cross-country.

He runs around the course easily and well within the time. That horse does like to go to his fences. And he's easy as anything to gallop—I can let him out, and he comes right back. Barrett has a smile on his face as we whiz across the finish line.

"That horse was gettin' it," he says. "I never thought much of him till just now. You've got a solid Prelim horse on your hands," he says.

That man loves a good gallop, and he has seen them so rarely with Calvin. A galumphing 18-hand Irish sport horse is not exactly a streamlined affair. Plus I'm usually waterskiing off my stirrups, struggling to keep the heavy-handed runaway in check.

As soon as Patrick gets back on the trailer, he takes another endless pee. My husband and I look at each other, eyebrows raised.

Barrett and I are ready for bed by noon, but we have to pack up and drive the two hours home. Our trip is marred by a conversation with John, who is engaged in a fight with his sister. The last thing I want to deal with after a good run the day before Mother's Day is a family feud, John retreating and Chance putting on the gloves.

I tell John that the maelstrom with his sister will pass. But how do I tell Chance that she's making excuses for her own fear of failure? Seven years since her graduation from Sarah Lawrence, she must feel discouraged, still answering telephones as a restaurant booking agent, auditioning for roles alongside thousands of other hopefuls, and trying to write competitive plays. She's gotten stung plenty. She suffers from the same disease I've got. Why not stop now?

John doesn't want to talk about the details; he just wants to hear my voice. I can tell from the strain in his own how hurt he is by his sister's accusations. Instead, he digresses.

"I'm trying to trace Charlotte's kids, but I haven't had any luck so far. The records are kind of hazy. Doesn't look like she had any more after she married Tracey in 1876. She lived from the time of Stephen's death in 1862 till 1876 alone with her children in our house."

Around White Marsh I go back to my attempted nap. But when I glance over at Barrett, he's heavy lidded and fighting his own lack of sleep, having been up and running for twelve hours. If he dies at the wheel, I want to be there for him. I don't want to be dreaming. I pinch myself awake and click my seatbelt.

Two miles from home, crawling up Blackrock Hill, "This is where his wagon overturned," my sleepy husband mumbles.

I get goosebumps at the thought of Charlotte's husband's fate, and how blindly ours have been linked to his tragedy.

Talk of death rouses Barrett. "I can see how this man worked," Barrett offers. "He timbers the top of the hill, rolls the logs down. Takes the wagon to the sawmill to drop off the timber, picks up a load of bark. Takes the load of bark to Scott's Tanyard. If he'd lived, he would have picked up a load of leather for the return. This guy never hitched his wagon without five strings tied around his fingers to remember what he had to do."

Once home, we open the trailer to a stream of pee running down the ramp, Patrick nonplussed by his urgency.

THE PHONE PARALYZES MY VOCAL CHORDS, ESPECIALLY WHEN IT comes to my daughter. Texting, I can fashion my words the way I want, with a little reflection and editing thrown in. It's about the illusion of control, which is my problem riding Cal: I don't have it. And Cal can't text.

Mom: *I've got an idea. I need more help and have been considering getting a working student. Why don't you come home for a while and work for me? You could use your spare time to write and figure your next step.*

Chance: *It is degrading and hurtful to me that you would suggest such an idea. New York is my home. Don't you ever suggest such a thing to me again.*

I've always loved Mother's Day—it's the one day of the year I can say anything I want without feeling guilty.

I talk at length to John, Mollie, and Barrett, but nothing assuages my worry about how unhappy Chance is, and about how much she blames her family—the ones nearest her—for all of her troubles.

I hack Calvin, Georgia trotting on ahead. His step perks up when we head down the farm road and pick up the pace. We turn toward Amos's Venture, find a trail here, a field there, wending our way and having fun going nowhere in particular. Georgia stays close, nose to the ground, stopping to investigate some tree branch or woodchuck mound, then racing to catch up. She takes a funny step or two with her left hind but works out of it like a good hunter.

Chance: *May I call you at 6:15 to wish you Happy Mother's Day?*

I bite my tongue when she calls. The subject of Barrett comes up. He's not feeling well again. I'm worried.

"Well, he sure felt well enough to write me two nasty emails yesterday," she says.

Chance is not the only one who responds viciously when afraid. Whatever it was that Barrett wrote, I'm sure it was his own frustration surfacing while trying to protect me. We've all been afraid lately.

I opt to say nothing. I can't handle what the response would be. I get out of the conversation as quickly as I can, sit on a trunk outside Calvin's stall, elbows on knees, head dropping to my chest, as if I were a statue, thinking.

It's another Black Dahlia dressage day. Calvin needs to be restricted from going forward until he is soft and waiting. Shiva needs to press his right hind underneath his body. Patrick must bend and give through his ribcage. I twirl small circles with him until I'm nearly dizzy, in an exaggerated shoulder-in, as I'm asking his hindquarters to step out in a leg-yield.

My body aches. No biking for me tonight. Instead, I head to the garden. I start yanking weeds and turning over soil as if I were possessed. I prepare the entire patch where the lettuces and peas will go. I'm still on my knees when the light starts to fade, postponing walking into an empty house without Daisy to greet me.

An email from Chance, sent ten hours ago, that I dare not open.

I'm celebrating with a vodka tonic and a guilt chaser: three great rides with the Ghost.

Julia: *Forgot to mention that the Black Dahlia was at the farm yesterday to give some dressage lessons.*

It's not too late to send this text, but it's too late for me to deal with his reply.

"The real question is why you lather these professional relationships with so much needless emotion," Barrett says.

I take another swig.

IN AN EFFORT TO REWARD THE CONSCIENTIOUS SET, WHO HAVE nothing better to do, the eventing rules change every six months or so. Patrick now needs an FEI passport for the Two Star. Damn the USEF! Used to be that a horse didn't need a passport until he reached the Three-Star level. As I begin the paperwork process, I stumble on the fine print: Allow six to eight weeks for processing.

I've got exactly one week before the start of competition.

At dinner hour, Barrett lies washed out on the couch. Huddled under the throw, he says he's cold, though he just took a shower. It's 70 degrees outside. I feel his forehead. I take his temperature: 100. I start texting and emailing everyone I can think of who can drive a rig or learn quickly. Only then do I call Barrett's doctor. I bring my husband chicken soup and tea, and tuck him into bed. He is either shivering beside me or getting out of bed to clean up his blood.

I am far from nurse-like. I was the same way with John and Chance—good about supplying ginger ale but weak on bedside comfort, and always yearning to get back to the horses.

BARRETT'S FEVER IS 101.2 THIS MORNING. I INSIST HE GET TO HIS doctor. I need him well enough by next weekend to drive Patrick and Calvin and me to Lexington, and do all the work of a groom once there.

The doctor puts Barrett back on a fistful of steroids and advises that if he's not markedly improved within twenty-four hours, then we head to the hospital.

I complete three seven-minute canters with Calvin and three sixes with Patrick, and both are game and driving in the final seconds. Patrick is particularly full of himself.

"That one has some get up and go," I report to Barrett.

"I know, I saw that at Plantation," he croaks. "He's a good turf horse."

There's something to be said for a man who knows his Thoroughbred biomechanics and functional breeding, as if it does make a difference who we come from.

BARRETT WAKES WITH CHILLS AND BLOOD. I BOOT UP SHIVA AND load him on the trailer. Fair Hill Horse Trials today.

"Don't forget the thermometer!" I yell. Barrett shuffles to the rig.

Out the driveway, turn right on Blackrock. In goes the thermometer. Halfway down Blackrock, he pulls out the lollipop.

"101.6," Barrett whispers.

"I'm taking you to St. Joe's."

It isn't so much the fever, but the awareness that Barrett's body could crash at any time. They call it consumption for a reason. We need to catch the first clue of that happening.

We pull into the hospital parking lot. I hog three spaces with the truck and trailer. I open one of the trailer side doors so Shiva can get some air and see the sights of this bizarre horse trial. He whinnies as I push Barrett toward triage.

Nurses hook Barrett up to an IV, get the fluids on board, promise him a room in an hour. He encourages me to leave, and so I leave.

Back at the trailer, a cue of doctors, nurses, hospital workers, and visitors are ogling Shiva, as if he were part of *Chevaux sans Frontières*.

I call the Fair Hill secretary to scratch Shiva, long past his missed trip down centerline. I take Calvin and Georgia over to Wilmot's Retirement. We meander through interconnecting fields and woods trails, Georgia dashing on ahead, Calvin with ears pricked, happy to be out of the ring. I note the off-again-on-again lameness in Georgia's left hind. For the hour that we're gone, I can almost pretend that everything is ok, that no plans will have to be changed or adjustments made, that Georgia is sound, that my husband is not dying.

I feed and turn out the horses, settle in for the night. Over wine, I call Barrett only to find him hot and freezing all at once, his fever spiking. I tell him to ring for the nurse, that I'll call him right back. I call the nurse's station: 103.6. The nurse tells me they've got double Tylenol on board. Tylenol? Good lord, I could have administered that at home. Why this high fever with IV antibiotics in his system? No good answer for that. She's a nurse—tells me what she is doing for the problem, not why the problem is occurring.

The list of poets who died of TB is long, but the list of everyone who died of it is much longer. I try to sleep, Georgia snuggling tight against me.

I ARRIVE AT THE HOSPITAL EARLY. BARRETT IS NO BETTER, NO WORSE. They've got ice packs on him, four on his legs, two on his ribs, one on each shoulder.

Barrett's eyes don't meet mine—he keeps glancing around the room, but we're alone.

"There are faces coming out of the wall. Children's faces," he says.

"Prolonged sweats and fevers are the window to hallucinations," his day nurse reassures me.

Midday, I return home to check on Marta's progress with the morning shift, and to get my rides done. I focus on the exercises that the Dahlia suggested—small circles of an exaggerated shoulder-in and haunches-out, slowing Calvin's collected trot rhythm, softening when he takes the outside rein. I use the corners to half halt with my body, fingering the rein as little as possible. Then, in that small configured circle, I leg-yield him toward the track—he lightens on the forehand, feels connected and through.

There's no one to share my good ride with.

Back at the hospital, I consider putting my plans on hold.

"Go to the event," Barrett says, without opening his eyes.

I text the Ghost, *Count me in for Tuesday's lessons.*

As I'm trying to fall asleep, I fret about Barrett. Then the horse. I have worked so hard to get Patrick ready for the Two Star. I've paid the entry, I've put the fitness work on him. I fall asleep, my father's words roiling around in my head: *Make a decision and don't look back.*

LESS THAN FORTY-EIGHT HOURS BEFORE THE START OF THE TWO Star. I feel the impossibility of what I want to do.

I have a great jump school on Calvin. At the hospital, there's a new line going into Barrett's body. A white paste of protein, fat, saline, and antibiotics. He's grumpy—a good sign. His fever broke in a huge sweat last night, he tells me. He's finally alert enough to complain. I'm so elated about the lost fever that I miss his rendering of the nurses' installation of a PICC line directly into his heart—how they levitated the bed toward the ceiling, how they spoke in incantations: "Inserting now, now, now," one said, as assured as the Queen of Swords.

We get around to the subject of Virginia.

"I'd be disappointed if you didn't go," Barrett says.

I climb onto his hospital bed to get as close to him as I can. What I'd really like to do is go to sleep until all of this is over, and Barrett is home and well. His mother arrives for a visit, so I pop up for pleasantries. She leaves, and then I do, too, when Barrett gets heavy lidded and I can tell he is done with visitors, even me.

I finish my rides and work. I have to wait till the light gets as heavy as my husband's eyes before April arrives to help me jump Patrick. I finally sit down to another meatless dinner of salad and baked potato and about twenty new concerned messages that have come in, including one from Chance, who wonders, as everyone does, if I need anything. I ask if she would attend my brother-in-law's sixtieth birthday bash in my stead at their home in Jersey City. My brother and Mark married soon after our parents' deaths. I zero in on my immediate dilemma.

Mom: *Do you think I should cancel my event this weekend?*

Chance: *Being an athlete is ten percent physical and ninety percent mental. If you are not in the mental space to do it, then don't. There will always be another Two Star. There will never be another Barrett. There will never be another man who loves you that much.*

THE DOCTORS HAVE TO FOOL BARRETT'S BODY INTO BELIEVING IT'S better than it is, because the good fight is killing him. One suggests Humira, yet they are concerned about adding a new drug into his medical mix, fearing the TB in his body. Humira blocks the ability of the immune system to recognize TB, while shutting down the body's negative responses to being autoimmune.

"That shouldn't be too much of a problem, should it?" I ask the doctor. "Can't you just give him more TB meds?"

The internist stalls. "Well, it wouldn't normally be a problem," he says, "except that apparently where your son was in India has the most virulent strain of TB in the world, resistant to all TB medications."

"But if John tested negative for TB," I counter, "then how could he have passed it to Barrett?"

"That's a very good point," the doctor agrees.

I call John to double-check that his TB test was negative.

"I never got one," he admits.

My whole body starts to shake. "Stop everything and go get one this afternoon," I spit.

I call Chance to vent, I call Jack to vent. Then my head explodes.

I call Barrett at the hospital.

"I did it," he says groggily.

"You did what?" I ask.

"They gave me eight doses. Four in each leg."

"Really?"

"Doc said I don't have any option," he explains. "I'm in no shape to undergo surgery. And that if we don't do something soon, I run the risk of going septic. I'm definitely in no shape to survive going septic."

I BAG THE TWO STAR.

I take Calvin to the top ring to get away from other riders.

Through my disappointment, I never get his body as supple as it felt the other day. Riding Calvin is like riding the Leaning Tower of Pisa—so tall and Gothic yet inherently flawed—fighting imbalance and gravity with a breathtaking fragility, as if suspended in the very act of falling.

For horse as well as rider, that's the one thing about eventing: it makes you face your flaws. You have to work with them, improve them, even make art out of them.

Barrett is sitting up in bed when I arrive at the hospital. He asks that we take a stroll. Ramrod straight, he pushes his IV cart down the corridors ever so slowly, chatting about farm business and life after St. Joseph's.

I return home and shut down for the day. I am making myself a late supper—yet another baked potato and salad, a jockey's best friend.

CHANCE: *I JUST WATCHED A GUY DO PUSH-UPS OVER A WOMAN'S MOUTH with his cock.*

Ah yes, my brother-in-law's birthday bash.

Mom: *Glad I'm not there.*

Chance: *It's inspiring. I think I'm gonna strip for cash from now on. You just have to look good, wear nothing, and shake your ass in people's faces.*

Mom: *I need to go do night check.*

Chance: *Ok. Take care. Rest up. I'll let you know which penis is the best.*

"BETTER KICK YOUR BOYFRIEND OUT," BARRETT SAYS. "I'M COMING home tomorrow!"

"Oh, that's wonderful, honey," I lie, making a note to cancel my plans with the Ghost.

Barrett's immune system was killing him. By shutting down his immunity, he's been saved—as long as he doesn't get sick from something that requires immunity. Ironic that such a contrary person would find his cure in being incurable.

He reminisces over an applesauce Jell-O recipe from his youth.

Here you go, his mother emails me. *I'm guessing on the size of the apple-sauce container.*

> *3 oz. pkg of raspberry Jell-O*
> *1 c. boiling water*
> *24 oz. jar plain applesauce*

Mix together the Jell-O and hot water until the Jell-O is dissolved. Stir in the applesauce till well mixed. Refrigerate till firmly set.

I was a product of the South ... Jell-O has cult status in Southern cooking ... the military ... again Jell-O heaven ... and a mother who had a career! Fast and easy was critical to that lifestyle. Enjoy!

JOHN ACCOMPANIED HIMSELF NIGHTLY ON THE GUITAR TO PHISH and Dave Matthews and Jeff Buckley songs behind his closed bedroom door throughout high school, before he left for India, and the sitar and sarode and surbuhar, and long treatises on the origin of sound.

Mom: *The CD of Paul Brady arrived. Thanks so much! I'm listening to it now.*

John: *Nice! Like it?*

Mom: *I love the music!*

John: *Yeah me, too. ☺ I've learned a bunch of his songs on the guitar. Did you listen to "Lakes of Pontchartrain" yet? Gorgeous.*

He tells me the children's names: Ida, Stephen Jr., and Amos. Charlotte Fowble has taken on a presence of her own at the farm. All my ghosts seem to be waiting for something to happen.

Mom: *Walking into the hospital now. I will be so glad when this is over.*

The doctors have changed their minds and decided to keep Barrett for another day. Just smelling the stale-sweet hospital air has put me in a foul mood.

Barrett is sitting up, chowing down on a baked minnow and a thimbleful of mashed potatoes. There are more calories in a Eucharistic wafer.

"I see Kate Chadderton is going to Bromont, why don't you ask her?" he offers, with his mouth full of something that once had fins.

"That'd mean I wouldn't have my own rig," I say.

"I guess it depends on how bad you want it," he says.

I get quiet, mulling over my options. Nothing sounds right to me without having Barrett along. Nothing sounds right without having my Barrett whole. Screw the competitions.

I leave him early to get back for an hour of mad biking.

I continue my text conversation with John over my own rations—sautéed sausages, baked potato with gobs of butter and soy sauce, and a loaded salad.

Mom: *I am having a really hard time with the prospect of stepping down from my sport.*

John: *Do you want to talk?*

Mom*: Not really, if you don't mind. I am much better on the screen.*

John: *Ok no prob.*

Mom: *I have worked so hard and I want it all to have meant something.*

John: *I think all athletes have to deal with that at some point, and you just need to find another expression for your sport. It can still be there, just maybe in a slightly different way.*

Mom: *But I don't know what that is yet.*

John*: Hey, my TB test was negative.*

That's my boy, saving the best for last.

I message Kate Chadderton to see if she has room for Calvin on her rig to Quebec. In the morning her reply is awaiting me: *Oui.*

BARRETT IS TAPPING HIS TOES IN THE HOSPITAL'S SIXTH-FLOOR VESTIBULE with a small stack of poetry books. He looks like such a hopeful little boy—he's going home. He rises slowly and we make our way to the elevators, where he pauses to catch his breath. I insist on fetching the car from the parking lot. Once home, he spends most of the day either on the couch or in bed. He makes a few stabs at his computer in between naps. When he's neither typing nor sleeping, he totters around the house like a crestfallen zombie, weak in his knees, pretending he's getting things done.

An old friend emails me that she can probably help me in Bromont. I text the Ghost to tell him that I have transportation options.

Julia: *I think I should do everything in my power to get there, don't you?*

The Ghost: *I am thinking about it. I would have loved to see you have the run this past weekend.* He is referring to Lexington, where I was also planning on running Calvin around the Intermediate track.

Later in the day he calls me.

"I think there's too much of a gap between MCTA and Bromont. That's five weeks he won't have run."

From my stubborn vantage point, I don't see how an Intermediate run at Virginia would have proven much, nor prepared Calvin any better for Bromont. Still, the Ghost's hesitation strikes a chord. It is a long way to travel under tenuous circumstances (no rig, no Ghost, and Barrett only a few days out of the hospital). The Ghost points out that the only solid run out of the five Advanced we've had this spring has been at MCTA. I probably need a few more good results before I tackle another Four-Star. Just because you're qualified doesn't mean you're ready to go. But the flip side can also be true: just because you're not qualified doesn't mean you're not ready. You don't fight with the army you want, you fight with the army you've got. As D. Wayne Lucas has said, "I've won a lot of Triple Crown races with horses that weren't *ready* to win."

The Ghost also advises not to give Calvin any time off, but to shoot for another Intermediate, and then Advanced at Jersey at the end of June, Intermediate sometime in the summer, then Advanced at Millbrook, Five Points, Plantation … Fair Hill International. He wants me to be on his same track.

If I go to Bromont, I'll need to leave a week from tomorrow. Border crossings can be tricky with one husband on a gurney and the other in the crossties.

"I WOULDN'T GO," STEPHEN SAYS.

"How come?" I ask.

"With today's courses, it's important for both horse and rider to keep honing their skill set, particularly leading up to a Four-Star," Stephen explains. "I wouldn't let any more than a month go by between events. It might be a little different with you and Calvin, though. He's a seasoned Advanced horse."

So he's on the Ghost's page.

I do my mental calculations. The gap between MCTA and Bromont is right on the edge.

"Plus," he goes on, "Bromont is a Gold Cup event. It'll be a selection trial for the World Equestrian Games. In the hands of the Rolex course designer, Derek di Grazia, it will definitely be a championship course."

Barrett says the only reason *to* go is that Calvin's had so much time off. That we've never competed him without drilling him, and that maybe the key is not to drill him.

Crooked as all get out, my stars.

I START CALVIN OFF SOFT AND SLOW, AS I'VE BEEN INSISTING ON RID-ing him lately. The Ghost wants more canter. I don't follow his advice. He jacks up the fences, and at the first four-foot oxer, Calvin stops, then crashes into it. He has all the scope for those bigger stadium fences at the slower canter, but the two of us have to be in sync. If I get a little ahead of him, or throw him off balance in any way, he can't leave the ground from the underpaced canter.

I dial up the canter, and for the remainder of the lesson, the horse is on the muscle and too far in front of me. I can get away with the bigger canter at home, but it would be a disaster at a show—all the rails would tumble. He just doesn't care enough about keeping them up, particularly as he gets faster. Once I've changed the canter, Calvin gets three strides in a four-stride line and is hard to rate and pull up on landing. Now the Ghost wants me to slow the canter. I either have too much or not enough.

I worry that the Ghost has run out of training ideas. Or given up on me. I consider calling Sally Cousins, known for her accomplishments on difficult horses, and who was so helpful to me with Redmond. Maybe she'd have some ideas for Calvin.

IT IS THE END OF MAY, AND STILL TREES ARE STRUGGLING TO LEAF out. My favorite crepe myrtle for one, which has grown against the house from sapling to stories high since we planted it almost twenty years ago, boasting hot pink blossoms from late summer into mid-fall. Its leafless branches worry me. As does my wisteria tree, as well as the persimmons that line the driveway and offer up their orange globes in late fall, providing Georgia's favorite game of jump and gobble. They don't seem to want to continue living. This last winter was a dire one for trees inclined to grow in a milder climate, tentative guests in our area, just south of the Mason-Dixon. The spring has been cold and wet, and these more southern trees don't want to show themselves until they can be assured of warmer weather.

IT HAS BEEN FOUR OR FIVE YEARS SINCE MY LAST LESSON WITH DOWN Under, and I'm a little nervous. I decide to ride good ole Cal first. Down always has challenging jumping exercises that resemble combinations you'd see cross-country: a skinny off a turn, bending three strides to a corner, then bending back the other way to a skinny chevron, for example.

Our rustiness shows up on cross-country. I don't do anything to balance Calvin at the first oxer, and he takes off long. Down wants me to develop more of a gallop farther out from the jumps and then steady close in. He complains about my reverse tendency, to coast far out and then surge to the fences. I make the correction, and Calvin is terrific for the rest of the school.

"This is what I need," I say to Down Under.

Down nods. Doesn't say anything.

Next up is Patrick. We repeat the difficult show jump exercises. Down says in his deadpan, "He can jump," which I take to mean he likes the horse. He asks me what breed and how old. "He's a good one," he concludes.

Down would still like to see more steadying closer to the cross-country fences, and I try to regulate the horse. That tendency to surge to my fences is exaggerated on Patrick because his canter is erratic. He is so eager to his fences that it can sometimes look like we're charging the enemy, rather than jumping a jump. Everything goes well in the cross-country part of the lesson, until we get to the final line: an oxer, uphill to a keyhole, bending downhill to a right-hand corner. The horse ducks coming through the keyhole, and I miss my line to the next fence. I cut the turn and come at the point of the corner too severely. Patrick accelerates the last couple of strides, then chips in and ducks out right. I come off, landing on my tush.

I'm still clinging to the reins from the ground, the horse standing over me. Down asks if I want a leg up. I decline, and get back on from the ground. My brain frazzles. I don't make any correction, and the horse runs out again. This time I hold on. Finally, Down puts a clod of dirt on the jump and tells me to go farther up the hill after jumping the keyhole and then come back on the point of the corner and jump the clod. This principle of jumping away from the point of a corner to avoid a run-out I learned years ago from Jimmy Wofford. And yet, when the going gets tough, I fail to execute.

I have got to slow things down. Make the necessary adjustments. Why let my emotions get in the way? Where is that mental toughness needed in this sport? "The best riders are impassive," I remember Jimmy saying, "because they don't let their feelings interfere with their riding."

I finally get it right. We jump the corner, and then we jump through the keyhole again, go farther up the hill, and come back at the corner and jump it again. And again.

"Ok, now go on to the water," Down says.

When we get to the two rolltops into the water, the rider ahead of me is lying on her back flat in the water, unable to move. "My horse stepped on my ankle," she says. She hobbles up, and a golf cart is summoned from the barn. Down rides over on his scooter. I'm still waiting my turn. But first he gets on the other student's horse and finishes the school, gets off, turns to me and asks how the water went. He couldn't see it from his vantage point.

"I didn't do it," I say.

"Why not?" he asks, speaking through his nose.

"Because Heather was lying in it."

The man scowls at me, as if I should have jumped it anyway.

I HEAR FROM MOLLIE: CANCER, IN THEIR CAT'S LUNG. JUST A COUPLE months left. We found this cat as a kitten in our woods maybe thirteen years ago. Pie lived as a barn cat for the next several years, until John and Mollie came to live with us for a spell before venturing off to their new life in LA. They bonded with the cat, and asked that we send her to them. We eventually put Pie on a plane and shipped her to Los Angeles, where she flew in the cargo hold along with two dogs, another cat, one giant goldfish, and eight coffins from Fallujah. "Would you mind putting her next to the goldfish?" Barrett politely asked of the cargo agent.

I HURRY TO RIDE CAL AND SHIVA, THEN RACE DOWN TO PENN Station. Chance's train is blowing its whistle. My daughter steps through the heavy wooden station doors, breathless and beautiful and ready to take command of my life. Her curly dark hair cascades down to her tiny waist. Her doll-like hands could fit in the palm of my own. Everything about her is petite in comparison to my long, thin yet broad-shouldered frame. An unlikely mother-daughter pair. No one ever guesses she's mine.

Chance is in a good place, despite warnings to the contrary from her father and brother. Her training for the New York City Marathon has revealed what a competitive runner she is. In fact, her whole life she has been running a marathon with her brother, competing with him for my affections. It is no accident that she has come home on John's birthday to distract me from it.

It is one of those rare spring days, 75 degrees tops, with a sun so brilliant and clarifying it almost hurts my eyes. Every inch of our eighty-three acres is caught up in it and magnified—even the shadows cast are chiseled and defined by the living sun bursting around them. The birds are jubilant with their various choruses. The crepe myrtle has started to bud.

It's a light horse day for me. I hop on Shiva for a brief flat school while Chance runs along the Gunpowder. Then it's an at-home day spent with my daughter, who doesn't want to go anywhere or do anything. She just wants to enjoy the perfect spring day on the farm—or so she says—as she plops herself in front of the TV, where she will stay for the bulk of the day. She explains that she doesn't have a TV in her Brooklyn apartment, so she wants to take full advantage of ours. I wonder if she's come home just to make sure I don't spend too much time on the phone with the birthday boy. I'm dying to get off the farm and would settle for going anywhere, as long as I'm able to break out of the enormous bubble—if only temporarily—that surrounds the farm and most days locks me within it.

Thirty years ago, the peonies were blooming at our old house on Wheeler Lane, and John's father brought a bouquet to the hospital. I always think of the peonies as John's birth flower, and equate their blooming with that day. This year, the plate-sized white ones I planted years ago are still tight fisted and waiting for an assurance of warmer days before they'll pop. I can only find pink ones in the online flower stores, so it's pink I send to California. I get a text from John thanking me, with a picture of their young cat, Dart, messing with the box the flowers came in. John doesn't say anything about Pie.

John: *There was rampant pediatric TB in Baltimore County between 1863 and 1866.*

I think of our bad luck year on this ground. Maybe there is something in the dirt.

I talk to Barrett and Chance about selling the farm, a prospect that fills me with dread. "All you have to do is walk on through it," says Barrett, referring to the metaphorical door. "You know what to do. It's interesting," he goes on, "your ride on Calvin. He's a horse that depends absolutely on the concept of balance, and yet in your own life you've spun out of control." He may be barely out of the hospital, but Barrett is back to being his old perspicacious self.

It isn't the farm that's killing us, it's my dangerous obsession. With Jupiter in my sights, I am burning up in my sun chariot.

Charlotte Fowble's Ghost

Hat in hands,
he comes to the door.
I shush the dog.

Morning, Melchor, I say,
wringing my apron,
smoothing my hair.

Watermelon rind
bubbles on the box stove.
"Stephen's dead," he says.

I had the land.
He had the dream.
First, he took the trees

to Millender Sawmill,
then hauled a load of bark
to Scott's Tanyard,

planned to be back
mid-morning with leathers.
The baby—

sickly these past weeks,
can't get the fever to stay down—
starts to howl.

I run to fetch Amos
from his crib.
Gripping the railing,

his little face puckered and drenched,
as if he already knows.
The other children

see-saw the tree swing
hanging from the front yard maple
like a ringing bell.

Last summer,
Stephen shimmied up its trunk,
rope around his waist,

buggy whip in his back pocket.
He clung to a sturdy branch,
fashioning loops,

as the world fell away,
our necks crooked,
in the direction of Jesus.

He pushed out
the knots with the whip,
tossed down the ropes,

like a herring man—
almost lost his footing.
Inconsequential now

if he fell
and lived,
or fell and didn't.

I hear Ida's pleas to little Stevie,
Higher, higher, as I scoop
the child in my arms,

run past the store to Zion.
Sickness and grief— cousins,
sisters, lovers—

whose sum is nothing.
As a wind rattles the schoolhouse window,
I watch agitated cornstalks

mirror my own commotion,
their tassels the color
of Ida's flaxen hair,

that she won't let me cut for anything.
A tall woman appears between the rows,
in black tights and riding boots,

hair whipping her long face,
searching for something
stolen long ago.

The wagon tipped, and he fell.
One wheel rolled over
Stephen's neck.

Bark flew everywhere,
shrouding my husband.
The horses trotted on without him.

We say our prayers,
forgive the universe.
Bless my children,

and the ones
that will come to me tomorrow,
and the ones that will never come now.

Who is this woman, looking long
and hard, after the children are put to bed,
seeing glimmers of me in the star lanes?

How will the corn get chopped?

Chapter Nine

Too Much Sunlight Makes Dracula a Dull Girl

ESTHER WAS ELIMINATED YESTERDAY WHEN HER HORSE REFUSED TO jump a stadium fence with a black box set under it. Still building core strength, Esther collapses forward when the horse gets sticky, which shuts the door. She ships him to me hoping I can open it.

I set a wooden box under a vertical. Esther's horse makes a move to stop. I sit back and kick. He stops anyway, but I make him jump the box from a standstill. After the correction, he turns his attitude around and jumps everything I ask him to.

We go out on a hack, Esther on Calvin, me on Shiva.

She asks if her horse can stay with me for a few days.

ROCKS AND NETTLES SLICE AND STING WHEN WE LEAST EXPECT. I know the Ghost well enough to know when he feels funny about something. What will I say, that Esther brought her horse here today? Surely he will smell discontent.

"That horse isn't forgiving enough for her," Barrett pronounces. His way of saying that the horse is not on the aids—either scooting forward when Esther puts her leg on, or sucking back. He won't accept pressure, preferring to move into it rather than away from it. He is not educated enough to be a solid citizen, and Esther doesn't yet have the skills to get him there.

One of our boarders raises her eyebrows as I'm leading Esther's horse to the wash stall. "How's he doing for you?"

"Oh, this is Esther's horse," I say, as if I'd have to explain that the chestnut I'm leading is not Shiva.

"I know, the Ghost told me he was coming here," she replies.

CROSS-COUNTRY SCHOOLING AT WAREDACA. I CANTER AROUND ONE bend to a Beginner Novice log with a snake carved into it, the head as one end of the log. The serpent catches Shiva's eye. He gallops up to it and ducks out. I sail off the saddle, landing on my back on the farm's hard frangipani clay. The horse stands over me looking perplexed. I'm on my butt clenching the reins, which have broken at the buckle. If I were in a better mood, the fall would be almost comical. I pop up, tie the ends, and stand on the viper's head to mount my trickster. We come again to the stupid rattlesnake, and Shiva over-jumps it as if it were four feet high, and rattling. We then jump most of the Training jumps on course, as well as a number of the Prelim combinations, including the coffin and water.

April's chestnut fares less well. She becomes perturbed with the horse's repeated stopping.

"Don't look at the ditch," I remind her.

The horse improves and finishes well. It's like that for us—April sees something and tells me, I see something and mention it to her. Both of us suffer from using one side of our brains to ride and the other to think.

Esther is waiting for us back at the trailer. I untack Shiva, cool him out, and get on Esther's horse. I squeeze him in front of my leg. This is an enormous piece of the puzzle. Without the horse's acceptance of the leg, the rider has nothing. When I first put my leg on, the horse spurts forward. I catch him with the reins and squeeze some more, until he puts his head down and accepts the energy created from his hind end into the bridle. I can see why the horse's tendency to run from the leg would unsettle tentative Esther, causing her to take her leg off and aggravate the problem further.

Esther's horse jumps around all the Beginner Novice fences with ease—once I get him forward and straighter. Esther is beaming—she seems to love it when I ride her horse. She doesn't know what to do about his entry at Seneca Valley Horse Trials in two weeks, though. She doesn't feel ready to compete him herself.

"Well, I'd be happy to ride him, if you can figure out what to say to the Ghost."

Stuck in rush-hour traffic on the way home, I conclude that I don't want to mar my relationship with the Ghost over Esther's horse. If the

Ghost is going to be upset, then let it be over my own decisions with my own horses.

The real question is why I can't take responsibility for my own riding. I know what's wrong, I even know how to fix it most of the time. But for whatever reason, I don't trust myself. And I have become so close to my Ghost that I no longer completely trust him.

An anorexic's worst nightmare: being interviewed by a food blogger. Jama Rattigan, of *Alphabet Soup*, sends me some questions. She wants to feature my new poetry collection, *Take This Spoon*, which combines recipes and poems.

> *Several of your poems examine the push and pull of the mother-daughter relationship. What are your favorite food-related memories of your mother and your daughter?*

Kill me now.

The Ghost's long, uphill, washed-out driveway drops off precipitously on either side. It's more of a straightness exercise than a driveway. I hold my breath for fear the trailer will run off the ribbon of asphalt and down into the crevasses on either side, steam or smoke rising from the depths.

Patrick and I work on keeping our rhythm steady to the fences. I dial up the canter with Cal, in an effort to find the pace out of which I need to jump the larger fences. No matter the canter, I have to keep him soft in the bridle.

I call Barrett on the way home. "Don't you ever check your emails"? I say. I've been forwarding Chance's emails to him for a week because I couldn't bear to open them.

"Hardly," he says.

We sign off, and five minutes later he calls back.

"Chance is in the *New York Times*," he announces. "Her new play was voted one of the top new plays written by women."

"Where?" I say, "In Maryland?"

"In the country," he says. "For her play *When We Went Electronic.*"

I pull the rig over on the side of I-95, set the brake. The emergency lights flicker like two crickets. My daughter doesn't answer the phone.

Barrett has agreed to go with Patrick and me to Middleburg Horse Trials. Which means I won't have to leave tomorrow and stay overnight, but can let him drive us to Virginia in the crepuscular light. At magic hour, we toast to Chance's news. I let my hair down and admit to my husband that I no longer want to event without him. I don't like going by myself, and I sure don't like going with anyone else.

"Wow, your hair is really long," Barrett says.

SINCE WE'RE THE FIRST ONES TO ARRIVE AT THE EVENT, IT'S UNCLEAR where to park. Patrick warms up reasonably well, marches down centerline, and executes the first couple of figures smoothly. We head down centerline a second time in preparation for a leg-yield. He pins his ears and won't move off my leg, hopping up and down rather than trotting sideways. I yank him over to the track with my reins and position him for a medium trot. When I turn onto the diagonal, he breaks into a canter and starts bouncing and flinging his body around. I somehow get him back over to K, try for the next leg-yield, which is worse than the first, then to an unsteady walk. He hops in the canter and runs sideways in the wrong direction. I'm waiting for the judge to whistle us out of the ring. Instead, she lets me squirm my way through the nightmare dressage test, until the final movement down centerline. Patrick plants his feet and won't go forward. I somehow shove him down the ring, and it's over. I salute and grimace toward the judge.

"What's a girl got to do to get eliminated around this joint?" I say.

"He is definitely not a happy camper," the judge admits, shaking her head.

"That was the worst thing I've ever seen," says my husband, who rarely offers a criticism of what doesn't come naturally to me, like dressage.

"This one doesn't get to jump today," I reply.

I take Patrick back into dressage warm-up to try and get some obedient work out of him before we pack up and head the 140 minutes toward home. I stew in the passenger seat. My horses. My life.

It's a brilliant spring day beckoning to be ridden. Instead, I catch up on correspondence and pay the electric bill. When in doubt, try to owe less. When in great doubt, bet.

Everyone in the world is hoping for a Triple Crown winner this year in California Chrome, except for Barrett. Near post time, our TV satellite has problems with its signal from NBC, so we turn to the racing channel, only to find that they are not permitted to air the race live. Dear God, will this day never end? The racing channel can't air the Belmont? Instead, we listen to the race commentators without being able to watch the race—a ridiculous situation, almost as ridiculous as not being able to coax Patrick down centerline. After the race, the camera switches from some backstory about the young chestnut colt to the commentators at their semicircular table. One has his forehead planted on the desktop. "Jay, we're back on," says his partner. Jay lifts his head, takes the paper in front of him, balls it up, and throws it straight at us. That's how we know the colt lost.

"Looks like someone else had a bad horse day," Barrett says, a few hundred dollars richer.

THIRTY YEARS OF PILLS. SOME THAT WORK, SOME THAT DON'T, SOME that work for a while and then quit, some that require a constant adjustment of the dosage. It never helps when the taker forgets to take, or decides she no longer needs to take, and the tower of sticks tumbles into another messy pile.

THE BAD HORSE IS RELATIVELY OBEDIENT. YESTERDAY MAY HAVE BEEN a fluke. Maybe he got the bit over his tongue. Maybe he was holding in a pee. Today I've switched his bit to Shiva's soft Nathe so that he can't come up with an excuse.

But at the ten-minute mark, Patrick starts rearing, refusing to go near the corner by M. He pushes violently against my left leg instead of away from it when I ask for a leg-yield. He hops up and down, then practically throws himself on the ground rather than go into the left rein. I whack him a few times, and he puts his head down for a pass or two, then starts up again. I whack him to get him at least in the same zip code as M. Hitting him only makes him madder, so I spin him in small circles till we are both dizzy. These antics and our corresponding furies go on for over an hour, until we are both wringing wet and Patrick's trot turns into a pained shuffle. He's barely picking up his feet, but he still has the energy to throw himself around rather than accept my aids.

Barrett pulls up to the dressage ring in the tin can, just as I am resigning myself to failure.

"No clean-up, no grain, in the round pen he goes until he can mind himself," I say.

I strip off his tack and throw him in the round pen.

Over the course of the afternoon, I start to wonder about his teeth and stomach, the possibility of Lyme disease, the suitability of Depo-Provera as a calming agent, and other medical intrigue. I text Rachel, asking if she would drop off some powdered doxy and Depo in the morning.

"I may also want to check his neck and jaw," she suggests.

I cruise by the round pen. Patrick has his body pinned up against the far wall, trying to avoid the sun. I take him to my barn's wash stall to hose him off. I offer him grain sprinkled with a few dusty doxycycline pills, then squirt a tube of omeprazole down his gullet, before turning him back out with an armload of hay.

From depression to anger in a heartbeat. That's why they call it a mood disorder. Apparently I'm the one who needs the round pen. No bath for Julia. No baked potato.

I LUNGE RHAPUNZEL FIRST, THEN CAUTIOUSLY GET ON HER. WE walk, trot, and canter in the indoor. One of our hunter-jumper boarders leaves the barn to go on a walk with her horse. Nicole's idea of a trail ride is an amble around the farm, in part to protect her horse's legs from bad footing, in part because trail riding is not in her bones. I ask if I can tag along. We march down the split between the steep paddock and the mare barn field, Nicole's mare on the left, Rhapunzel and I on the right.

"I love riding between fences," says Nicole, "Makes me feel so much safer." I nod in agreement, but think otherwise: *Unless you're claustrophobic.*

We reach the top of the hill and turn right. I'm still on the inside next to the fence, Nicole and her mare on the outside. Nicole talks about her painting progress on the cross-country fences. What is the name of the jump she calls a mushroom?

"It's a lamb's feeder," I say. "I'm not sure why, but that's what it is."

"Maybe because the lambs crawl under the mushroom?" she suggests.

Nicole's horse gets a little too close, and my boot brushes the fence. Feeling the pressure, Rhapunzel bolts, throws herself sideways across the field, and starts bucking. Caught off guard, I am late getting the mare's head up. By the time I process what's happening, I'm clinging to the side of the saddle. I come off, hit the ground hard, and the mare bucks off before galloping down the hill toward the barns.

"My god, are you all right?" Nicole panics, jumping off her horse. "You're bleeding!" she says.

I'm still on the ground.

I reach up, feel for my nose, blood streaming out of it. I struggle up with Nicole's help.

"On my god," she repeats, hugging me now, "I feel so bad for you."

"I'm ok, I think." I can see from a distance that someone has caught the horse, but no one has sent the gator for me. No one actually saw anything, except Jan, who watches over everything at the farm with a puzzle-solving, flat eye.

Jan is holding my renegade at the bottom of the hill. I limp down to the horse, take her from Jan, then into her stall, where I attempt to get back on her, with Nicole's help. As soon as she feels my weight in one stirrup, the mare flies back into the corner of the stall.

"Hold on to her," I say, and try again.

Same response. The horse's eyes are huge and white. "Don't do it, Julia, it isn't worth it," Nicole advises.

I call Barrett. "Where are you? I need you," I say.

A few minutes later, he's at my side.

"I think we need to put her down."

"What???"

"Rachel thinks her problem is neurological," my husband goes on. "I've wondered myself for months."

"Then why the hell did you let me get on her?"

My head starts pounding. I mop my nosebleed with a dirty hand towel.

Curses fail our relationship—Barrett has never been able to rule me off a horse for any reason, while I've spent years contradicting him for having unproven hunches that later turn out to be fact.

The Black Dahlia arrives at the farm.

Both Cal and Shiva go well in their lessons. The Dahlia says she wouldn't mind seeing Patrick today, though I wasn't planning on riding him with her.

I get on him during her last lesson. A few minutes in, he starts hopping. The Dahlia suggests that I overbend him to the inside while asking his hindquarters to move to the outside, thereby giving his hind legs a place to escape to. She thinks I've become too rigid and demanding, driving him into the contact.

"Cut the sleeves out of his strait jacket, Julia," she says.

I have to show him that there is a way out. Here hind legs, move over a little so you can reach farther with them. Here, Rhapunzel, come off the rail so you don't feel squeezed.

But no matter, Rhapunzel's reaction was extreme, and it wasn't the first time. She has been lame and some version of unrideable her whole short life. I hesitantly agree with Barrett: she is too dangerous to work with. She has already put Daniel and me in the emergency room.

"RACHEL AND I TALKED SOME MORE ABOUT IT," BARRETT SAYS. "IT was the right thing to do. The woman who picked her up was very nice. Quiet and respectful."

How hard must it have been for Barrett to hold the young horse as the deadly pink barbiturate went in. The filly that he made. Selected the sire, took care of her in utero for eleven months, then foaled. I remember when she was born. I always remember when they were born. Wee hours. Barrett called down to the house. Took a deep breath, blew out an apologetic sigh from the back of his throat. "Chestnut filly," he admitted.

I'm not all that interested in racing. I like having the babies around, but about as much as I like having a family of cardinals flitting around the bird feeder outside my office window. Some miracle to marvel at from a distance. Eventing takes all my attention, and I have nothing left. I may not have had room in my head to include racing, but I had no problem cashing the winning purse checks. Barrett always wanted a buddy to share his love of racing. He resents all those win photos without me in any of them. He gave up trying to woo me over to the darker side, until he gave up himself. And then Rhapunzel was born. Her three pasture mates—all fillies born days apart—have since become stakes winners. Unlike Rhapunzel, who had a paddock injury as a yearling and never went to the track. Who hurt Daniel and then me last fall, when she bucked me off and ruined my shoulder. And now yesterday. More than just a screw loose. A young, nearly feral, questionably sound, neurological mare. It isn't lost on Barrett—if he were a horse, surely he would have been put down last November.

Still, it is never easy to drop a horse. To wait until the heart stops beating and the eye glazes over, and the last gasp spasms of the enormous body have quieted. Barrett foaled her alone, and he is alone when the needle goes in. Meanwhile, I'm at my desk watching birds lined up on the garden fence.

"Who was her father?" I ask Barrett when he comes back down to my aviary.

"Light the Fuse."

I WAKE TO RAIN AND DODGE STORM CLOUDS ALL DAY. ABELINO AND I choose where to put the new cross-country jumps. Abelino immigrated from Monterey to jockey horses and eventually started a business helping local farmers. He has acquired a good collection of farm equipment, including a bobcat, which we need for this heavy lifting. We are only half finished when he is called to the hospital. One of his hands on another job fell out of a tree and broke his neck.

Later in the day, an Englishman finds me in the wash stall as I'm bathing Calvin. Paul leased Redmond in his retirement and grew fond of the (by then) plump, fuzzy chestnut. He was devastated when Redmond died.

"I have something for you," Paul says, "a gift."

I follow him out to his truck. "It comes in three parts," he says, moving to the truck bed. "First, a bag of cement," he says, holding up the bag. "Second, a post," and he produces a post. "And last," he says, opening the truck door. He reaches in and pulls out a big black sign that announces, "Redmond's Way."

"As in, he did it his way," Paul explains. "It's a year today," he goes on. That fact had slipped my mind—the day a year ago when we found Redmond dead in his paddock, struck by heart attack or stroke, we would never know.

I am not a sign waver. I want Redmond to hold up my printer and sit next to me in my office, his ashes tucked away in their mahogany box, our relationship still just between the two of us and a toner cartridge.

My love for Redmond was different than Paul's. I was almost jealous of his feelings for my Fair Hill horse, as if he didn't deserve them. He didn't know the Redmond that I knew, didn't live what we lived through together. No one else could have that with Redmond. Still, Paul came into Redmond's later life and fell in love with the lovable, overweight, overgrown pony. And now mourns him.

Paul digs a hole, lays the cement, erects the sign on the mound leading into the farm.

"EARIE DIED LAST NIGHT," BARRETT PHONES FROM THE BARN.

One of the mares got cast in her stall, waking Marta and Roberto in their loft. When they came to help get the horse up, they discovered Earie curled up asleep in the wash stall. Or so they thought. When he didn't respond to his name, Marta found him to be already cold, as if the horse's problem announced the cat's demise.

I couldn't get within fifty feet of the one-eared, feral stray when he first showed up ten years ago. We used a snare pole to catch him and get him fixed. He let us inch a little closer each day, until he was purring and rubbing up against us for attention and food. He wormed his way into the house by figuring out how to use the dog door, and we let him stay. A few years ago, he developed a thyroid condition, which required a daily pill. Giving pills to cats usually ends with a gob of cat spit in the eye and a few nasty scratches. First I had to find him. Earie's daily pill quickly became last on my list of chores, a hit-or-miss operation. The news of his death lets that slimy old rodent Guilt through the dog door.

"Where should we bury him?" I ask.

"Bury him? I didn't know you'd want to bury him!" Barrett says.

I panic, imagining him already tossed in the dumpster, and the dump truck come and gone down the road to the landfill. Guilt is now breathing heavily over my shoulder. "Where is he?"

"Relax, I've got him in a plastic bag. I'll bury him on top of the hill next to Bentley."

THE FOOTING AT SENECA HORSE TRIALS IS DEEP AND GOOEY FROM the recent downpour. The region has a base of clay and "Seneca Red" sandstone that was used to build the Hirshhorn Museum in Washington. I muck my way around the cross-country course and doubt that running today is wise. Still, if I don't, Advanced at Jersey in a couple of weeks won't be likely. I need this Intermediate run under my belt before tackling Advanced again.

The Black Dahlia asks if I'd like some help warming up for dressage. It's exactly what I've been wanting—coaching at the events. I light up with only a little hesitation in my voice.

"It'll make me nervous, but I'd love it if you did."

"I don't want to make you nervous," she says kindly.

"No, no," I say, "I love being nervous."

The Dahlia suggests I let my eyes wander to promote relaxation. Calvin comes together, and we go in the ring and have one of our best tests ever. I smile at the judge afterward and she glances up and even gives me the A-OK sign with her fingers. A first for Calvin. We score a 36—not terrific, but not too shabby either, particularly for us at Intermediate—we're fifth after dressage out of a large field of twenty-four.

As soon as I round the first turn in show jumping warm-up, Calvin slips.

"What did you put in?" I ask Barrett, referring to the size of stud.

"The biggest ones you have," he says, bristling. "If you need anything bigger, you shouldn't be running," he adds.

It's true: Barrett has studded the horse well for Seneca's yielding turf over an unstable wet clay base—but there's still no traction. Slipping and sliding, the horse never has his feet underneath himself. Four rails.

I almost don't go out of the box, but my evil twin shows up and I decide to run. When we get out on cross-country, Calvin takes hold with his big cuppy feet, and the faster speed and momentum plus the straighter lines help his traction. He jumps great for the first part of the course. We gallop uphill to the woods, and I have to duck under a branch to get my line to the bank combination's first jump—a little ramp, four strides to the bank and bounce out. The bank is tiny, and very wet. Dodging trees and saturated ground to get there prevents us from putting our eyes on the bank until a split second too late. Calvin slips up the bank, can't get his feet underneath his big body, and chests the out. I hit the saddle, my air vest explodes, catapulting me out of the saddle and onto my feet.

Calvin stands like a terrified statue. We both hate the gunshot of the air vest activating. I give him a reassuring pat, and we walk back toward the trailer, my drive deflating with the vest.

Dieting

1.
My mother was always on a diet,
or about to be.
One brother was fat.
The other, a bodybuilder.
Yours truly, the anorexic,
addicted to not eating.
Father was the only one
impartial to food.

2.
We are always eating,
or about to, or just done.
We are hungry, we are sated,
we are wishing we hadn't.
We are making up for it,
or planning our denials,
or confessing them.

3.
I surround myself with cats
who kill and eat, dogs who eat
what's killed, and horses
who eat what's given to them.
Self-consciousness doesn't ruin

their appetite or enjoyment.
They don't judge what they consume,
or long for what they won't allow themselves.
They don't confuse who they are
with what they eat,
fearing they won't be loved
if they're fat, or don't cook,

or overcook, or nearly kill themselves
by making up for their gluttony
with fasting.

4.
They nicker
when I enter the morning barn.
Ears pricked, they come to the pipe gate,
and watch me, and wait, in the evening.

As wet bran slops onto their noses,
they lap it up with simple,
unfettered relish, then quietly munch
their flakes of dessert—
contentment,
its sure, steady rhythm.

I'M MAKING A MOVIE ABOUT MY POEMS. A GOOD TURN FOR SOMEONE who doesn't like to go out to dinner, let alone give poetry readings. I've been wood-shedding for the last twenty years and am rarely seen in poetry circles. Too much sunlight makes Dracula a dull girl.

I scout locations—outside of Calvin's stall, sitting on a bucket, on a log at the water jump.

"I think of you as a private person," the Ghost said to me the other day. Which makes my life at the farm deeply ironic: there is always a circus of Saltimbanques in my backyard.

"I am in person," I explained, "But on the page I'll say anything."

My phone chimes.

Chance: *No, Mom, I do not want to be your production assistant.*

THE GOTH POSTPONES MY VIDEO RECORDING IN ORDER TO VISIT A Civil War graveyard. Abelino scratches our appointment to place the rest of the cross-country jumps. I pull Patrick out of his stall. He's dead lame on his right front.

Rachel, thick into an emergency, shows up later in the day. She digs in the hoof with a hoof knife. Pus rivers out of a thumb-sized boil.

"What's that?" I ask.

"A bad dressage test," she says. She finds a big corn on his right heel beginning to abscess.

Instead of prayer, I rely on the old horses. I want to rub and rub on the ancient ones, who will lean into my rubbings and won't need teeth to smile.

I come back from my ride on Shiva to find that Barrett has already turned out the oldsters. My plans for grooming them get canned. I turn my frustrations with the day's unfolding lack of events on Barrett, who has to take all my hits, as he's the only one who has promised to put up with me for better and worse or, more accurately, for worse and worser.

"You're the one who gave the bank barn to April," he says, "when I was lying sick in the hospital. So don't talk to me about consulting with you first before turning out the Viejos."

When we first moved to the farm in 1995, we found old cattle stanchions in the dank building a person had to crouch to enter. We renovated the barn to accommodate my horses a few years in, as an escape from the boarding operation. One worker nearly lost his life when a knee wall collapsed as he was digging out the foundation. Then the bats moved in.

"Huey and Surf were perfectly happy in the bank barn," Barrett goes on. "You're the one that messed up their schedules."

"Don't do that to me," I counter. "That's another issue."

"No it's not," he disagrees.

"It's just a communication problem," I say, and then, my famous solution: "We need to have more meetings."

"We don't need to have more meetings. You don't converse, you dictate. I'm not typing an interagency memo every time I do something normal."

He's got me there. We are often going in so many different directions that we don't schedule enough scheduling time. If you have a scheduling problem, how do you figure out how to schedule the time to work it out?

"Look it, I don't want to argue with you," I admit. "Can't we please just table this? I *am* going to see your friend Linda Zang tomorrow. Does that count?"

I turn to the weeds that have overrun our backyard, front yard, everywhere yard. I focus my attention on the high ones at the front of the house under the evergreens next to where the cars park. Attack the most visible first, and all that.

"Come look what I've done," I call to Barrett, who is at last struggling to get some writing done in his office. I always love to show off my weeding accomplishments. Probably because it happens so rarely.

He drags himself out of the house to look at how I've tidied my garden thoughts, rearranged and cleared the space for whichever old ones need a stall for the summer. His stare splits me in two.

"You pulled out the butterfly flower," he says, pointing to a vibrant orange bush twenty feet away, parent of all the seedlings I yanked out of the earth just now, smearing the frosting on my husband's mood. "Now what will the Monarch butterflies eat after their long flight from Mexico?"

"Oh no!" I say, and then, "I'm so sorry." Words both of us have been waiting for all day.

BARRETT WAS HANGING OUT AT LINDA ZANG'S BARN IN 1990 WITH A friend who kept horses there and was in a racing partnership with Linda's husband. Barrett tried for over twenty years to get me to take lessons with her. I finally got around to it. But it has been a while since I've seen her. Bless her—Linda gives me license to let my arms move around on a longer rein, opening my inside suppling rein to encourage Calvin to soften, lengthen his neck, and come rounder. She has me open the outside rein when I need to move his shoulder over and get him straighter. Others would have me sit like a stone with my hands close together and get all the work done with my seat and legs. Linda allows me to use my hands. She warns that as long as I soften and bring my hands back to neutral position after I widen them, then I can use them all I want. A couple of times she even says to me, "Pull on the left rein!" One potato, two potatoes. "Now soften."

"Don't tell anyone I said that," she whispers.

There's truth in both methods. If I had to say, Linda probably crumples her toilet paper, whereas the Black Dahlia, I bet she's a folder, skilled in the art of origami, wiping her tush with paper swans.

BARRETT BUSIES HIMSELF IN THE FEED ROOM, TAKING POT SHOTS AT Patrick's farrier.

"If he'd taken the shoes off when he was supposed to, we wouldn't have this problem," he says. "Not to mention Rachel's assessment that the fucking shoes were too small," he goes on, smoke twirling out of his head, "and that he was cut too short and shod too aggressively last cycle." Barrett is dying for Patrick's problem to be the farrier's fault, ever since the blacksmith started showing a reluctance to work on tricky horses and obsessing about moving to Montana. What he doesn't concede is that Rachel often thinks out loud, throwing out random dire possibilities when she is trying to get to the diagnostic root of a problem.

When the farrier shows up, he's got more bad news. Patrick has two new abscesses brewing in both front feet that the vet had missed.

"It's gonna take a few days," he reports. What he means is weeks.

"This horse," I say, as if that explains anything, "he misses more events," I go on, just shy of expressing my desire to send him to Montana with the farrier.

I soak and wrap both fronts, give him some bute, latch the stall door so he can't hang his head over the spaghetti strap. He rests his muzzle on the stall bars.

I run to my psychopharm appointment to get a renewal on my scripts—god knows I need that, though I typically get antsy in the infrequent sessions, always feeling I'm wasting everyone's time by what I'm not revealing about myself. I can't even sit still for a therapy session.

In the evening, Patrick can barely turn around in his stall and doesn't even want to come out to graze.

"I'm kind of worried about Patrick," I admit to Barrett over cocktails. "Do you think he's trying to founder?"

"That's what Rachel was worried about," he says, discouragingly. "You don't think I'd be this mad about the farrier's ego for nothing, do you?"

I can't find my phone. The last thing I want to do is get in the truck and drive off the grid to West Virginia for lessons with Jimmy without it.

I try to con Barrett out of his for the day.

"What if *I* have to call *you*?" he says. Really, they should charge admission for tours of my husband's mind.

The drive isn't as bad as I'd remembered, though I'm constantly imagining the rumbling signifying a flat with no way to call for help. Instead of telephoning everyone I know so I won't fall asleep at the wheel, I hatch a new plan: to continue on with Calvin, shooting for Fair Hill International in the fall, and then to retire after that. Both of us. There. I've said it: I am going to retire.

My work mode takes over at the clinic. Jimmy reminds me to keep coming to my fences without so much checking with the reins—"Don't take back to keep coming forward," he says. "Too much tugging produces front-rail knockdowns. If your horse is in front of your leg, you can afford to miss." Which is probably why the Ghost is fearful of my slow, balloony canter with Cal—not only does it produce time faults, but I also have to be so damn accurate.

Calvin tries hard with a more forward canter and doesn't touch a rail. "He sure knows how to jump," Jimmy concludes, with a smile.

Shiva is a different story. He's a perfect student in the class, but his form is still lacking.

"He needs to study page 46 of my book *Modern Gymnastics*," Jimmy says with a wink, referring to his very own Bible. "The exercise with the low wide oxers. A lot of people are under the mistaken impression that a horse who tends to dangle his legs needs to get snappier with his front end and learn to jump up around his fences. But they're wrong. This type of horse needs to learn to open his shoulders and jump across his fences. He's a project," concludes Jimmy.

"Don't I know it," I say. "He's done a lot at Training level, but I don't think I should move him up until I can get his form sorted out."

Jimmy nods in agreement. "I wouldn't," he confirms my suspicion.

When I get home, Barrett and I run around the barn lifting up trunks and calling my cell. Barrett's phone starts ringing. He looks up dumbly at me. "You're calling me!" he says, with feigned confusion. "Oh hi," he says all velvety-baritoned. It's my shrink: I'd left it in her office yesterday. "Where would you like to meet?" Burt Lancaster continues. "In front of the bank at Greenspring at 5:00? See you there," he says, snapping his phone shut.

Rachel shows up with her X-ray machine and good news: there's no rotation in Patrick's coffin joint, and no significant navicular changes. He's got the abscess in the one foot, paper-thin soles on both.

His recovery is going to take some time.

I MAKE A VODKA, TAKE TWO SIPS, AND DUMP THE REST IN THE SINK. I admit to Barrett my retirement plans. His eyebrows—the few hairs he has left—go way up. "Yeah, I even wrote about it this morning," I say.

"You've been writing?" Barrett asks.

"Work to get Calvin to Fair Hill this year, and then retire." I offer, in lieu of an answer.

"I'd rather go out on top," I explain. Sad to think what my "on top" is. At least I know what it means to myself. It means I didn't go on past my ability to improve. I want to get better, but I don't want to struggle for the status quo. Or struggle as I slip. Or get hurt and be forced to stop. The trick is to leave myself wanting more. Push the lamb's leg away when I'm not quite full.

I sit down at my mother's piano, which I inherited after her death. I raise the dusty key cover, spend some time plinking out a few notes of a Bach invention I used to play. The Bechstein resonates with crisp, bell-like tones.

SHIVA TIPTOES INTO THE MUDDY TRENCHES OF THE DRESSAGE RING at Surefire. I can't imagine a more obedient test, despite not being able to get near the mucky corners. I keep my gloved fingers crossed that he won't slip and go down.

He receives a mediocre score, with only a 6 earned for obedience.

Shiva, Georgia, and I settle into the living room at the back of the trailer. I turn Shiva loose to enjoy his freedom in the overgrown box stall, while Georgia and I walk the course. The dog's hind end lameness is worsening by the day, and I regret encouraging her to come along on the walk. She is limping when we get back to the trailer.

We have hours till our jumping phases, so I take my time with the detail work of getting myself and the horse ready. We are backed up against some trees, tucked away from the hubbub. I enjoy the quiet and the time spent alone with my horse and dog, who seem to relish getting all of my attention.

Show jumping is a little harder for Shiva, but he tries, jumps all the jumps the first time, with two knockdowns. On the cross-country course, he takes a serious look at the first combination on the course—two large skinny logs set downhill with two strides in between—as well as the water. Surefire's water is always a bit spooky, set in a depression among some dark locust trees. It feels more like a wallow than a water jump. I have to ride positively forward to the bright marine-varnished log perched at the edge of the water. I feel him backpedal, but I'm able to keep myself in a defensive position and my heels dug in, my whip tapping his shoulder and my voice clucking in rhythm to his canter. He finishes the course.

We get back home to the sun collapsing from its sky, Calvin in his paddock, peering over the fence at us. *Where have you been?* he says, not directly to Shiva but to the shadow that is following my chestnut.

"For a dumb horse, Cal sure is smart," says Barrett. I'm not sure how to take this remark. Does that mean for a dumb horse, he has moments of intelligence, or rather that all horses are dumb, but he is a smart one? I'm too tired to ruminate on anything but grape juice.

THE GOTH STEPS OFF THE LIGHT RAIL IN HUNT VALLEY.

"I see you finally made it back from Seattle," I say.

"Yeah," the Space Needle was really cool," she says, barely moving her lips. She's wearing fingerless tawny gloves.

We start in the woods. Georgia interrupts our progress by rubbing up against the Goth squatting with her camera in the desiccated oak leaves. Just yesterday, we found out that Georgia has torn her ACL as well as ligaments in her ankle and will require surgery. I wasn't crazy. If you think you see a lameness, it's probably there. If you sense a problem, there are likely two or three lurking.

We move to Indian Run, where Georgia splashes through, then plunks herself down under the steeplechase bank into water, possibly expecting to be a prop for the camera, or for another jump.

When we get to Calvin's stall, I can barely coax the horse to stick his head out of his window for a treat, let alone be backdrop for the reading. The Goth seems more interested in panning the camera at singular maple leaves and copulating dragonflies than catching a few blinks of the obvious horse.

"My hands are so hot," she says, peeling off her gloves, finger by finger. And I see why she wore them: the backs of her hands are covered with an angry red rash that looks like psoriasis. Everyone in my life seems to have immunity problems.

I keep reading—at the dead red oak at the top of the hill where we buried my first event horse and where crows congregate in the early mornings, under the apple tree by the mare barn. After she splices and edits, The Goth will post the reading on my website and Facebook page to help promote *Take This Spoon*. My readers won't have to leave the comfort of their sofas to attend a poetry reading. Plus, insects on the wing. And maple leaves.

I AM IN SEARCH OF THE BOXES OF MY MOTHER'S OLD PIANO MUSIC. IN the cramped, stink-bug-infested attic, I can't stand up straight for fear of hitting my head on the splintery rafters or on one of the rusty nails protruding from those old beams. After bonking my head a few times, I find the boxes I'm looking for with Bach's French Suites and Scriabin's Etudes.

I wonder if Charlotte ever came up here after her husband died. Maybe she had an old trunk filled with mementos that she liked to sift through. Or maybe her retreat was a way to escape the demands of three young children with no one to share the parental duties with. I imagine she'd like to sit, looking up at the beams and remembering her brother and father and Stephen raising and hammering the roof as they made for the young couple a home to live a whole life in. By this point, no doubt, she would be crying.

What to throw away and what to keep. I sort through piles of horse gear in the bank barn in preparation for April's move. There's a lot of nostalgia tucked into the recesses of my storage cubbies—faded ribbons, photos of long-grown foals, and daughters riding ponies. It's hard for me to surrender this space to someone else, but it's a decision I've made in order to bring April closer to me.

GLUE-ON SHOES HAVE PRETTY MUCH DESTROYED PATRICK'S FEET. Rachel says it's time for heart bars, to protect the frog and the heel. Barrett votes for aluminum shoes or turning him out for the summer. I say plain old-fashioned. The farrier says Bozeman, Montana, is beautiful this time of year.

My mind is fried. But hoisting myself onto Shiva's back, I know I'm where I want to be.

"I need to ride," I say to Barrett, who's holding the horse for me as I mount.

"I know," is all he says.

Both Shiva and Cal are good for the Ghost. I try out the bitless bridle on Shiva, and he responds well to it and jumps rounder with less head flipping.

"I have the blues," I admit to the Ghost. The Ghost knows how much age is an issue for me. He must have once felt the limitations of aging, too, but he is beyond that now.

"How so?" he asks.

"Oh I'm just wondering—you know—how long to keep going. Do I just keep going until whenever, or what?"

"As long as you're still enjoying it," he answers wisely. "I still love it," he says. "My dog and I were perfectly happy on our way to the barn at 2:30 a.m. on Surefire morning."

I cannot admit to same.

"It's been hard for me when I don't have help. I love it when Barrett comes, but he just doesn't have the stamina anymore," thinking of Seneca weekend, Barrett dragging his heels to warm-up, forgetting the fly spray, being worn out by noon, and having to pass out in the back seat for an hour.

I don't admit the mounting dread I feel before each event; fear of failure, my constant companion. Always lurking—years of hit or miss with Calvin, years of rails and falls, countless bad dressage tests and getting run off with, the recent stops and run-outs. Why am I still riding such a difficult horse?

The answer stares me right in the face every day in the barn.

A NIGHT OF STORMS KNOCKING OUT POWER. A BRILLIANT MORNING. I write a thank-you note to the world:

> *Dear Paul,*
>
> *Can't tell you how many people have come up to me to compliment the new sign—It is sure to become a landmark. No one will ever know what Redmond meant to me and what he chose to be for me. I appreciate your love of him. I respected Redmond more than any other creature I've ever known. We weren't made for each other, but we were each other's best shot at greatness. He was a Love, and he shared that with you.*
>
> *Thanks for your kindness,*
>
> *Julia*

DOWN UNDER NAILS ME FOR LETTING MY HORSES RUN AT THEIR fences.

"There's a real problem in your training if you can't get him to come back to you enough to get the two strides."

He's referring to the short two strides between two small trakehners in his cross-country field. When I start from a show jump canter, the two strides are easy to get, but after a gallop, not so much. It doesn't help matters that I don't have Calvin's cross-country bridle, and hence not the brakes I need. Using Calvin's hackamore cross-country is like trying to lead an elephant with a dog leash. Down won't let me make excuses, though, and he hates talk of bits and bitting. He gallops all of his horses in a snaffle. Then again, he doesn't gallop an 18-hand elephant. Lucky him, he's a man, with his center of gravity through his chest line rather than his hips, so the snaffle doesn't require as much arm strength.

We continue to a bending line involving a corner. My lesson mate has more trouble with this exercise, so now it's her turn to be admonished.

"I'd save my money and not compete him for a while. The horse needs more training," Down says to her.

"What about me?" I ask with a joke in my voice. "Retire?"

"Why would you want to retire?" says Down. "You're just starting to get good."

I hose Calvin off, chatting with my lesson mate about her winter digs in Ocala. As I'm walking back to my trailer, I see the Ghost's rig parked kitty-corner to mine

"Can't be," I say under my breath. I run through my Rolodex of eventers' trailers. Most other professionals' rigs are plastered with their sponsors' ads, except the Ghost's. He makes a point of looking as anonymous as possible, the odd phantom out. Ironically, his rig stands out in its blankness—reverse advertising.

I dash around, wrapping Cal and throwing things back on the trailer, intent on leaving before the Ghost gets back to his.

The Ghost: *Just saw a cute horse today you might like up in the barn where I teach in New Jersey.*

I am fingerless with relief.

"I don't know if I can do Jersey by myself," I admit to Barrett over coffee.

I stand at the sink, my eyes welling.

I spend the morning riding Shiva and Patrick and packing the tack and traps for the weekend, saving Cal's ride for when we get to the horse park, so that he can get accustomed to his new surroundings and be as relaxed as possible for his dressage test tomorrow.

I leave the farm merely a half hour late, and though I've picked a non-rush hour, I still get stuck in traffic south of the Delaware Memorial Bridge. When it lifts, I take a wrong turn: I'm headed on I-40 East to the Trump Taj Mahal in Atlantic City. What could be worse? I get turned around and Braille my way to the New Jersey Turnpike, whose relentless traffic gives me plenty of time to stew over what I should be doing with my life and the angst of why now. Why, after all these years of being possessed with eventing, why now?

"Everybody should do what they're good at doing," Barrett pontificates from home. "You're good at training and riding these hawses," he says, stretching out my passion as far as possible, "so you should be doing what you're already doing. You have to compete," he starts to explain, but I jump in, "so I have a measure of where I'm at."

"That's right," he agrees. "You have to know where you are before you can go further."

"Kinda like, now that I've found the Jersey Turnpike, I can come home?" I ask playfully. "And you should do what you're good at," I go on.

"And what's that?" Barrett asks.

"Being a con artist. What's up your sleeve?"

"Chance is coming home in a few weeks. She wants me to do some research with her for her play about the dead jockey."

A SCORCHER OF A DAY. CAL MAKES AN EFFORT IN THE TROT AND walk work, staying relaxed yet forward. But when we pick up the canter, he strikes off on the wrong lead—a Bush League boo-boo in an Advanced test. And then both of his flying changes are hysterical.

I change tack for show jumping in 90 degrees. Calvin's round starts out well, but as soon as he hits the out in a six-stride line at fence 6, he stops trying and starts hitting rails. The next four poles tumble as he gets increasingly against my hand. In Calvin's fear of doing the wrong thing, he does the wrong thing, and then tries to run as far away from his mistake as possible. He won't confront himself any more than I will. My angst carries me into the evening and is my dinner companion back at the Radisson, where three servers with thick Jersey accents hang out at the bar with me and complain about their beer-swilling husbands and cranky toddlers at home. They want to know if I am learning to ride and do I have a horse at the horse park. Their eyes get big when I explain how I drove the horse from Baltimore. We are enthralled with each other through my overdone T-Bone and something to wash it down.

I'M A LITTLE BLEARY EYED AND A LOT EXHAUSTED, IN PART BECAUSE of wedding revelers at the Radisson last night.

"They just don't stop," the hotel receptionist says when I trudge out of my room as the first sparrows are tuning up.

Just seeing Calvin gives me confidence. I rummage around in my backpack and pull out the bride's garter I caught last night. I boot up Cal, slip the lacy doughnut over his hoof, positioning it just above his bad hock for good luck. They are running early. Before I know it, we're struggling at the first turning combination when I take one too many tugs and Calvin puts in six strides instead of the planned five. I remind myself not to be such a control freak and to let him come forward to his fences. After that, the run smooths out until the back quarter of the course, when I get tired exactly when he's running the hardest and is most strung out. We have one other iffy jump when Cal launches at a big oxer, but he still clears the fence easily on about a sixteen-foot stride, does one more combination, and finishes the course. I'm hot and exhausted, but very happy. A one-eighty from yesterday. The same old Cal I had at MCTA—the horse who would jump anything that gets in his way.

It takes me three hours to cool him out, ice his legs, pack up all my gear, strip the stall, wrap him, and load the trailer. I head down the Jersey Turnpike toward home with my salty head still in the fire.

Chapter Ten

All Beaches Are Nude Beaches if You're a Dog

In spite of my bark, I pack three bags, unsure of what not to wear in Bethany Beach, three hours to the east.

At the boardwalk, a huge sign warns: "No dogs at any time allowed on the beach," with a red slash through a picture of a Lab that looks exactly like Georgia.

"Ah-fuck-it," I say to my husband, "I'm taking her anyway. It's one of the main reasons we came here, to introduce Georgia to the ocean. She's had nearly as bad a year as us." I tighten the leash and close my eyes. "She's my therapy dog."

Georgia seems overwhelmed by the ocean. The waves come in, and she runs back with a worsening hitch in her stride to her daddy, plopped near a carved sand turtle, his doppelganger.

It's late in the day. The three of us sit close together on the nearly abandoned beach and look out to the water. The world stretches into nothingness and my mind goes with it, pulled from its troubles and daily-ness, engulfed by an immense womb.

And so begins our time at Bethany, named after the biblical village outside of Jerusalem where Jesus and his donkey made a pit stop en route to the Crucifixion.

Mr. and Mrs. Ah-Fuck-It shimmy to the edge of water, skirting hundreds of sunning bodies, beach bags and toys and drinks, playpens and umbrellas. We plop down on a napkin of soggy sand, next to half-completed sandcastles and children squealing up from the waves with their plastic buckets of brimming water. Barrett sits mesmerized by the older boys on boogie boards showing off their fancy tricks riding the building waves, maybe seeing his younger self. I hunker down with Brian Morton's *Breakable You*, a Romeo and Juliet tale about an American Jewess and Arab, and her broken family. I love to get lost in other worlds when I'm toasting on the beach. Here, we get boardwalks and funnel cakes, salt-water taffy and frozen custard, oiled bodies and umbrellas dotting the sand like giant mushrooms. It's downright democratic.

BARRETT'S MOTHER BUILT A BLUEBERRY HOUSE TO KEEP OUT THE birds, a long arbor constructed of wire mesh and two-by-two's plunked in the middle of the backyard. When hunger pangs come, we go outside and stuff our faces by the fistful, then pick gobs of fruit to add to our protein shakes. Two cardinals were trapped when we first arrived. Barrett and I shooed them out the door.

"Why bother," I said. "They're in bird heaven."

"All birds need water," my husband reminded me.

I ponder this as I grab another cluster of berries and strip them off the vine. In a couple swoops I have enough for the blueberry crisp I'm planning for dessert. Stuffing myself, I feel like Violet Beauregarde—Barrett will have to roll me into bed to squeeze out the juice.

The first hurricane of the season bears down on the East Coast. The Outer Banks are getting pummeled. I can only hope that it reaches Bethany. I adore bad weather. Like holidays, it takes me out of the norm, gives me an excuse to either focus on the fireworks or switch on the Weather Channel. I love to turn away from my daily list to watch the trees get quiet and anticipatory, then all riled up before a good dump. A control freak's finest hour is surrender. Tomorrow is Independence Day, and Hurricane Arthur is upon us. Orgasm.

I wake in the night to some whooshing and pitter patter, go back to sleep, then wake again to a morning that got away with some heavy rain but nothing for the record books. No fallen trees or limbs in the backyard, but a glimmer of sunshine on the horizon. Too bad: it might be a beach day after all.

Blue on Blue

We duck through
a hobbit-sized door
into a feast of blue,

guarded haphazardly
by chicken wire and wooden slats.
Like us, one ravenous jay

has found a way in,
drawn to his own hue
in the vegetable kingdom,

blue on blue. Like Midas
to gold, branch to branch,
gorging on fat, juicy berries,

hanging in bunches,
heavy as grapes.
Trapped by too much,

and alarmed by our intrusion,
he flaps spastically into wire.
We strip them in clusters—

so many, I ache
to fill my mouth
with spit, made into wine.

THE RAIN RETURNS TO WASH OUT OUR FOURTH OF JULY PARADE. THE
wind picks up, and the trees are in a frenzy. It's a good day to visit Barrett's
grandmother, quartered at a nearby nursing home.

She is sitting in her wheelchair when we arrive, dressed for company, lips touched with red, her blue eyes still fierce in their beauty. "Come here," she says. "Just looking at you makes my eyes feel better."

I've brought the blueberry crisp both of us passed on last night, so it will seem freshly made. Her eyes get even more intense when we tell her where the blueberries came from.

We chat a while, mostly about members of Barrett's family I've never met. Barrett seems a little flat, and Nan even flatter, though I suspect that's basically how she is now.

"Where's that blueberry crisp?" she remembers.

I fetch paper plates from one of the nurses, and Barrett and Nan dig in while I pass on the late-afternoon snack.

Others down the hall also have Fourth of July visitors, and a couple are sleeping soundly, as if it were the middle of the night.

Georgia makes the rounds, visiting the suffering old ones room by room. Everyone seems glad to meet her, even the cranky nurses. She livens the place up, and I fantasize about a business model that would involve traveling to nursing homes with Georgia as a way to cheer up the dying. Georgia curls up at Nan's feet. One bad leg can always find another in a crowd. Nan's are bound in special stockings and Ace bandages to prevent the worst of their swelling.

After a while, Nan gets quiet and seemingly vacant, and I can tell she's tired and has had enough of company.

"What time is it?" she finally asks, a bit anxiously.

When Barrett tells her it's a little after 4:00, she says it's almost time for dinner.

"Everybody starts congregating outside the dining hall about now," she says.

We roll her down the hallway where her friends are already waiting for dinner, some in their nightclothes, asleep in their chairs, a couple ga-gaing at Georgia, others slumped and staring vacantly into space. I don't know what I was expecting ... a small crowd dressed for dinner with cocktails and hors d'oeuvres in hand? ... but that's not what awaits Nan. We say our goodbyes and punch the elevator button. Georgia dashes in when the doors open, and lies down in her Wonkavator to await our descent into the circle of beach vacations and a waterfront dinner at a local bistro.

We lie spent and exhausted in the beach-house bed, musketry of minutemen in the distance, edging closer to our bivouac.

It takes me two seconds to figure out the rhythm of the waves—unusual, as I've been having rhythm problems with my riding for years. I wait until the next wave breaks, and then I throw the ball as far as I can. On this more remote fisherman's beach, where dogs are permitted, Georgia dashes out and heaves herself into the calmer waters between breakers to snap the ball in her alligator jaws. Another wave builds in front of her. She turns for home and back she swims, cresting the next wave, which brings her swiftly to shore. The fishermen and their families are amazed at our show, and clap when she successfully brings back the ball. We play like this off and on all afternoon. Georgia can't get enough, though I start to worry that body surfing will be too strenuous on her torn ACL. Didn't the vet say swimming was ok? I throw caution to the waves, and we continue to play in the ocean, meeting her fans on the beach, reading, sleeping, thinking of anything but Calvin.

Barrett is in his own world on this "vacation," having already finished reviews of new books by Mira Gonzalez and Mark Wunderlich, and is now working on his third. I'm enjoying our dog without the constant distractions of horses, boarders, bills, my angst-ridden self. Out she gallops again, and then swims as though her little engine will never stop, her shoulders vigorously churning above the surface of the water.

When Georgia gets up from her nap back at the beach house, she can't put any weight on her left hind, and hops as though she lost a limb.

We make one last stab at the beach. Vacations are always the sweetest when you know they're about to end. They're good for taking chances, too, which suits my character. I continue to allow gimpy Georgia to enjoy the waves.

Dorsal fins break the surface of the water.

"Sharks run solo, don't they?" I ask Barrett, for reassurance.

"I think so," he replies. That's good enough for the likes of me. I dive back in with my dog, get tossed back to shore. I turn, strain my eyes toward the horizon. A couple of dolphins breach their intelligent bodies. The school makes its way along the shore, combing the shallows, gorging on the day.

Others realize it, too. Little fishing boats materialize from the horizon while surfcasters lining the beach hoist themselves out of their lounge chairs and run for their lines, ever hopeful, probably theorizing that a hundred or so dolphins know more than their fish-finding gadgets. Barrett and I are more interested in the dolphins. Occasionally one pops up a little higher, shimmying his body in satisfaction, having just slurped down a kingfish. We watch the animals bring playfulness to their work until we skip our own way off the beach.

I HATE BEING HOME BECAUSE I HAVE TO BE NICE TO PEOPLE. PATRICK is still sore in his heels. He's sound at the jog in hand, so I hop on him for a few spins in the indoor. He feels good. The trick will be to keep him that way.

I try the bitless bridle with Shiva again. He continues to take to it well, and the Ghost suggests that he swap places with Patrick on Saturday at Loch Moy, to see if the new bridle will work in a competition environment. I plan on using it for show jumping and then switching him over to a bit for cross-country.

I tighten the hackamore chain for Cal. From what he saw at Jersey, the Ghost posits that I need to come around the corners with a skosh more power, so I can settle the canter in the lines, rather than coming in softly and then humping to get to the next related fence.

"You were at Jersey?" I say.

"I knew you were going to be disappointed," he says, "but so much of your show jumping round was good. If you come into a line too weak, then you have to chase to get the striding, and Calvin gets flat and jumps at his fences rather than around them. Positive capability—that's what it's all about."

LAURA RELATES AN UNFORTUNATE INCIDENT THAT HAPPENED WHILE we were away. Laura is one of those sylphs who gets tinier as she ages, as if she were slowly disappearing. I hear the tall version of Patrick having gone after his pasture buddy, the broodmare, Romantic Notions. Patrick ran her around the paddock until they were both heaving. When Marta caught the horses, they were spent. Since Marta was in the middle of the afternoon shift by herself, she threw the horses in stalls, left them drenched and blowing. Laura insisted that they pull out the hot horses and hose and walk them.

"Glad I was here," Laura says. "Marta is a hard worker, but she doesn't know anything about how to deal with a hot horse."

I cringe, thinking about having left the horses in the hands of people with inadequate horse sense.

"But we didn't," Barrett says. "Laura was here."

TONIGHT WE DRESS UP AND GO OUT AGAIN—A DINNER WITH OLD friends at a local restaurant that requires a sport coat after 5:00 p.m. Barrett dons a tie but omits the jacket. The maître d' approaches with several house jackets to choose from.

"Damn," Barrett says, "I couldn't remember whether you had a rule about jackets or underwear." He chooses a lime green number.

Blue is a wine boss and directs the ordering. I'll spend the evening trying to cover my glass before Blue tops me off. One glass can easily turn into three or four if I'm not quick enough. Barrett orders a dark beer— better for his existential gastronomy. Blue makes a fanfare of ordering— and ordering too much. We're all gluttons of something: pain, food, wine, horses, climate denial.

Our waiter breathes heavily through his enormous frame, grips the little pen and pad with slightly tremulous fingers. He hovers above the four of us, squashed together in a plush booth, with bench seats that are too low for the height of the table. My nipples press against the edge, as if they were seated at an enormous brassiere. I can't even push my chair away.

None of us wants to talk about Blue's nephew, recently killed in a car crash.

"Any offers on the farm?" Allie asks instead.

"People aren't buying big farms right now," I say.

Her thick Chardonnay gaze insinuates it's looking like we don't want to sell, or we would have already.

"Our desire's got nothing to do with it," my husband says. He rags on our realtor.

The dinner pianist starts to play "Piano Man."

"Then fire her," I spit.

Our friends shift in their seats. Barrett is seething beside me. These are friends we've known so long that we feel comfortable enough to spat in front of.

Blue, in bowtie, metro-plaid sports coat, and jeans, rips off a piece of bread, lodges it in one side of his mouth, talks out of the other. "It would appear that the two of you want the same thing, but are frustrated you're not getting closer."

Barrett and I glare at each other.

"Now, now," Blue offers. "You should be kind to your husband after his recent brushes with death." I have an image of Blue leaning against Barrett's sixth-floor hospital room window. "Hello, hello," he'd said cheerily upon entering the sick room.

"Jewels," Allie interjects with her pet nickname for me, "Would you ever consider stopping the shows? You could always just ride your horses at home."

I look at her blankly.

"Barrett needs you," she goes on.

I've known these friends for so long, but they still don't understand my passion for eventing.

On the short trip home, silence. Finally, "That dinner cost us what Bethany cost," Barrett says.

"What do you mean—the entire week in Bethany?"

"Yep."

We did not know yet that Blue would be dead in a year.

BARRETT'S NOT TALKING TO ME. DITTO ON MY END.

I pop Shiva over a few of our cross-country fences. A deer jumps out of the corn. Shiva sees it before I do, scoots sideways, and spins. I'm on the ground, clutching one rein while Shiva stands docilely over me, pretending it was an accident. *Damn it. I'm going to feel this tomorrow.* I hoist my left foot in the stirrup and pull myself back up.

We have a good school despite a run-out at the narrow chevron—it's more of a Preliminary effort, but it still eats at me. That, and my fall. It's never a good day when you fall off a horse. Today's lesson is that I can never ride Shiva unaware. There are surprises around every corner—children in gingham pinafores running across bean fields, cross words to your well-meaning husband after you've had a couple snorts of firewater.

I warm Calvin up long and low, all three gaits. I shorten the reins, and he's right there for me. He's so forward that I feel his back come up and he's really working now. I give him a few half halts, but I remember to soften right away. Butter in my hands. At least Calvin's talking to me.

SHIVA STRUTS DOWN THE BARN AISLE TO HIS STALL. HE WAS GOOD IN all three phases at the first Loch Moy Horse Trials, including stadium. He skipped around the challenging Training cross-country course. The disappointment was dressage. I was sloppy with my fifteen-meter circles. I never was very good in geometry and now more than ever have trouble walking a straight line. Still, we were fourth after dressage, third overall, in a field of twenty-two.

Barrett wins a prize for a poem about a former girlfriend, and we celebrate with pizza. Our hurts never last long. But I'm just jealous enough to suggest an early bedtime. I wonder if he'll call me Tanya. We douse the lights.

Calvin: *Get some rest. Remember, I had the day off today.*

CALVIN WINKS AT ME AS I TACK HIM UP FOR A HEARTY TRAIL RIDE. We bump into a couple of riders on the driveway, and instead of my usual aloof, I ask if I might join them. They seem pleased—they know I will take them places they've not dared go.

"What's your plan?" I ask.

"Thought we might have a bit of a conditioning hack," one of them says.

"Rambo hack it is, then," I say.

I take the lead. When I look back, both horses are struggling at the canter to keep up with Calvin's trot, a look of determination on their riders' faces. One of them likes to small talk—a lot—so my plan is to go so relentlessly she won't be able to speak.

It works. I stay in my own head, weighing the pros and cons of moving Shiva up to Prelim next weekend. He's ready, and Loch Moy II promises to be on the soft side—but I'll have Calvin with me, too. His welfare is my main concern.

I text the Ghost. I can't seem to brush my teeth these days without asking his permission. Barrett makes a face.

"Just do it," he says. "Own it. He's ready."

I wait for the Ghost.

A MIDNIGHT TEXT.

Chance: *Mom, I'm on my way to the hospital. Call me.*

Which I do every half hour till I finally reach her at 5:00 a.m. She is back home in bed, trying at last to get some sleep—if her phone would stop ringing. Translation: you're bothering me. Apparently, the Pulmicort that her ENT prescribed did not mix well with the marijuana lozenge a friend gave her at a party last night. The vertigo she suffered for a year has boomeranged. So much for her pee sample. When I talk to her midday, she's still dizzy. No one believed her, she complains, and wrote her off as a paranoid pothead. All night she lay on a gurney, waiting for the marijuana and Pulmicort to stop interacting, while the woman in the next booth kept moaning, "I don't exist, I don't exist."

"You've got to write this down," I say to her brightly. "It's your next play."

I tell her my own stories of too much cough medicine, lidocaine toxicity, dizziness from marijuana highs—anything to make her feel that her difficulties are not unique and will pass.

Unbeknownst to me, Barrett tells her about Ventipulmin, a Pulmicort-like drug some trainers give to racehorses, which can increase heart rates and cause heart attacks at finish lines. Just what she doesn't need to hear.

Chance, you exist. We exist.

She tweets. *The title of my new play: Postcards from the Hedge. Leave it to my family of writers to tell me to write it all down, when I'm in the midst of a medical emergency.*

LIGHT CREEPS IN WITH ITS CANE. THE CARDINALS GET MORE ACTIVE at the feeder outside my window. Time to pick up a hoof.

To keep myself awake driving to Down Under's, I text Chance to persuade her not to die. She is convinced she is going to—even two days after her initial vapors. We text for a while about various drug reactions. I respond to my daughter's plight with sympathy, remembering Barrett's advice not to give her advice. Which I bristle at, too—I don't want it any more than she does. Chance doesn't want my help, yet she needs to know I'm there for her.

In Sleepy Hollow, the familiar horse-drawn plows of the Amish tell me I'm in Ghost Country. My paranoia takes over. I toss the phone to Georgia and cringe at every dark sedan and rig until I arrive at Van Tassel Farm.

Down is always hard on me. He wants me to stop holding my horses at the fences, letting the fences hold them instead. I'm not sure how to accomplish this with Calvin, as nothing ever seems to back him off.

"You've got to build more canter," Down reminds me, "then steady at the fences. You always begin too slowly, then rush at the end."

Riding dyslexia. I need someone to video my rides and play them back in reverse.

Calvin is foot-perfect in the ring but a bear on Down's cross-country course. I have less control in the hackamore, and Down nails me for not being able to regulate my strides within a line.

"You need to land, half halt, and regulate the four steps between those two jumps, not just go along for the ride and hope it works out."

It's true: I have no half halt in the hackamore on cross-country. Nor much turning. Several times I have to pull Calvin off fences that we're not supposed to jump.

Calvin has all the talent in the world, but without the fortitude of mind to realize his potential. Both of us lacking inner calm, self-confidence, Jimmy's sprezzatura.

My teacher acts nonplussed when he sees Shiva's bitless bridle. He's meeting my youngster for the first time. Though I mention needing to improve his form over fences, Shiva does surprisingly well in the ring with Down's exercises.

We head out to the cross-country course.

"Would you mind if I put a bit in his mouth?" I ask, as politely as I can. The students in the class smile, but Down keeps a stony face.

By the time I join them, the other horses have already started jumping, and I have to hurry to catch up. Never a good plan. I jump the logs Down tells me to jump, then head for the little rolltop on a mound, forgetting that Shiva is often afraid of what he can't see on the other side. We canter quietly up to the rolltop, and he stops. Ugh. I circle back around, and he stops again.

Shiva repeatedly throws himself down the mound sideways and backward, rather than jump the jump. Down himself finally gives me a lead. Once I get him over the jump at the trot a few times, we proceed with the lesson. My mind is rattled, so I don't ride well thereafter. I miss at a little trakehner, climbing up Shiva's neck and getting ahead of my horse.

"Can you tell me what happened there?" Down asks, testing me, as if he's not sure I would even know.

Lessons with Down are at best humbling. He finds the rider's or horse's holes and exposes them, then challenges the rider to fill them. I suppose his philosophy is that a rider has to make mistakes in order to improve—and somehow keep her ego intact.

"He'll be all right," Down concludes, referring to Shiva. "He just needs to be ridden forward to his fences to learn to put in the extra stride so he'll jump around his fences rather than at them." My instructor makes a motion with both of his arms, swinging them simultaneously behind his body like a swimmer preparing for a dive.

It's a miserably hot, humid day, and between the drive and two horses to ride, I'm toast even before I head home. I slink down in my seat between Tarrytown and Sleepy Hollow, driving behind my axle.

DROPPING TEMP. DROPPING MOOD. MIDDLE OF JULY, AND I ALMOST need a sweater. Birds and commuters at it again right outside my bright window. Cloudless, too. Horses grazing on wet morning hillsides.

Passion can be so much drudgery. Down trains my head: the Ghost trains my heart. It's another Sleepy Hollow day with the Ghost. Two-timing stabs me in the gut. The catbird in the octopus tree, ever encroaching on the house, flits from arm to arm, mocking my stupidity. My lack of courage. *Just talk to him. Either that, or stop what you're doing.*

"I thought a lot about it," the Ghost says. "I don't think it would be a bad thing to try out the bitless bridle one more time before moving Shiva up to Prelim."

I look at him blankly.

"The USEF sent around an email to instructors. Since two riders died last month, they're cracking down on anyone who has been on the watch list. They're encouraging instructors to take another look at those riders and reevaluate their riding and safety."

"That's right. I'm still on the list of bad riders," I croak.

We begin jumping. Both horses are lively today. Shiva attacks the Preliminary-level fences, and Calvin is his usual game self. The Ghost reminds me to keep my body back within the lines, and to maintain a connection with my horse to the base of each fence.

Is my Ghost losing confidence in me?

INTERMEDIATE AT LOCH MOY SHOULD BE AN EASY DROP-DOWN FOR Calvin. In dressage, he has his usual fit in the canter work. I resort to my hands, which makes him even madder. I put the hackamore chain on blisteringly tight for show jumping. He's better, knocking only one rail. The first six fences on cross-country are solid. They've dumbed down the water after two bad falls previous to our run. The track circles around the water before taking us through it. At speed I have trouble turning Calvin, who would rather be moving in a straight line toward a destination. As I yank on the left rein, Calvin slips behind, and I barely get him turned in time to jump the hut. The horse stalls as if to question the absurdity of the tiny bank, plops into water, and jumps the Preliminary second hut, as newly directed. He then tunes me out on the long run to a corner, bolts to it, and ducks out at the last second. I hit him once, circle around, and come again—he pops over it and we continue on. After the run-out, I'm deflated, while Calvin has gotten rank and unrideable, probably mad that I've hit him. He's running and leaving out strides willy-nilly. I manage to finish, rip off the tack, and dump the Myler bit in the nearest porta potty.

THE LAST THING I WANT TO DO IS RETURN TO LOCH MOY FOR A second siege.

Shiva stands in the trailer like a lamb. More like a sleeping lamb. He seems as exhausted as I am. When I get on him for dressage, I tickle him with the whip a few times to wake him up and get his motor going. Typical Shiva, he gives me a lovely effort, and I'm even able to correct my fifteen-meter circles.

His tiredness affects our weakest element. In show jumping, he won't respond to my attempts to get him in front of my leg. Our rhythm is consequently erratic, I have trouble seeing my distances, and we have two rails down. Always the rails.

Barrett calls to ask how it went. "Cross-country was a breeze," I tell him, hiding the rest.

SEEKING FRESH DISAPPOINTMENT, I TURN TO PATRICK, WHO GIVES me grief in our first serious flat school since his foot problem. He has a darker mood than I do and won't let me canter him. He runs sideways, hops up and down. My body rages. There are no keyboards to be found, let alone a good note before ending. He's got to be still hurting. I go lightly, then put him away, get Cal ready for a hack. Head on over to a neighbor's farm. Trees lying where they fell, pastures overgrown, fences in disrepair. I get off my mountain to lead him across a rickety bridge that has a few baseball-sized holes in it. I stupidly test its strength with my own weight before I lead Cal across. I don't have to look far for a strewn log to hoist myself back on Kilimanjaro. It's the one thing with horses I could always do well; God grew me long legs for something. We head deeper into these overgrown woods, as if my purpose were to get lost. Paths that once existed are no longer, fields that Chance and I galloped across are congested with scrub.

Purgatory is not a place you go to—it is a place you become.

We head down a steep hill on a precariously rocky path, where a tree is down and no way to get around it. My cell phone rings. It's the vet. Georgia is on the table, and I need to make a decision. Knee replacement or stem cell? The tear is about 50/50; it could go either way. Cal dances under me. "Let's get going!" he whinnies impatiently.

"I'll call you back in five," I tell the vet. "I need to talk to my horse."

I end the call, pat Calvin's neck.

"Surgery," Cal says. "She's a big dog."

THE TECH LEADS GEORGIA OUT INTO THE WAITING ROOM. SHE HOPS across the room on three legs, turns her head away, refusing to look at me, as if I were the one responsible for her misery. Barrett and I lift her into the back seat, and I crawl in beside her for the ride home. As we struggle our way up I-95, I catch a glimpse of Barrett's red eyes in the mirror, and mine start stinging, too. I wish I could take on some of my dog's pain, or at least explain to her what is happening, and that one day soon she will be whole again. "It was a perfectly fine broken knee," Georgia says, "and you ruined it."

At home, we situate her on her dog bed, strew an armful of favorite toys. She still won't look me in the eye. I leave Barrett in charge, and go out to confer with housepainters before tacking up Patrick for his first jump school in weeks.

The Ghost shows up bearing a peace offering. A hackabit rig, which is what it says it is: a hackamore with a bit attached.

"It'll stop a train," he says about the powerful segunda bit with a shank on the hackamore the length of Calvin's show jumping hackamore. Loads of leverage.

I manage to stay on Patrick through his exuberance, thrilled as he is to be jumping again for the first time since his foot trouble. He is aggressive, but he's jumping well and feeling good.

I gallop around the back field on Calvin, pressing him into a two-min-ute lick, to see what kind of control I have with the new rig. The Ghost's hackamore, while powerful, is not as strong as my own. We decide to pair my hackamore with the Ghost's segunda and try again later in the week.

I don't tell him about Down Under, I don't tell him about the Black Dahlia. He asks if I've ever been to Boyd Martin's farm and his new cross-country course. I'm relieved to say I haven't, and he suggests that we take Calvin there to try the new rig.

"How about Tuesday?" I say. Next week is Millbrook, and I feel a need to get the experiment done quickly.

"It's been another dark night," I admit to him. "After Loch Moy, I wanted to throw in the towel."

The Ghost looks right through me.

"Anyway, he's what I've got."

BARRETT AND I START OUR NIGHT SLEEPING UPSTAIRS. I SOON MAKE my way downstairs around the baby gates Barrett has installed to spend some time with Georgia, before coming back up as Barrett descends for the graveyard shift.

I dream that an exercise rider who trains with the Ghost shows up with a horse for sale. He seems like a nice one with good gaits, a decent jump, a kind attitude. A little over at the knee, maybe, and narrow in the chest. The Ghost likes him quite a lot, thinks I should proceed to the next step. I like the horse, too, but I'm not in love with him. Not sure I can live with the scraggly tail—a lush tail, sign of heart and longevity, though I'm making up the longevity part. Got to have some legitimate basis for demanding a lush tail. As I'm combing through it, it starts to fall out in huge wiry chunks, until there's nothing left but a hairless tail bone protruding from above the horse's ass.

I wake and come down to give Barrett a break, but he says he's getting up anyway, so go back to bed. At 6:00, I get up for good. Barrett is snoring on the couch, one arm draped around Georgia, who snoozes on the floor beside him, as close to him as she can get.

I SNIP THE GLADS OPENING UP AROUND THE GARDEN, THE ONES WE planted as bulbs this spring—lavender, crimson, pale yellow—and bring them into the house. I lie down next to Georgia, scratch her ears, her back, her tummy. Housepainters thump and scrape outside.

Charlotte, in a long cotton day dress and kerchief round her neck, is standing under the old maple. "I wouldn't have picked that color," she says before disappearing into the shadows.

Rachel shows up with Cal's Tildren, a drug used to treat lameness in horses suffering from hock arthritis or navicular disease. She's still testy about a scene the other day at the farm: someone's horse colicking, another vet called, Rachel showing up in the midst. She rummages in her truck for her IV set, then recommends I send Georgia to the vet for her rehab. Her dogs have Obamacare; I've let mine lapse. She tells me stories of a Rottweiler breeder who lets the dogs be lame for the rest of their lives when their stifles blow out. She warns me about giving Tildren injections too frequently. I've opted to re-administer after only seven months. Rachel disagrees with my insistence.

"Well, his bloodwork is fine," she admits. "But I've had one horse go bad, and he got really sick. Was on fluids for days. And I mean days."

That's where all of her IV catheter sets probably went.

"But isn't it ok if you administer it slowly? That's what I've read, anyway," I offer tentatively. "Can't you slow down the drip?"

"Well, I can't stay," she says. "you'll have to pull out the line yourself."

I'm waiting. And waiting. I pass the job to Barrett so I can join the band of boarders already in the middle of an inefficient jump setup on top of the hill in our jump ring, commandeered by one of our hunter-jumper residents. After over an hour of helping out, everyone scurrying around but accomplishing little—mismatching jump standards, mis-measuring lines, and someone hopping strides because her left leg doesn't reach as far as her right—I return to the barn to find Barrett standing on a bucket in Calvin's stall, adjusting the line of fluids running into the horse's vein. The line keeps shutting off the drip. What should have taken forty minutes has already taken over an hour. Well, at least Rachel got slow. I disappear to finish my rides, and when I return to Calvin's stall hours later, he is still tied to his chest bar, head down, grazing on what chaff he can reach. Barrett had left him tied, as per Rachel's instructions, to keep his head up after the drip so he wouldn't develop a hematoma at the injection site, but so much for keeping his head up. And who knows how long he's been tied like that, while Barrett raced to Penn Station to pick up the Brooklyn jockey.

MY DARK FRIEND COMPETES WITH CHANCE FOR MY ATTENTION. MY tolerance is busy keeping them both at bay. We go to the spa. Chance doesn't want to shop for clothes afterward, as is my suggestion; instead we go to Wegmans. "The only thing Maryland has that New York doesn't," she says. We slalom our way between tables mounded with stalagmites of organic fruits and vegetables, while formations of tiny American flags leftover from the last holiday sway from the ceiling like stalactites. We buy Chance food and cosmetics, plus sockeye, tomatoes, mozzarella, almond milk, and ice cream. Then haul bag after bag of groceries into the house, skirting the housepainters, whose brushes are still wet.

Before we start dinner, I sneak two sips of a potent vodka tonic, then hide the rest behind a bag of wilted parsley in the frig, pretending that Barrett will finish it, though he hasn't drunk vodka in years. I'll dump the rest down the drain either later over dishes, or in the morning as I'm fetching my cranberry juice. I refrain from filling my tumbler of Chardonnay to the brim, fearing criticism from Chance. Instead, I secretly roll a joint then take hop-along for a walk. Georgia looks incrementally better, as if the first step toward health is to become good at hurting so much, though she is still not able to bear weight on the leg, which is swollen and stapled shut.

I make the mistake of setting the table in the dining room. As a family, that's where we always ate dinner together. Later, Barrett will remind me that most likely the room brings back memories of too many dinners with the four of us. Invariably, the subject of her brother and Mollie floats up.

Chance brings up the subject of the ring.

"Now wait a minute," I say.

"Well, you didn't even ask me—you just gave it to him," she complains.

"Your grandmother told me that she always saw her engagement ring going to John's wife-to-be," I remind her. "Think of the wishes of the dead."

My mother wanted all of her jewelry and clothing to go to Chance and me, with the casual stipulation of her engagement ring. Little did I think that Chance would care that much about Mollie *not* getting anything that once belonged to my mother. Maybe she sees Mollie as the one who swooped in on her brother and took him away from her. Chance doesn't realize that John had already made the break by the time he met Mollie.

I put down my fork, looking at her as coldly as I can. No matter what I say, a ruckus will follow. I don't have the strength nor inclination to put up my dukes. Instead, I retreat upstairs for the night.

"I thought you'd never come," Darkness says.

THERE ARE FLAKES OF RED PAINT EVERYWHERE. THE PAINTERS ARE almost finished, which means it's time for me to start putting back in order the frowsy landscape that surrounds Charlotte's farmhouse, fresh coats of

Battleship Gray and a bright-red tin roof fit for a spaghetti Western. I can't wait till the first patters of rain, a sound sure to soothe me.

I spend the day icing Georgia's swollen leg and waiting for Chance to need me. I suggest that we go to a movie, or on a hack, and when neither suggestion captures her, I try to entice her to go for a walk on the Gunpowder. Nothing works. She wants to "hang."

"You can't sit still, can you?" she says critically.

I want to do something fun with my daughter. Instead, I go outside and yank some ragweed and dandelions. It feels good, relieves the tension inside, makes my tongue less sore from biting it.

Georgia still won't put weight on her leg. The bag of frozen peas and my sitting with her bring me a sense of peace and accomplishment as she settles into the ritual. Three times a day, following her PT exercises— stretching the leg out and holding it for ten seconds, repeated fifteen times. At least I'm getting something worthwhile done, in this time of waiting for my daughter to want me.

Patrick and I head out. I dare to trot him on good ground, and I'm relieved to find him sound. After weeks of being crippled with sore feet, he is starting to come around. I've entered him in the Fair Hill Horse Trials.

Hopefulness is the sweet kiss of death.

The prospect of dining out is the first time all day I've seen Chance excited to do something. She raves about the Manor Tavern before we arrive, remembering the dinner we had there last summer with Silas, who has recently dumped her for the second time.

"My husband will have the Mandarin chicken, and I'll have the canoe."

"It's quinoa, not *canoe*," Chance corrects me.

"We get that all the time," the waiter says kindly.

Chance drives us home. I'm exhausted, but my daughter is just revving up. She spends the next hour changing into a diaphanous lime-green swirly thing, and loading on more eye makeup, before she leaves for the tango festival—her chief reason for coming home, though she has already missed the first two days, including the workshops and lectures and last night's Milanga with an *orchestra tipica*.

I wake to Georgia whimpering between us on the bed—I've forgotten her late meds—so I haul myself up. An hour later, the thudding of wheels on the drive. It's 4:30 a.m. Barrett, just getting up, goes downstairs to greet the stranger and make coffee.

From upstairs, I hear profuse apologizing.

"I'm really sorry, Barrett, I didn't know what to do."

I'm awake now. Barrett returns to our bedroom. "What was that all about?" I ask.

"Chance had a flat and drove the car home anyway," he reports.

I HUSTLE TO GET MY WORK DONE BEFORE CHANCE RISES. I'VE RIDden two horses before light hits her eyes at twelve o'clock.

"God, he worked well today!" Jan exclaims from the shed row, referring to Shiva's usual good efforts on the flat.

I pivot from barn to house, checking on Georgia and Chance. I find Chance at the kitchen counter munching away. Our bad tone continues. She's worried about the flat tire and the possibility of having fucked up my car. I explain what I thought was the obvious thing to do when your car has a flat: you pull over and call for help, or change it yourself.

"Didn't they teach you how to change a flat in driver's ed?" I ask.

She shakes her head no. "I'm from New York; I don't really drive anymore," she explains.

"Then you shouldn't be borrowing people's cars," I say, the taste of iron infiltrating my mouth.

Chance hasn't budged from the kitchen counter since she has been home, refusing to sit on the slip-covered couch where Georgia spends her afternoons. I ice Georgia's leg and return to the barn to finish my rides. When I come back to the house, Chance is sunbathing by the pool, where she claims she has been for the last few hours.

"Have you gone swimming yet?" I ask, innocently.

"The pool's disgusting. It's all green, and there's stuff floating at the bottom."

"It's just algae," I say. "We get it every year. You know, organic."

She pulls her sunhat down over her face.

I do some weeding around the pool.

"You really can't sit still, can you?" she accuses me again, muffled under her sun hat.

I ignore her, continue my satisfying work, yanking weeds, making things better. A white lily has multiplied and bloomed, its flowers so heavy they are toppling over. Its perfume wafts my way.

"Come look at this!" I say to Chance. "It's one of the lilies your grandmother sent," referring to the Easter lilies my mother would gift us every year. Barrett planted the spent stalks, and here they are again, a decade and a half later, busting out all over our backyard.

"I can smell them," Chance says from her chaise, without moving an inch.

Barrett runs out to pick up crabs. Chance has insisted on a dozen and a half extra larges, though Barrett can only eat one at best with his condition, and I'll probably not be able to eat more than two, due to the heavy-handed Old Bay seasoning.

"Mom, can you come here a minute?" Chance calls from the top of the stairway, having just gotten out of the shower, a towel wrapped around her tiny damp body.

"Is this really bad?" she asks, showing me her rosy cleavage, where the sun has made an impression. Her New York City skin is pale as china, and unaccustomed to wind, sun, rain, or snow. It is inside skin. Mine is outside. Hers definitely doesn't ride horses, pick stalls, weed gardens, swim, or drive a car.

Later, as we're pounding and picking on our back patio, hurrying to beat the thunderheads headed our way, Chance asks why Barrett and I aren't eating crabs. She's on her fifth or sixth. Barrett and I have each had one.

"I can only have one," Barrett says, which makes sense to Chance, considering how sick he has been. She glares at me. "Kind of hot," I say, the smallest of allusions to my new intolerance to spice.

Chance's accomplishment for the day is a homemade raspberry pie for dessert. Barrett and I are still famished, so we dig in to the tart, luscious pie.

The scent of my mother's Easter lily follows me up the stairs to bed.

"I'm really upset about what I've done to my body," Chance says, entering the safe zone of my bedroom. She is deeply earnest about her irresponsible cleavage. And though she might never admit it, she needs to be close to me.

"It will be ok. It'll turn brown," I say, "and then it will be beautiful."

CALVIN IS RANK AND IRRITABLE FOR THE BLACK DAHLIA. I attempt to school the Advanced test that I am supposed to ride at Millbrook on Friday, but because his mouth is bothering him, too, he flips me off with every stride. I do everything I can not to rely on my hands and to use my body as leverage. The Dahlia's instructions don't even help.

I lay out all my leverage bits to decide which ones I'll try before Millbrook, but with Calvin's mouth ripped open, I may have to run him cold.

Julia: *I won't be able to cross-country school tomorrow.*

The Ghost: *I hope everything is ok.*

Julia: *Family complications.*

CHANCE IS WRITING A PLAY ABOUT A JOCKEY WHO DIED IN THE starting gate at Santa Anita in 1971. Alvaro Pineda and his horse are the main characters. She and Barrett visit the Maryland Breeders' Association to do some research. When they pull back into the farm, I'm walking out of the mare barn, tacked up and ready to mount Patrick.

"Bring him here so I can pat him," Chance commands from the driver's seat, her tiny foot resting on the brake.

"Who's this?" I test her, teasingly, holding Patrick, a dark bay with two white socks and a white umbrella on his forehead.

"Calvin," she says with assurance.

"Wrong," I say—the worst word I can utter to my daughter.

"Calvin doesn't have any white on him," I go on, like an idiot. She won't feel criticized, she'll feel invalidated, as if my asking her a horse question when she's been writing a play about horses is meant to undermine the integrity of her art.

Barrett gets word that he has won a fiction prize from *Salamander Magazine*, yet again for a story about an old lover. I suggest we celebrate with crab cakes and a yummy wine, a treat he has not allowed himself since getting out of the hospital in May.

Chance doesn't want to pick the twelve remaining crabs. She suggests that I buy already-picked jumbo lump from the store.

"Why would I do that, with all those uneaten crabs in the frig?" I ask, bewildered.

"Because that's how we've always made them before."

Apparently I don't pick them right and leave bits of shell. She then vanishes upstairs when it's time to make dinner. She doesn't want to make crab cakes my way. She lists the ingredients she wants in them, but leaves the scene before they're made. I turn to Oprah's recipe and bag the mayonnaise, hoping to satisfy my health-conscious daughter.

We sit down to dinner. Barrett forks a crab cake.

"Who's this?" he says to Chance.

"Calvin," Chance replies. They both crack up.

"Do you like Calvin?" I ask.

"Stop trying to trap me," she accuses.

"How am I trying to trap you?"

"Because you ask me if I like Calvin, and the only answer you'll accept is the one you want to hear," she says.

A mountain of weeds encroaches on the house.

"You're always trying to suffocate me," she goes on.

"Watch it," I warn her, "not over dinner. Not at my table."

"Your table?" she asks incredulously.

"Yes, my table." I am an advocate of the Hospitality Code: be gracious to those who ask you to sit down at their table to share a meal they've cooked for you.

We silently shovel forkfuls of Calvin and baked potatoes into our mouths, tasting like crumpled paper or wool socks, seasoned with the bitter atmosphere that has settled over the four oak planks we call a table.

"Why is she being like this?" I ask Barrett, under my breath.

"Because I won a prize," he explains.

THERE ARE SOME FIGHTS YOU CAN NEVER COME BACK FROM. THE one after your husband has an affair, for instance. You have just found out you are pregnant and now realize the baby is doomed. Or the one when your daughter is so unhappy with her life, and she blames you with all of her hurt heart.

Chance finds a text from Mollie on my cell charging on the phone stand. Something about Chance's miserable posts on Twitter and are we all right. Chance madly punches buttons on her phone.

"What a bitch," she says. "I'm blocking her, I'm unfriending her right now."

"Chance, she's family," I say. "You've got to get ahold of your anger."

"So what? She is a mean person."

"She was only writing out of concern for us," I say.

"The two of you have been talking about me behind my fictive Internet persona."

We wrap ourselves in tissue paper and crawl into the tin can to drive thirty miles to Penn Station. The left front tire thumps against the bent rim with each revolution. Chance needs to catch a 7:30 train back to gloomy Manhattan.

Our confinement does nothing for our argument, or our desperate need to get away from each other.

"Chance, I really think you need to get some help. You've got to get control of your temper. Or maybe go back to school, find a new career, join AmeriCorps. Do something to get out of yourself."

"*You* need to get some help," she spits. "Ms. Marijuana Alcoholic, smoking pot to change your mood, or whatever."

"Get out of the car," I command, veering over to the curb, a couple blocks from Penn Station. "I won't be talked to that way. Nor will I help support your life in New York anymore, if you are going to treat me like this."

"What, so you're cutting me off completely? I thought the extra money was to make up for the inequity between John and me."

"This is not about John. This is about you," I say, trying to steer the conversation back to my troubled daughter.

"I hate John, and I hate you," she says. "I worked a shitty job for eight years. I take a month and a half off, and now you're complaining about how I need a job?"

"Get out of the car," I repeat.

"You're kicking me out?" she asks incredulously.

"Get out of the car," I say a third time. "Either that, or I'll take you to Shepard Pratt, where you can spend some time with your Aunt Zelda."

She gets out, yanks her bags out of the back seat. I pull away, looking straight ahead, though I can't miss out of the corner of one eye, her running up to the passenger side window, her face distorted in an Edvard Munchian grin, waving violently and screaming goodbye. Then giving me the finger.

All of my mouth sores have ripped open.

I LEAVE EARLY WITH CALVIN FOR THE GHOST, CHECKING MY CELL phone every few miles. I walk up to the jump field, my head bent over the saddle, still glancing at my phone to see if there's any word from Chance: Nada. The Ghost is waiting for me in his ring.

"In or out?" he asks.

"Either way. Maybe a little of both," I say. Jumping in the ring will help put Calvin back together, but jumping out will offer more diversity and be a truer indicator of where he's at.

Calvin tries his big old Irish heart out on the lumpy hill.

"Just don't let go in front of the fences," the Ghost reminds me. "Keep your elbows soft. Keep a connection, but a soft, flexible one."

This is what is so hard to do: to hold Calvin steadily, but in a forgiving way. A little like parenting. Supportive, but not forceful. Soft, but not abandoning. Why is it I could never learn this when raising Chance?

296

"I'd leave it at that," the Ghost concludes, after we've come through his four-foot-plus uphill triple without fault.

By morning, I'm packed and ready to roll. I call Barrett at the barn. "Let's go!" I say, mustering as much enthusiasm as I can.

"Nan died last night," he replies, "a complication from a bout of pneumonia."

"That's a good thing, right?" I say, tentatively.

"I guess so," he says. And then, "I'll do whatever you want," he says with hesitation, "but I think it's a mistake to go." I can tell he doesn't mean because of Chance's bombardments, nor Georgia's recovery, nor even his grandmother's death; it's because he doesn't feel Calvin and I are ready for Millbrook. It's a Gold Cup event, and there will be plenty of FEI officials there, happy to run around on their golf carts watching us, particularly if we make a mess of dressage. Deep down, I believe he's right; it's just so disappointing. But I know if I shake up either Calvin or myself, then it will be impossible to bring us back again. I think of Jersey Fresh. There are one too many strikes against us.

I pull the plug on Millbrook. I tell the Ghost there's been a death in the family.

I flat the old crab in a hackamore, working on changes and parts of the test I won't be riding this weekend, and then it strikes me. In the same way the Ghost does not want me to turn him loose in front of the fences, I cannot turn him loose at the critical moment in a flying change. I have to keep my giant horse underneath me, not let him pull ahead. Elastic support. A relationship with boundaries that can breathe.

Oh, Chance.

Chapter Eleven

Make the World Smaller

CHANCE WRITES SCATHING TEXTS. I HAVE NEVER SUPPORTED HER, I love her brother more, I only think about myself, I am painting her in a corner. She will either suffer or end it. She never wants to speak to me again.

I call her father.

"I'm in therapy myself. I can't sleep at night," Jack says.

I write back to Chance. I'm sorry she feels this way. I love her.

She says if I loved her I wouldn't *manipulate* her. I am why she feels like shit every day of her life. *Because to you, I am never enough.*

My daughter. My beautiful, vibrant daughter.

I DO THREE SETS OF FIVE-MINUTE GALLOPS ON CALVIN TO TAKE THE place of his Millbrook run. I flat Patrick. Deal with some farm issues.

Chance: *Please forgive me. I have been going through a really hard time. It can be very lonely not to have a support system and spouse.*

Maybe Chance is taking out on us what she would otherwise have done with Silas, or because of Silas. She is flying apart like the Challenger, the way she did when she was in high school. But that was high school, when you're supposed to fly apart.

I hop on Shiva for a quick hack. The horse spooks at jostling rows of cornstalks. He flings himself sideways. I hold on, but my saddle slips to starboard. I land on my feet, gripping the reins. I hoist the saddle off and back on, cinch the girth tighter, and mount from the ground, Shiva twirling circles around me. If I had a gun, I'd shoot him. "White or dark meat," I'd say to Barrett, handing him a rib.

When I get back to the barn, Barrett's off running errands. Even Marta and Roberto are gone, which leaves me alone on the farm, for once in the bluest of moons. I close my eyes and listen to the silence, feel the absence of humans and cars, smell the smell of nothing but horses, gaze across acres of rising pasture. Forgive me, Chance.

I MAKE AN IMPOSSIBLY LONG TO-DO LIST FOR THE DAY, TO DISTRACT myself from troubles with Chance. It has sixteen items on it. Surely I won't have time to think about my sadness.

Chance is overreacting to things that don't make sense.

How terrifying must it be, not to have a built-in editor of your emotions, so that whatever crosses your mind comes out. We all have chilling thoughts, but we learn to keep them to ourselves, to not let hysteria rule us, to dress frankness with kindness and consideration. Chance must be miserable with her inability to do this. I'm the opposite: I keep secrets, which is its own agony—won't say what's on my mind, while silently judging the person I'm chatting with. I am my own specter, my own dark father. I might betray you.

It is Calvin's day off, which is never fun for him. Barrett says, "A horse needs to learn three things: when he's out, he's grazing, when he's wearing leather, he's working, and when he's in a stall, he's resting." It sounds simple, but it takes some horses years to figure out.

Calvin looks at me longingly over his stall guard. But he needs a chill day after his gallop yesterday. He needs to snooze in the back of his stall, without pressure to perform. To allow himself to shut down. Which is, I realize, what I've been doing these past couple days, in my decision to distance myself from Chance. I need space and time to gaze over my stall guard at life going by without her.

A PILE OF STEEL AND COPPER AND BRASS AND CHROME—NEW BITS to try on Calvin. I can't ride him without thousands of men and women—bless them—who pull shifts deep in the mines digging out ore. I choose the Professional's Choice bit similar to the one I've been using but with a significant port in the mouthpiece. I walk Calvin around the farm, then switch to another long-shanked western bit that has ornate filigree on the shanks, making us look more like we're about to rope cattle than jump cross-country fences. I study the six bits carefully, deciding the pros and cons of each before I put them in his mouth. I've got to be careful, as I've been working hard to heal his mouth sores, and I don't want to do further damage. My experimenting will have to be slight; I'll only be able to test the bits at the walk and trot and guess the world from there.

A TEXT COMES IN AT 6:00 A.M., FROM SOMEWHERE IN A COUNTRY shaped like a boot.

Jack: *Am in dolomite wilderness, with limited service till tomorrow. Chance very hateful to me last night and cut off our communication.*

Barrett scurries around the house with a green canvas duffel slung over one shoulder, stuffing miscellaneous food items inside. He's on his way to his mother's beach house to help her sort through his grandmother's things, and to prune and weed the backyard.

I lean out my office window, taking a photo of the dead weeping cherry we painted yellow. I'm avoiding the subject of our daughter, which I've done all weekend.

"Pretty bad when you have to take food to your mother's," Barrett jokes, stuffing in his pills, his peanut butter, Triscuits, bottles of dark ale for his amber digestion.

"I'd have a field day," I say. Protein bars and shakes, pretzels. Licorice, my latest passion. Four sticks every night for my own shade of amber.

"Better than those hard candies that took your teeth out," Barrett says.

I have to get a molar removed tomorrow. It'll be the first time off the farm since I took Chance to the train station last weekend. I stuff my life with so much work that keeps me bound to these eighty-three acres.

"Bye, I'll see you tomorrow," he says to my back. There are three yards of mulch in the truck bed. I'm already at my desk, typing away. Won't budge for nothin'.

"Bye hon, love you," I say to my computer screen.

This is my dolomite wilderness, I write to Jack. I send him the photo of the yellow tree.

CAL'S RIGHT DRIFT SHOWS UP AGAIN, UNINVITED. THE GHOST PUTS a rail on the right side of the fence to get his attention. And it does. My horse's body becomes as straight as the pole he's trying to avoid.

A horse trial in a different time zone sounds like a good idea, after missing Millbrook. The Ghost agrees to ship the horse for me to Kalamazoo. He also recommends that I enter him in their CIC Four-Star division, as show jumping will be before cross-country in that format. Unlike Barrett, he believes this sets Calvin up for a cleaner show jump round. The plan is for Barrett and me to fly, as Barrett wouldn't be able to make the long drive.

Tonight, sleeplessness gets the better of my travel plans. I worry that the trip will make Barrett bleed, I worry about the expense, and I question my own will. My worsening neck pain doesn't help my resolve. It would be so much easier to give up the dream now. I have plenty of excuses. How does a rider who runs out at the corners of her own life prevent her horse from doing same? For some of the top athletes, returning to Fair Hill International is as easy as buying the next horse. For others, it is like trying unsuccessfully to get pregnant and give birth to another child after having had a perfectly normal first pregnancy. Some women can't get pregnant again. And some riders can't get back to Fair Hill. Some things are just not repeatable.

THE FRACTURED TOOTH IS IN THE WAY BACK. THERE'S NOT MUCH left of it, and it doesn't hurt. My dentist warns me that one day it will. The tooth fragment must come out.

This isn't my first rodeo when it comes to tooth pulling. My parents both had bad teeth, which did not bode well for mine.

Dr. Emmett is an amateur bodybuilder. Maybe a handful of years younger than me, he's in top shape. Which is not a bad thing for the guy who yanks teeth for a living. It's not exactly like he has to put one foot on the chair for leverage, but there is some brawn involved, particularly with a stubborn molar that has been nearly razed at the gum line. He knows me as an equestrian who still jumps big fences, so he thinks I'm tough and doesn't offer me a sedative, nor could I take it if he did, as I've come without a groom to this show. I sit back, take a deep breath, and start fluttering my foot for distraction. The beautiful swan assisting him dons her mask.

"How did your arms get like that?" she asks me as the dentist draws up the Novocain.

"I wring turkey necks," I say.

Sting. Slow burn. Then another—smack into the palate.

"She's an equestrian," the tooth puller grunts. He's into it now. I hear a loud crack from somewhere deep inside my mouth and then a satisfied "Awww, good" from Dr. Emmett. Now that he's broken it up, he can pull it out in segments, like a foaling dystocia. Here goes. "You're going to feel some pressure now." I close my eyes, thinking of long slow waves. Very blue. I conjure my self-sedation, Rasta woman that I am.

A few more twists and pulls—a hoof, an ear, a shoulder—out it comes. Then another needle and long thread, the cat's cradle of flesh being sewn, the satisfied look on Dr. Emmett's intentionally scruffy face, which I am just now noticing. Not bad looking, actually, despite the exaggerated muscles in his arms. No criticism there. In the same way I want my gynecologist to have small hands, I want my tooth yanker to be Hercules.

"Girl or boy?" I quip through a mouthful of cotton and blood and spit.

He hands me scripts for an antibiotic and Percocet, which he says I probably won't need, and sends me on my way. I brag to Barrett how easy it was, how I can't believe my doc would hand out Percocet for such a tiny ache.

I wake in the middle of the night, the Novocain worn off, my mouth throbbing. My neck seconds the motion, and the bill passes. Pain is as political as it gets for me.

"I don't know why you're such a freak about eating opium," Barrett says, from his own version of sleeplessness. "He gave it to you for a reason."

I roll over seeking my own milk of Paradise. But there isn't any. I'm too sore to even get out of bed to take one of those evil pills. Barrett is still too shell-shocked from driving around Delaware with his grandmother's ashes in the back seat to get me one.

"I kept wanting to put the seat belt over her box," he says.

I'VE BEEN AVOIDING OUR CELLAR. I DON'T GO DOWN THERE UNLESS I have to. Three-quarters of it is carved into gabbro bedrock. I have to duck to pass through, cobwebs clinging to my Ariat shirt and britches and helmet hair. I spy two boxes in the far back corner next to the fuse box: one I think contains bits. The other is unfamiliar, possibly leftover from the last century—maybe a wooden crate of old baby clothes, coated with inches of dust. I'm more interested in getting out of there than finding out.

The rain picks up outside. I hoist the bit box and climb the crumbling stone stairs and slam the hurricane door shut.

I want to try the long-shanked Mikmar I think might be in the box before the weekend's event. I can tell how light Calvin is at the walk and trot, and how much pressure I have in my hands. If I feel much of anything at those slower gaits, the bit won't hold him at a gallop. I narrow the box of six down to two.

I take Shiva out to the cross-country field to fire his engines before his Prelim event this Sunday. He jumps all the big stuff, and then we head down to Indian Run, where I aim him at the Prelim rolltop into water. We both hold our noses, and he launches and frogs the landing. He bounces back to the barn, his whole body chuckling. Shiva leans into the crossties in the wash rack toward Barrett. He can't wait to tell him the news.

The long day and night close their legs on me. I return to my St. Augustine ways. The Richland office wants my entry fee. I pull out my credit card and perch it next to the keyboard. I'm tired of ending up at the bottom of the division, tired of the effort and expense of running Advanced tracks, not to be competitive, but just to say I did it. I need some measure of my daily grind. Not all goals are about strategy, and not all knowledge is for the sake of power. What would happen to this record if I gave up now? My daughter and I … we are both as stubborn as the leg on a dead mule.

At Fair Hill Horse Trials, Calvin is civil in dressage, but show jumping is in the field next to cross-country, an impossible setup for him. He pulls five rails in his excitement to get to the cross-country course.

"I'm so sick of it," I say to Barrett, who is trying to get me and my equipment turned around for our cross-country run.

"I'm not sure this horse can show jump before cross-country," Barrett says. There's a quaver in his voice that I've noticed recently.

I continue to adjust the western bridle for Calvin's cross-country run. Riders trot by us on their way to warm-up, all of them having show jumped in their cross-country bridles, as if sharing a secret about which I am forever green.

Calvin runs around the Intermediate cross-country track. The bit works.

We get him back to the trailer, cooled out, iced, and wrapped. Almost immediately, I have to return to cross-country to walk the Prelim course. It's big and daunting.

Shiva is good in dressage, Patrick so-so. Shiva, however, unravels in show jumping with four rails. He wants to either fall behind my leg or scoot away from it.

He's good out of the box and jumps the first few fences well. But when we come to the rolltop before a downhill bank with a blind landing, he stops, and I opt to retire.

I have to turn right around and go out on Patrick. He jumps show jumping well, despite two rails, and then eats up the cross-country course. I'm happy with Patrick, disappointed in Shiva, and exhausted overall. As Barrett predicted, the weekend has been too much for us. Three horses at a single event is no longer possible.

Barrett retreats to the house to rest while I unload the tack and start cleaning and organizing. I give Calvin a bath, pack Patrick's feet, grain them.

When I get back to the house, Barrett is standing in front of a dark TV. He can't find the remote and doesn't know how to turn it on.

"They made a TV show about John and Mollie's house."

"What?"

"Yeah, some political-spy drama. They needed a house for the set design."

John: *I stepped out of my bedroom this afternoon. Ali Garter was pointing a handgun in my face. And scowling.*

"It's called *Legends*," Barrett explains.

Chance: *Do you have time to talk?*

Mom: *Yeah. Do you know who Ali Garter is?*

Our conversation goes nowhere fast. She has the same old gripes, weaving a fabric of my wrongs. I'm always mad, she's never good enough, I make her feel worthless—so far off the mark that there must be something else at the bottom of her complaints. When we get to the subject of her brother, I hear coins jingling underneath her anger.

I tell her I can't talk anymore. I tell her that I love her, but I just can't talk.

A COMEDIAN KILLS HIMSELF AND IT RAINS ALL NIGHT. IT'S A SAD DAY for us triers, for depressives and mothers of depressives, for drinkers. The wisteria trees are winding closer to my office window. How many years before they touch the glass, obscure my view completely? My family of cardinals flits from tendril to tendril, reminding me to check the feeder.

I take Calvin on a long, easy hack. His legs are cool and tight after his run. We luxuriate in Baden's stream, walking west to the deepest section that will come up above his hocks, where Simon once broke through the ice on a frigid January day. I had to dismount in order to haul him from sure death, drenching myself in the process, then re-mount and gallop home, the dog re-instilling circulation through blessed movement. I had to immerse myself in tepid bath water and gradually warm it up once home.

Barrett calls from the Baltimore Historical Society.

"I found a map," he says.

"A map?" I say, more interested in the quiet that surrounds me than any geography lesson from my husband.

"General Meade made a map of friendly homes that might quarter Union soldiers. It was for his march to Gettysburg. In Maryland, if you lived by water that flowed to Washington you tended to sympathize with the rebels. If your water flowed into Baltimore, you tended to support the Federal troops. Still, there was a lot of kin interspersed on the differing watersheds. Meade had to check each family, to know how they sided."

"What are you saying?"

"Charlotte's house appears on the map."

I call Richland Park and pay my entry. I schedule an MRI for my persistent aching neck, buy plane tickets, arrange a rental car, meet with the Goth, pay a few bills. I don't hear from Chance.

The ocean at night is a wolf. I dream of drowning. I am with my baby girl. She is on a child-sized raft, asleep, in a frilly dress. I am in the water, trying to guide the raft to some distant shore. And then I go under, crawling into the wolf.

Glads

For Robin Williams

I planted them from scratch—
too much to ask
of the dormant brown bulbs
and my black thumb.

They shot up as reedy stalks,
and stayed that way.
No flower, no color.
Nothing to say I tried.

But one morning at my window—
a tower of orange ruffles,
already toppling from their burden—
so much beauty on such thin stems.

Every day, a different hue
to cut and fill the ample vase,
and pluck the spent ones.
Greedily, I brought them in.

I wanted to lie down in the dirt,
and forget about ambition,
my mother's everlasting push

for perfection—

till the last ivory petal,
translucent as a mouse's ear,
pricked and listened
for my footsteps.

I PRESS TO GET MY RIDES DONE BEFORE MY RESONANCE. I DUTIFULLY arrive fifteen minutes early to fill out the five-page questionnaire, then hunker with my iPad to order Barrett some underwear. I choose bright blue, adorned with a rooster and a bull, and red ones with lucky horseshoes stamped every which way, attempting to have some fun with the TB lodged in his gut. If you're going to bleed, it's better to bleed on some light comedy.

I wait an hour and a half before I'm called. I strip and change into my napkin while they warm up the oven.

"You've had one of these before, right?" the technician asks in a smoky Indian accent.

I lie down on the freezing table, and he stuffs a couple of cotton wads next to both ears. His female counterpart offers me a thin blanket, before they send me on my way. I'm lucky if it's 45 degrees in this morgue.

The intense clicking and thumping and grinding go right through me. When they pull me out, I'm disoriented, with a pounding headache. It takes me a moment to get my sense of balance when I stand, unassisted by the man who subjected me to the tunnel.

They keep me waiting another twenty minutes while they prepare a CD of my spine, and when a new technician finally appears in the waiting room, he is bearing a clipboard with the same questionnaire I filled out at the beginning of this ordeal. Only it's blank.

"I'm sorry, but we lost your forms—the receptionist must not have clicked *Save* after she scanned them." He's impossibly cute, with a mop of curly dark hair falling every which way. And all of about thirty.

"You've got to be kidding," I say, wondering what might have happened if I had metal plates somewhere in my body, or was allergic to the material the damn machine is made of, or was a raging claustrophobic.

"Isn't someone supposed to review the forms before they send me through that contraption?" I ask.

"I'm sorry," he repeats.

This one's just come on duty. I can't get too mad at him. He has had little to do with my experience here besides bring me blank forms to fill out. And giving me something to look at. I hightail it out of there, wobbling in the intense sunlight that greets me, my head raging with echoes.

Once home, I change into my little cotton jersey skirt and polo shirt, part of a new clothing line I've fantasized: loungewear that doubles as dresswear. This number is top on my list of comfort clothes. I slip it on, have my usual wine, eat to my full, and fall asleep in it.

The next morning, I wake at 6:00. Barrett's already been at his computer since 4:00. I waltz into his office.

"All ready for the next day," I say, waving my arms in a downward motion and spreading them across my shirt. Ta-da! "Nary a wrinkle. I could make millions!" He looks up from his screen and smiles at me.

"You should call the line *Decent Exposure.*"

Good morning, lovely husband.

CALVIN YAWNS THROUGH HIS GYMNASTIC LINES, AND I'M THRILLED with his easy effort. Barrett is on the ground setting fences.

"Looks good to me," he says.

Not true for Patrick. He gets mad as a hornet when I ask him to negotiate the same gymnastic lines as Calvin, figure-eighting over the narrow panel set on the short side, which forces the horses to get deep to the jump, as do the two panels set at twenty feet apart with the raised guide rails. After a few semi-tries, in which Patrick flings his body over the obstacles rather than jump them, we come to the figure-eight exercise again, and he runs out. I hit him, we come again, and he runs out again. There's a crowd in the shed row, which always happens when I'm having trouble with a horse and need to discipline. Whack-whack, which only makes Patrick incensed that I would hit him. Barrett lowers the fences, and I do my best to end the school on a good note. But I'm already disappointed and a little perplexed by the horse. I wonder if his feet aren't bothering

him again. I ask Barrett to jog him for me after we're done, and the horse
jogs solid and square.

I flat Shiva and spend the rest of the day getting ready for the jumper
show we're hosting this evening. I run around like a mad woman until
the trailers start pulling in, and then it's hours of making sure everything
runs smoothly. My official job is timer. April is judge. After four hours
of timing every round, my head is ready to explode. Woofie plies us with
glasses of white wine. I don't dare drink and deal with time. April guzzles
my wine when she's done with hers, gets a little loud in her tipsiness—and
starts to make mistakes. She misses a couple of rails, calls out a few incor-
rect placings. I'm able for the most part to catch the errors. And, what the
hell, it's just a schooling show, right?

CALVIN ON A GALLOP. THREE SETS OF SIX MINUTES. CALVIN LOVES
this part, particularly in the hackamore, when it's easier for him to piss off
with me. He goes for the avalanche effect downhill, to outrun gravity. The
uphills make it easier for me, as he slows. He listens to me when he has to
work harder. What goes down must come up. Happy and blowing as we
wend our way back to the farm. The walking, the long bath, the grazing,
and the wrapping. He loves all of it.

The silence from Chance continues.

Barrett has won a third literary prize in two weeks: this time, publi-
cation for a chapbook of new poems by a hot indie press. I had no idea
he had thirty pages' worth of old loves. He wants to talk, which is the last
thing I want to do. I'm pooped and sore from my long day of perpetual
motion, salivating for my nightly jolt.

"So you better check and make sure that Middleburg isn't the same
weekend as Brian's wedding," he says when we're both floating around in
the bathtub. Sheer heaven after my day.

"I don't want to talk about it right now. Not on the second floor." Our
household rule—never talk business on the second floor.

"We've got to talk about it sometime," he says. "You go full bore all
day every day, never time to talk, and then it's cocktail hour and you don't
want to talk," he complains.

Shades of Chance's complaint. Yelling at me through the passenger side window before she harrumphs off to the train station, fury in her satin duffel.

My Calvin. Seven hundred dollars an ounce on Baltimore Street.

WHEN CONFRONTED WITH A WHOLE COURSE, TAKING OFF THE MARtingale doesn't seem to make a difference to Calvin. Clunk, clunk, clunk. Each time he skims a rail, I halt and back him up. When that doesn't work, I start growling at him. I rein-back, and he gets emotional, starts dancing in place. He knows what I want and that I'm unhappy with him—he just doesn't give a damn. He is jumping well, but he is not jumping high enough. If we were at an Advanced competition, today would be a five-rail day. Barrett strips off his front boots and puts a couple of guide rails up, and Calvin starts to jump more cleanly. We finish well enough.

What could I put on Calvin's front legs to make him pick them up a bit higher? His form is fine—it is good, actually—he just needs to be tighter with his knees. Or is it his shoulders? I'm desperate to find a canned solution to Calvin's sloppy jump. I conjure training paints and blisters, even Bigeloil and whatnot, but they are all illegal substances. I catalog natural agents like rubbing alcohol, Sore No More, witch hazel, pepper sauce, menthol, wintergreen, Bengay, Biofreeze, ginger. Ginger salve is what Saddlebred trainers use under their horses' tails to make them pick them up before they enter the ring. What if I were to combine tincture of ginger with water, and spray it on Calvin's legs? I don't admit Jimmy's much simpler conclusion: front-rail knockdowns are from riders interfering too close to the jumps.

AT LEAST A DOZEN TIMES TODAY, I STOP MYSELF BEFORE REACHING for my phone to text Chance. I remind myself to return to the possibility tomorrow; I can't bear a potential fight once the sun goes down. Instead, I rub ginger salve on my elbows to soften them for my eight-ounce curls.

"Patrick's stock just went up," my ever-hopeful husband says, studying a recent issue of *Thoroughbred Times* over his cabernet.

"What do you mean?" I ask, a little desperate for any good news.

"His cousin, American Pharoah, just won the Del Mar Futurity Stakes."

"Does that horse have a shot at the Derby?" I ask.

"Not a chance," Barrett says.

I RUN AROUND PACKING CALVIN'S TRAPS FOR HIS TRIP TO RICHLAND. It's doubly hard this time—I have to fit everything in trunks and bags, as my rig won't be making the journey. I include a whole bag for bits alone. Not to forget his magnetic blanket and Equissage, towels and wraps, sheets and blankets for the more northern clime, show clothes, boots for us both, passport, and health certificate.

Somewhere in the course of my manic day, it occurs to me I haven't been to Michigan before. We're heading to Kalamazoo. It's kind of fun to have a city with four syllables as your destination.

I clip Cal from knees to coronet bands, hoping to make his legs more sensitive to rails, like the jumpers do. He looks as though he has knee socks on, but I'm hoping the new clipping will blend in by the time he canters down centerline on Thursday.

I return to my office to call the Imaging Office to get the results of my MRI. They have no record of my getting one. I email Chance. I tell her that I love her, no matter what, and that I wish things weren't so weird between us. I also tell her that I'm on my way to Michigan. I always want Chance to know where I am.

John was not the one Chance was in competition with. The horses were. I was always anxious to get to the horses, either riding or taking care of them, or going to an event. It was a juggling act when John and Chance were younger and still living at home. There were the kids, and there were the horses. I tried to split my time fairly, but somehow the weight of it was always spent with the horses. While Chance concluded that I doted on her brother because I loved him more. Oh Chance, you were so wrong. You should be jealous of Calvin, not John. Of Redmond and Huey and Surf. Jerry and Little Sister, Beans, even Picante. Little Red and Piper and Gideon. The names fall off the page.

BEFORE THEY HIT THE ROAD, CALVIN JUMPS WELL IN THE GHOST'S ring with the usual gymnastic exercise, and Patrick puts on his Superman cape and jumps better than ever. He feels jet propelled, with hard, thumping landings.

My trainer looks at me quizzically. "You're kind of holding your arms funny," he says, "like a chicken or something."

"I had an idea of putting tincture of ginger on Calvin's legs to make him pick up his fronts higher. I rubbed some on my elbows to try it out." What I don't tell her is that I also rubbed some on Calvin's cannon bones to see if it made a difference. The Ghost is a freak about drug rules, and since Richland will be an FEI competition, the most stringent rules will be in effect. Meanwhile, nothing happens on my own arms besides conveying a pleasing aroma.

"It's corn oil on the legs with boots over it that does it," he says.

"Corn oil?"

"Yeah, the oil heats up under the boots and burns their legs. But if they find you doing that, they will set you down for a long, long time," he explains. "That's why they run their hands down the legs when they weigh the boots, to see if there's anything on them."

But starvation doesn't test. The latest craze: don't feed your competition horse several days before an event to calm him down and make him more obedient. We are all a bunch of hypocrites. Do everything you can to enhance your horse's performance, as long as it doesn't test and you can get away with it: joint injections, Legend and Adequan shots, shock-wave therapy, laser and magnetic therapies, icing to mask pain, all kinds of natural calming medications, and, more recently, not feeding your horse for five days leading up to a big event. And all for a better dressage score.

I load Calvin's show stuff onto the Ghost's rig, get him settled in his temporary stall, and head home with Patrick from Sleepy Hollow. My neck is killing me, and my mouth is salivating. No starving in store for this one.

ON THE WAY TO THE AIRPORT IN THE MORNING, I DOUBLE-CHECK the tickets. It's 9:30, and our flight leaves at 10:55. Wait a minute. I blink, blink again. The ticket says 9:55, not 10:55. I can't believe it.

At the Delta ticket counter, the attendant looks like she's got a marble in her mouth. She studies the screen, won't look me in the eye. My watch says 9:40.

"You've missed the 9:55," she says sternly.

"Even if we run?" I press.

"They're punctual about closing the doors, and you couldn't possibly get through security in time," she says, still not looking me in the eye.

We wait for the 1:00 Delta flight to Detroit. Barrett buys a small stack of Charm City postcards and writes Allie and Blue, John and Mollie, Chance, even Edwin Forrest, about how great it is to be traveling nowhere, calling attention to Fort McHenry, "O! Say Can You See," the Battle of Baltimore, and the new topless restaurant on the Block.

Once we're an hour late in Baltimore, we're an hour late all day, and have that stressed sense of hurry. We miss our connecting flight to Kalamazoo. There's only stand-by available on a later departure. We rent a car and drive another two hours to Richland Park.

We arrive at 6:00 in the evening. The Ghost has almost finished at the barn. He has done the in-barn check for Calvin and gotten him settled in his stall. He has even walked him around the dressage ring to familiarize him with it.

The Ghost offers to warm me up for our dressage test.

"Where's your copy of the test?" he asks, bleary-eyed from the long overland drive from Sleepy Hollow.

"Top of my trunk," I say.

The Ghost opens the trunk, rummages around, pulls out the Tupperware container of Limoncello.

"For Calvin's legs?" he asks, tilting the droopy side of his face in my direction.

Maybe Chance's pee will do the trick.

I FIGHT THE SOFT MATTRESS AT THE BEST WESTERN IN KALAMAZOO with Barrett squeezed next to me. A two-foot stick is lodged in my foot. I slowly pull it out, inch by excruciating inch. There's a shoot of green leaves at the end of it, like the root of a boil. I pull and pull, and it painfully comes out, leaves and all. It is Calvin, I realize, even as I'm dreaming the dream, that I'm slowly pulling out of my foot, as if the horse is ingrained in my body. To ride him I must give birth to him.

I wake up sweating from my nightmare, needing to tell my snoring husband about the horror of an 18-hand boil I'm extracting from my foot.

It's 4:00 a.m., an hour away from rising. But we're now an hour early, trying to make up for the day before. Not quite time to get up and drive the half hour to Richland Park. Not yet time to feed, muck, walk, ride, bathe, and braid Calvin, get him tacked and ready for dressage.

The Ghost keeps Calvin and me focused and busy, right up to the time we canter down centerline. Calvin stays with me for the entire test. No blow ups, no bouncing at the walk, no running away from me at the canter, round and obedient for most of the test, and I'm happy, really happy, on finishing. I thank both FEI judges. I'm smiling as I exit the ring, I'm patting my horse, and dismounting and hugging him.

My small audience is smiling politely. No one is sure who should comment on the emperor's new britches. It was an ok test, and I am ecstatic.

"I don't even care what the score is, I'm really happy with that," I say to Barrett and the Ghost. The Oxford-educated voice of God emanates from the burning bush to announce my score: 73.5. Barely qualifying.

Calvin was a good boy, I try to convince myself. I look up at the sky. "He didn't kill anybody," I say.

I WALK THE CROSS-COUNTRY COURSE WITH THE GHOST IN THE morning, deciding to go all the long routes and take the "easier" options. That should be my first clue that things aren't right, and that maybe Calvin and I aren't ready for this Michigan track.

I walk the Four-Star show jumping course. It's big and technical, set on unlevel, oxen-ploughed turf—the worst possible scenario for Calvin. The irregularity of the footing, combined with my electric seat and a horse who doesn't care if he touches rails, spells failure.

Five-Star rider Jon Holling returns to show jumping from stabling. "You're in exactly the same place as you were a half hour ago," he says.

"Yeah, well," I offer, extending my gaze to the difficult last line: a maximum-height oxer, seven bending strides to two tall, airy verticals, four strides to a last four-foot oxer and the finish line. All downhill.

The Ghost shows up.

We walk it twice. "Hold out on the turn from fence 1 to 2," he advises. "Slice fence 2, keep the engine around the turns, and don't let him stall, particularly coming into that last line. Watch the long one-stride in the triple combination."

We head back to stabling to get ready, my head spinning.

"You're going to need more canter than you'd like," the Ghost says. "That slow canter would be fine if it were in a ring, but on terrain with those big jumps, it won't be enough."

I return to the arena to watch a few riders go. The first competitor is Jon Holling on Proper Timing. Two rails come down. The Ghost puts in a beautiful clean round on his gelding. The Black Dahlia appears at my side as the Ghost is jumping. "Keep coming around the turns," she reminds me, and then, "You ok?"

"I'm fine," I lie, trusting that the blood clots forming in my legs won't break off and travel to my lungs.

Barrett and I return to stabling to get Calvin tacked up. Down to warm-up we go. Calvin seems relaxed, and I get him started with a little bit of lateral work. I wait till there are only four riders in front of me in the order of go. The Ghost arrives in warm-up on another horse just as I'm jumping my second oxer. I ask Barrett to make it bigger. I jump it twice. The Ghost barks at me. "It's not going to get much better than that. I wouldn't jump anymore."

"But I haven't jumped at height yet," I bark back.

"How many jumps have you jumped?" he asks me, suspiciously.

"Two," I say, and continue warming up.

Calvin seems a mite slow to react to my leg, but he is relaxed and jumping well. I try to find the correct canter, and then I ask the Ghost if it's enough. He nods his head yes, and I enter the ring. I approach the first fence in good rhythm and balance, and he clunks it. I'm in trouble. He clunks fence 2, leaves up 3, and from then on I lose count. I press with my outside leg around the turn to the triple and even remember to counter-bend him, and to hold out on the turn. Still, he jumps in a little flat, lands dead, and doesn't make the effort to jump out of the one-stride, tries to put in two, and stops. For a moment, I think it may have been my fault: I didn't put enough leg on, knowing that the distance was long. But then again, it's awfully hard to put your leg on a horse who's pulling rails. In fact, I'd started to hold his front end off the jumps in an effort to encourage him not to hit them, and this strategy caught up to me at the triple.

They blow the whistle, reconstruct the jump, and I re-approach the triple and jump through it, and the Liverpool, which is the only jump he makes an effort to actually clear, and then the last difficult line to the finish.

"That's thirty-two jump and sixty time faults," God says.

I exit the ring. Barrett is waiting for me. I draw a knife across my neck.

"He's done," I say decisively.

"You went about twice as fast as you needed to go," Barrett says.

"What are you talking about? I had the exact same canter in the ring as I had in warm-up, and it served me just fine there. The Ghost said that on this terrain, that's the canter I needed to have. He just doesn't want to do it anymore."

I want Chance.

I hold it together till we're back in stabling and we've stripped his tack. I head to the Ghost's trailer. I need to be alone to assess the last ten years riding Calvin, chasing a dream that disintegrated a half hour ago, pushing a horse with all the talent in the world, but neither the head nor heart to go the distance.

The Ghost joins me in the trailer.

"We need to find you a new horse," he says. "It's time." I'm surprised by the comment, and yet I'm not surprised. My vision is blurry, and he keeps wavering in and out of focus, as if in a dream.

I don't disagree with him. I never do. Which is part of the problem in our relationship: I am the good girl, determined to please my father, never contradict, but only agree with the past and do what it says I should do. I never learned how to be my own Ghost.

I go through the motions of organizing and cleaning, wrapping Cal and taking him for a graze, then feeding him. Barrett and I return to the hotel room.

I try to change our plane tickets, but that would cost the moon. We'll have to hunker down in Kalamazoo for two more days until our scheduled flight leaves.

We stumble on a wine bar in downtown Kalamazoo, sit on one of their couches, and order a slate cheese board and Migration Chardonnay for me, plank salmon plus a dark craft beer for Barrett. Barrett changes the subject to our plans for Patrick and Shiva, and how Calvin's retirement gives the room to focus on the younger horses. I confess to Barrett that the Ghost had recommended I buy a new horse. He winces, as I knew he would.

"Where's the story in that?" he asks. "There's a story in Shiva and Patrick, there's no story in going out and buying a made horse. And you really aren't rich enough," he adds.

I doubt either Patrick or Shiva is an upper level horse—Patrick doesn't have the feet for it, and Shiva probably has a version of Calvin's mental problem. What difference does a dream make? What good is it to push in a sport, when your daughter isn't talking to you?

We return to our room and collapse into bed. I'm woozy from a combination of Benadryl and Chardonnay. I dream fitfully, then wake with a jolt, my thoughts already formed.

"I wonder how Houston would have turned out," I say to Barrett, just as I'm surfacing from a drowning sleep. The horse who came with Calvin. The one who died.

Barrett hears me from the edge of nowhere. "He would have been a good one," he says.

CROSS-COUNTRY DAY AT RICHLAND PARK WITH A SCRATCHED HORSE means sunglasses and a ball cap. I use my spare time in the morning to ride Calvin on the flat, practicing the flying changes that we won't need again, and medium and extended trots, which have always been mediocre and still are. I am terse with Calvin this morning, and I'm sure he feels my disappointment. I'm at the close of a bad marriage, having finally decided to end it after years of promises and regrets and apologies that went nowhere. Calvin, the unfaithful husband who is mortally contrite after the next affair, and the one after that. I take him back in and he tries hard to be good for a few months, only to stray at the corner or narrow brush oxer when temptation winks.

Neither money nor love was enough to get this job done without the right horse. A ten-year endless cycle of falling away and coming back that has been broken finally at Richland Park. I take off Calvin's tack and put him away.

The decade wasn't worth it. The wrong horse died.

The rest of this sad day Barrett and I spend helping our fellow eventers in the vet box cool out their heaving, dripping partners. Barrett is happy to help Kate Chadderton. Her truck broke down and she caught a ride to Richland with a friend. She's alone in the vet box with her hot horse after successfully completing the Three-Star course. Barrett stands next to her holding a bucket of water. The Ghost runs around cross-country like the old campaigner that he is. I grab his horse's shank while Barrett quickly throws ice water on the horse. The Ghost's horse is almost as big as Calvin, and it takes him some time to cool out enough for the vets to allow him to go back to stabling.

The loudspeaker at the start box goes on the blink, and so I wait in audible darkness while Barrett takes the horse back to the barn and the Ghost returns on his next mount. I wait and I watch, though I can't hear much, except the chatter of excited riders and grooms as their horses come off cross-country after what turns out to be mainly successful goes. First Buck Davidson, then Down Under and Boyd Martin, Jon Holling, Sharon White, the Black Dahlia, Daniel, Stephen, and Ian Roberts and his son Waylon gallop home smiling—even Kittie Wilkins comes back with a huge grin on her face. Everyone is thrilled and tired and satisfied. Well, not everyone.

We feed Calvin, pack up, and head back to the hotel, leaving the Ghost the care of his horses, as well as Calvin, who will make the return trip with him tomorrow, while we catch a flight back to Baltimore.

"I'll tell you one thing," Barrett says.

I know what he's about to say before he says it, and pull the words right out of his mouth: "He's kicked out of the family tomb."

"I want him gone," I say. "I sure hope your idea of trading him for hay works." Last night, long into his second ale, Barrett proposed that we attempt to get a year's worth of hay by trading Calvin for it. Bruce Fenwick is a big guy. He needs a big horse.

I sulk on the bed, worn out and exhausted from the current disaster.

I wish I could agree with Barrett that it comes down to management, but I can't. Even with all the talent in the world, Calvin never had the mind to make an upper level horse, and whatever mind he had was blown at Bromont. He never was the same horse after that Four-Star. It has taken me this long to admit it. I tried to force him into being another Redmond, which wasn't possible. Calvin is not that kind of horse. When you push horses beyond their scope and ability, they start to say no.

When you expect too much, they move to Brooklyn.

I write Chance asking to visit her in the next couple of weeks, having no idea if such a trip will fit into my eventing schedule. I don't even care if there's a conflict. I wait expectantly for a half hour or so, but my phone remains silent.

Barrett and I retreat to a Starbucks near our hotel to kill some time before our flight. A small girl—maybe eight or ten—is waiting outside the café doors, in a bright blue-spangled skirt cut just above her brown, sturdy knees, t-shirt and dark glasses, waiting for her father to emerge from the store, Macchiato and muffins in hand. I wonder where she has come from—surely no church service, more likely a dance class—it makes my heart ache to remember Chance at this age, always in some pink tutu or purple leotard, waiting *en pointe* for her next class or performance. The in-and-out sun sparkles off the girl's skirt as she twirls impatiently once or twice, her father still waiting for his name to be called at the counter.

Chance once waited like this for me, an impossibly long time ago, the same old sun but a different era.

I can't take anything back.

THE YELLOW TREE WAITS FOR US BACK HOME, ITS BRIGHT BRANCHES showing off their balletic flair. And Georgia is waiting for us, eager to show off her willingness to put more weight on her bad leg. The air is cool, tight and autumn-like; just seeing Charlotte's house, I can breathe again.

I sit down at my mother's piano. I call the musician in the family. We talk about practicing, about Bach.

"We should learn some music together," I say, the idea just occurring to me. "Let's pick a piece, then record and send it to each other."

I'm the planner. John's the dreamer. We're a good team.

"We should learn Bach's Prelude No. 1," I suggest.

Makes sense. Start at the beginning. Come to the X.

"The Bach of the Month Club," John says.

I find the prelude in the cupboard under my living room bookshelf. My old sheet music is turning yellow and fraying at the edges. I start plinking away, and it comes surprisingly easily for me, though my arthritic fingers ache after a half hour.

I'm restive all night, have another sleepy conversation with Barrett.

"I can't bear losing both Calvin and Chance at the same time," I say. "I need to step back. Even when my parents died, I kept on pushing. I don't want to do it anymore. I don't think I want to compete anymore."

"I know," he mumbles.

"Maybe if I give myself time, I'll get some perspective. I've never allowed myself that before."

"I know," he mumbles.

"I need to separate the issues: losing Calvin and Chance, and the prospect of losing the Ghost."

"I know."

And then more sleeplessness awaits me, lies down beside me, prodding me in the back with her swollen fingers to stay awake, keep at it, keep fretting, until the fretting leads to thinking clearly. But it doesn't. It just leads to more of itself.

THE DARKEST OF CLOUDS, THOUGH IT'S BRILLIANT SUNSHINE BATH-ing the farm today. The air crisp, the light penetrating and exaggerating everything it touches.

Barrett heads up to Sleepy Hollow to pick up Calvin. Blessed man. I can't do much of anything at the barn until he returns with my caravan of shit. I loaf around at the piano for a long while in the morning. I've almost got the Bach prelude down, so I leaf through what's lying on the hood—some sheet music of Natalie Merchant's. I pause between tries, stretch out my knobby fingers. They actually don't hurt that badly. *These are the days.*

I never was much good with modern music and its syncopated rhythms, so this song is a challenge. I rummage around in our bottom-most cupboards to find some early keyboard music.

I don't want to go to the barn. I don't want to talk to anyone, or see everything that needs to be done. I sit on the bench until my hands ache from their new exercise and my eyes do, too, from squinting at notes in the poor light of the Ancestors' Room.

CALVIN LOOKS OUT OVER THE FENCE IN THE FRONT FIELD WHEN HE sees me coming past on Shiva. No doubt he's confused he wasn't brought into the barn today. I turn away from his longing. Up the hill I go for my first lesson with the Ghost. As soon as I see him, I melt. Big sloppy ones, the kind even my sunglasses can't hide.

I tell him I want to make a change. I tell him I'm thinking of getting out of the sport altogether. Or taking a break, maybe I need to go away for a while.

"You have a lot of options," the Ghost says, "you just need to figure out a game plan. I've worked my way out of my depressions for years. So many mornings I wake up before my alarm and think I can't get out of bed. I put one foot in front of the other, then another, and before I know it, I'm on my tenth horse."

"This is it for me. There won't be any Fair Hill for me now," I say.

"Well, not this year," the Ghost says.

I look at him through my dark glasses. He is wavering in my shaded sunlight. We both know the unlikelihood of my getting there on another horse. I'd have to buy that horse, and even if I could, buying made horses has never worked out for me.

"I'm turning fifty-nine this week. Let's be realistic."

I walk back down the hill with Shiva. Cal is exactly where we left him, at the fence line, watching us. *Finally*, he seems to be saying, *finally, you accept who I am.*

I hear back from Chance later in the day. She is uncertain of her schedule for the next few weeks and has little free time to see me.

HAPPY BIRTHDAY TO ME. I CELEBRATE ANOTHER YEAR BY SETTING A jump course that looks a lot like what we had in Richland. April joins Calvin and me. I try to re-create the slow canter that earned us our few successful show jumping rounds this past year. So far, April and Barrett are the only ones who buy this strategy. I think Chance would agree, too. Show jumping was always her forte on her pony, Sunny Delight. A good show jumping round was a thing of beauty to her. "Make it pretty," she would say to me. Translation: smooth, clean, rhythmic, effortless. And for Calvin, add slow. Maybe it's a generational discovery, April and Chance sharing approximately same ages.

"Almost tranter," April says.

"That's right," I remind myself. That's a good way of thinking about it, of feeling the correct show jumping canter for Calvin. One of my dressage coaches once said about Cal's gaits: that his working trot was more like a regular horse's medium, and his collected trot like their working trots, due to his size. So why wouldn't that hold for his canter as well—that a normal horse's collected canter would be like Cal's trot? But it takes a lot of guts to go into a 4'3" maximum-width oxer at a snail's pace.

My birthday is made with this jump school, and all the rest is icing.

Up at 3:30, leave by 4:30, arrive at Loudoun Horse Trials by 6:30. We pull into the show grounds and park next to the Ghost's rig.

I think it's him zooming by me on his scooter, as I'm making my way to the start box in the semi-dark. I have a question about how to ride the first combination, but he is nowhere to be seen once I'm back at the rig.

Patrick is reasonable in dressage, only has one rail in a tough show jump course on hilly terrain, and sails around the Prelim cross-country course, lickety-split. He may be a pill ninety percent of the time, but he's a go-getter on course.

It's hotter than it's been all summer, and we're unprepared, without enough ice to keep horses and humans cooler—no generator, just one dinky fan in the rig aimed at Patrick. I'll sweat through three shirts before the morning is out. I'd rather be elsewhere, maybe at my piano, or on the couch with a thick novel about the Holocaust.

Stop. Stop now. While we are still in one piece. There's a time to be a ghost, and a time to come back to life.

Chapter Twelve

Blue Angels

You must say words, as long as there are any, until they find me, until they say me, strange pain, strange sin, you must go on, perhaps it's done already, perhaps they have said me already, perhaps they have carried me to the threshold of my story, before the door that opens on my story, that would surprise me, if it opens, it will be I, it will be the silence, where I am, I don't know, I'll never know, in the silence you don't know, you must go on, I can't go on, I'll go on.

—Samuel Beckett, *The Unnamable*

"Mom, I need to talk."

Chance confesses that Silas left her before her last visit home. Why does she always go for addicts? She answers her own question: because she feels worthless and unloved.

"Will anyone ever love me again?" she asks.

I say yes, you will love again, and be loved again and again, imagining the phantom children she will either have or not.

"Even my own father doesn't love me," she says.

"That's not true—he loves you," I say.

"He said he cared about his own life more than he cared about mine."

"That was just his therapist talking," I say.

I remember the young man who became Chance's father telling me over endless glasses of afternoon wine at a bar in Tempe, Arizona: his art would always be more important than any person. I would have to accept that if I wanted to stay with him. And I did, until our children became more important to me than his art. I would build this farm for them, even if they didn't want to go to school with straw in their hair. Even if my being an eventing freak scared them.

I want to tell Chance to get out of the city, start a new life, go back to school, learn a trade, or find another career option. But if I say that, it would seem as if I didn't believe in her. I tell her to forget about Silas. It's impossible to get back to Fair Hill with a drunk artist. No life can be built around that.

"I love you," she says.

FAIR HILL INTERNATIONAL WAS SOMETHING TO PUT MY SIGHTS ON fifteen years ago with Redmond. Did I really want to do it again, or did I just not know where else to focus? Or how to gracefully step down from the sport? Shouldn't it be more about the horse than the event? Time to figure out how to live without spinning circles. Time to open my eyes wider at the world.

Calvin waits at the gate for my footsteps, my outstretched hand offering him a treat. Or with his head over the stall guard, ears pricked, maybe pawing a little impatiently. *Hey, what are we getting wrong today? What are we not doing? Let's not go for a trail ride, not catch the sunrise, not pop a few logs in our way. Let's not see if Georgia wants to come with us.*

I SIT AT THE PIANO. AN HOUR FLIES BY. BARRETT COMES IN FROM the barn, interrupts my Bach.

"Animal, vegetable, or mineral?" he says, referring to his impending grocery run.

"Spirit," I say.

COOPER GOES OVER CALVIN AND NOTES PAIN IN THE HORSE'S LUMbar region as well as slightly swollen front ankles, which tend to carry fluid this time of year from the pounding on hard ground. When he palpates the right leg, Calvin flinches, jerking the leg away and knocking Cooper to the ground.

"Let's see him move," Cooper says, struggling to right himself. At similar ages, he's about as creaky as I am.

Calvin jogs sound, but bobs off lame upon flexion in both front legs.

"I want to ultrasound that right front before we go any further, just to make sure there's nothing going on with the suspensory," Cooper says.

Cooper spots tiny black spaces that shouldn't be there in the ultrasound picture. Small tears in the suspensory ligament that should look more like the gray, grainy, well-knit fibers that surround them.

"At least there's no hole," Cooper says.

"I think A-Cell is the way to go," he continues, "and then slow, con-trolled exercise, twice a day, walking under tack."

I gulp.

"If everything goes absolutely perfectly, you may have a spring season. But it would have to be pretty perfect."

Spring. Which means, in my past experience with similar injuries, that the horse would only get started with moderate training in the spring, making him ready to compete come summer. He'll be sixteen then. I'll be turning sixty.

I agonize over what I should do. Rehab is grueling work. I don't want to go through it again, at least not with Calvin. I realize what little heart I have left for any effort with this horse. Barrett agrees with me that turning him out is probably the way to go. He's felt for some time that the horse needed a break. Now the break has found us.

I MEET FLEUR AT A HOT YOGA STUDIO. IT'S MY FIRST ATTEMPT AT yoga in a sauna, and my first go-round with any yoga class in several years. I snap my yoga pants over my hips, and Daniel saunters in.

"Fancy meeting you here," I say. We both laugh.

The heat is intense. By the time the hour-and-a-half session is over, I will drink an entire liter of water. I attempt poses that I can't negotiate with my stiff joints, while the nearly naked diehards around me contort themselves in 110 degrees. I'm counting the minutes.

I pull myself up from the mat one more time, aborting the *shavasana*, and escape into blissful air conditioning. In the lobby, Fleur confesses that not only has she been doing yoga all her life, but that it took her several months before she could make it through an entire session of hot yoga without taking multiple breaks.

"My cardiologist railed at me about the idea, but I just took my pulse a lot and made sure I went out of the room for breathers. I can't believe you made it through on your first try," she says brightly.

It didn't occur to me there was another option.

That's me: sticking it out when I am dying on the inside and nearly passing out from heat. That's me: running a horse Advanced when all the cards in the deck are saying "Pull up!" That's me: lousy jockey, fantastic Marine.

"I can't imagine why Fleur is so stiff in the tack. She's unbelievably flexible in yoga," I say to Barrett, once home.

"She's scared," he says.

IN DOWN UNDER'S TIGHT RING, PATRICK'S TWO-RING WATERFORD IS too much bit. He handles himself fairly well, until Down jacks up the heights on a serpentine line of verticals. I lose momentum in the first turn and Patrick plows into the vertical, sending the whole fence tumbling. On our second attempt, he jumps it and we finish the lesson.

Waylon Roberts is warming up a horse in the ring as Shiva and I strut in.

"Is that a bitless bridle?" Waylon asks. Silence from Down Under.

Shiva negotiates the same exercises that Patrick fumbled. Down asks if we want to finish with some cross-country.

I excuse myself to put a bit in Shiva's mouth. My fingers grope and flutter around the leather straps, and in no time I'm back on, though it feels like I've kept the Maestro waiting a small eternity.

The fence troll is waiting on the backside of a chevron to pounce on Shiva. He ducks out right. Down tells me to hit the horse on his drift side. I whack him once and Shiva jumps the fence on the second pass.

"That'll do it," Down says flatly.

I walk over to my instructor, who has already mounted his motor scooter, using one foot as a kickstand. I'm smiling thank-you, but he's not done with me yet.

"Julia, what are your goals for your riding?" he asks in his antipodal twang, mispronouncing my name so that it sounds like "Julie-Error."

I'm baffled by the question. I stutter as I try to express an honest answer. "Ever since Redmond, I've wanted to get back to Fair Hill. But that's looking kind of dim right now," I apologize. "But I'm not really sure anymore. I guess to improve."

As soon as I utter it, I feel like an idiot. I'm in a barn where riders are on their way to competitions in Europe. My quest for knowledge and rituals of grief are child's play.

"Look it, you're a seat-of-the pants rider. You're really brave, aren't scared of anything."

I squirm in the saddle.

"But you lack foundation. I can take your money if you want, but you won't learn anything here, just going through the exercises. You need to go back to basics, and I don't really have the time in a group lesson."

I look at him. Barrett looks at him. Even Georgia is looking at Down.

"You get the exercises done, but you don't do them well. Half the time your horses go around upside down. You have absolutely no foundation," he concludes by repetition.

I start to tremble. "Down," I muster, "I've spent the last twenty-five years working with the best ghosts I could find."

"Then you haven't been studying with the right ones," he says.

I take it, and I wilt.

"If you look at the really good riders, you have a sense when they're coming to a fence that it is going to work out well. They don't rely on big bits or bitless bridles or any fancy gadgets, they just go out and jump the jumps. With you, I can never tell if it's going to work out or not. You need to find a jump instructor who can give you more attention. I can't do it in a group lesson," he goes on, ruthlessly. "You need to go back to poles on the ground. No jumps. Until you can see your distances consistently. Look it, I've got to get going."

Down cranks up his scooter and whizzes off, leaving us alone on the cross-country course. I'm choking as I head back to the trailer.

AT 4:00 IN THE MORNING, I BEGIN ANOTHER DROWSY CONVERSATION with Barrett.

"It would be so nice to have something go right for a change in my horse world. Just the tiniest piece of good luck. I already miss riding Calvin."

Barrett surfaces from REM. "If you make horses responsible for having things go right in your world, you're in trouble."

"Maybe that's the fatal flaw," I say.

"Well, if you're going to worry about finding the fatal flaw, then you have to also try and find eternal beauty."

"I already have that," I mumble.

"You've got that nailed, huh?" he says, the question mark in his voice still thick with sleep.

"Yeah, I've got that one down," I say. The smell of Calvin's neck, the hacks with Georgia trotting by our side, this man, waking beside me.

CALVIN STANDS IN OUR FRONT FIELD'S INDIAN RUN STREAM underneath the willows. No matter how much the world has changed, I can look at an eighteenth-century map from when the Wisner family owned the land all the way to Butler Road and still find this stream on it. It was why Charlotte's dad chose this place. And partly why we did. The tart spring water bathing Calvin's sore ankles is probably a better cure than any A-Cell injection. Attentive when I ride by his pasture on Shiva or Patrick, he is obviously confused about his different status at the farm. And maybe a little jealous, too, that my attentions have shifted. I tell people I'm not going to bring him back after the cold water has done its magic.

I SPEND SOME TIME ON THE BACH PRELUDE AND THEN SWITCH TO "Sellinger's Round" by John Bull, then "Maid with the Flaxen Hair" by Debussy, ending with "Landslide." One hour turns into two, then three. Time doesn't matter the way it did when I was younger and forced to practice. I lose track of it now. That's how I know I'm on the right path. When you find yourself checking your watch, you're in the wrong game.

Barrett and I listen to Stevie Nicks at dinner hour, that enveloping time when everything is done with our day. We listen, and sway into each other as the song sends a spark up our spines. At first we are hugging like two old friends—the musky smell of his neck, his disheveled mane of hair, the vague smell of horses.

I KEEP NEXT TO THE PIANO'S MUSIC RACK A PHOTO OF CHANCE—SHE'S maybe three or four—in a long white nightie, holding a balloon and looking wistfully at the camera as if she doesn't know what to do with her prize. It was one of my mother's favorite photos. It sat while she was alive exactly where it sits today. I tried to keep things that way, because, in my mind, little Chance always belonged there, watching over my mother as she fingered the keys. Little Chance is beautiful and sad, exactly as she is today.

The John Bull variations come slowly; the notes go every which way in an endless configuration. One note at a time.

IT'S MY FATHER'S BIRTHDAY. HE WOULD HAVE BEEN NINETY-FIVE. After my day is done, Georgia and I walk down to the water jump in the front field. Calvin and Surf and Huey join us, then follow us back to the gate. Georgia skims the fence line. She's a smart dog; she'll stay near her escape in case one of the horses chases her. I turn around, and Calvin is at my back, still confused about his new schedule. I put my arms around his giant neck, breathe deep the smell of all the Calvins. I look over at Huey, whose eye has that gray, sunken look of a very old horse. And Surf Guitar. Suddenly, I am back in northwest Pennsylvania, hopping on my pony bareback, galloping around the perimeter of his field, leaning over his neck to steer him with my hands gripping the halter. I put my head in his white-and-tan mane melting in the growing darkness to black—and a half century flies by, right here, right now, drinking the wind.

I AM ON THE STREETS OF BROOKLYN, MY EX IN HIS BOWLER HAT COVering an absence he won't let the world see, his wife beside him. We struggle to the tape that prevents us from going any farther. Thousands of spectators line the streets. I install the app to follow her progress, and especially so we won't miss her. She and her father have made careful plans. When I complain of hunger pangs, Jack urges me toward the nearby bagel shop, while he and his wife position themselves at the appointed place, at mile 8. "How will I find you?" I ask, a bit nervously. I scan the masses around us; I've already gotten lost once in the New York Subway system, trying to follow Jack's directions. None of the taxis or buses are running. He motions downward, opening his leather coat; he is wearing a bright red, beautifully pressed Oxford—part of their plan.

"She's at mile 3," Jack says, frowning into his phone. "She's slow; I don't understand why she's so slow." He even knows her running expectations.

I start to panic. "It takes a long time to get off the Staten Island Bridge," he reassures himself, and us. "There are so many runners in each wave, you end up mostly walking the first couple of miles."

I vaguely recall Jack's own NYC Marathon run, maybe twenty years ago, which he ran with Bruce.

I relax a little, take some shots of the little girls in the family next to us, their parents helping them hold out miniature hands so the first runners can low-five them.

"I think we may have missed her," Jack reports minutes later. "The tracker says she has already passed us." The three of us look at each other, crestfallen.

We strain our eyes, the masses thickening in this first wave of the more elite runners. I get texts from John, from Mollie, and from Barrett. Everyone is tracking Chance's progress.

My tracker says she's almost at mile 6, John reports. *Oh my god, this is so exciting.*

She's making good time, Barrett texts.

Jack's worry settles. "She'll be waving a red bandana," he says. Then I get it. Ah yes, the red shirt. Pamplona. San Fermín. The running of the bulls.

A red speck in the distance grows into my vibrant Chance, who a year ago decided to train for the nearly unattainable with her pony legs and fervent desire for things slightly beyond reach.

As she comes into focus, I see the bandana and huge red sunglasses. Chance is sporting Kinesio-taped legs to help hold together the various injuries she has sustained during her months of training, a professional job that from a distance makes her look like she's wearing patterned stockings. Her mouth wide open, she is nearly skipping up the left-hand side of the street toward us (*I run on the left, and plan to run on the left,* she had advised in her long, thoughtful prerace email), waving her red flag, arms open, heading straight to her father, ostensibly to pick up an energy snack, but in reality to give him a hug before she runs on.

SOME IMAGES STAY WITH YOU FOR THE REST OF YOUR LIFE. YOU know it when they happen. Oh my god, this is it. Remember it. Silly to remind yourself, though, because you've already tucked it away. Maybe you collect five of these over a lifetime.

We subway to Central Park, fight our way to the rail at mile 26. The first-wave runners are starting to appear. The party we witnessed in Brooklyn has morphed into a different gathering, with a somber, almost funereal tone. Many of the runners' once graceful, efficient forms have fallen apart. Their body language says it all: feet shuffling, trying to leave the earth as little as possible, overly active spastic arms trying to take over for the legs, some runners bent at the waist, upper bodies slightly ahead of the legs, collapsing toward the finish line. Most every one of them is struggling in some way. One runner is foaming at the mouth, another has a bloody face. Several are walking, gripping their cramping legs and sides. They have only two-tenths of a mile to go, and some cannot take another running step. We urge them on: "You can do it! You're doing it! You're almost there!" "Bravo Italia," Jack calls over and over. "Just a few more steps! Looking good!" I echo. We take direction from their running shirts: "Cassie, Brent, Jarrod, you go!" Some are still smiling, most grimacing in pain. A few glance our way when we call to them, a couple runners now walking look through me as if I can't possibly understand the horror.

We wait. My throat starts to hurt from all the screaming, and we wait. A few of the Achilles runners go by, pedaling recumbent bikes with their artificial limbs, in wheelchairs, or blind, all having started the race long before the others in their own special wave. It briefly crosses my wandering mind whether any of these impaired runners were victims of the Boston Marathon bombing. Now that's stubborn.

She's on Fifth Avenue, John texts. I can feel the excitement through his words.

"She's slow," says Jack.

"Don't tell me that," I say. My heart is beating hard. I'm screaming my head off for the other runners' progress. "You're almost there! Keep going! You're almost there!" All of a sudden, I'm screaming for Chance, I'm screaming for myself, for my ghosts, and for my competitive life, so fast running away from me. I'm screaming at the time left and lessons learned and courses run successfully, and those I failed at but was nonetheless successful in the trying. I'm yelling for my life and the lives of those I love, that I want so much to be imbued with meaning.

She's picking up speed, Barrett writes. Thank god for Barrett.

We wait.

And there she is, still running on the left. Arduously now, but chugging along at a slow trot, still in decent-enough form, though the earlier glow is gone. She begins to make her way up the hill. Pushing and pushing, and still running. I position my camera. I scream and I scream. She glances over slowly and sees us, as if just moving her head to the left is too much effort—no smile, only the most essential movements—and then she looks again, her left arm raises, and she gives us a thumbs up as she trudges past us toward the finish. An anonymous runner on her right lifts his hand, touches her back in encouragement.

"I think she's hurting," I say to Jack.

"Of course," he says, "of course she's hurting."

Runners wrapped in their New York City Marathon tarps file past us, looking like bedraggled soldiers, or deflated angels, solemn, most with heads down, many limping, all walking impossibly slowly, their blue wings trailing behind them. We strain to catch our first glimpse of Chance, but we will have to wait a long time for her to make it to us. But she does, eventually, still sporting the red dime-store glasses, consumed by the tarp and the completion medal she wears around her neck.

"I was slow," she will later complain. "My wall was a horrible cramp I got at mile 18 from drinking too much water. I had it for two miles. It finally went away at mile 20."

She bends her legs in place, trying to shake out the pain. A sea of blue around us.

"I learned all about cycles of pain, I can tell you that. And that what was bothering me before wasn't a problem. My knees and calf were fine, it was other stuff I least expected. My groin and stomach. I learned if I just kept running, the pain went away."

I try to hug her, but she recoils. Even that doesn't bother me.

"Please. Everything hurts," she says.

Her father and his wife leave for another engagement. We walk to the subway. People look at Chance and smile as she passes.

"You're a hero for a day in New York when you run the marathon."

We struggle to find correct change for the kiosk in the dungeon. One of the subway workers waves us through.

"Oh, that's so nice of you," I say.

My daughter frown-smiles and shakes her head under her blue hood. "They're supposed to do that for the runners," she explains.

We train back to Brooklyn and shuffle the few short blocks to her apartment. She finds she has forgotten to lock her door. We walk in, Chance admonishing herself, relieved to find her hole-in-the-wall still just a hole-in-the-wall and not a crime scene. "Too bad I was so slow," she says again, stripping off the tarp, only half complaining, "but I finished my first marathon," she concludes, with some pride.

"It's not about the ribbons, honey," I tell her, and instead of chiding me for my saccharine advice, she smiles, thanks me for my support. Her phone is texting and ringing. Barrett calls, and her brother calls. I busy myself admiring my new memories as they talk, and a half hour later, Chance and her brother are still at it.

"Maybe you and I should run the LA marathon together," Chance suggests. "You're built for it way better than I am, with your long skinny legs." She is bubbling with pride and excitement, even as she crouches over her spent body.

"I was thinking," she says to me after she has finally gotten off the phone with her brother, "that in my career, where only twenty percent of female playwrights ever get produced and how awful the odds are to attain success, how cool is it that I set out to do something a little later in life that I'd never done before, and I did it. I actually did it." I smile to myself. *A little later in life? My almost thirty-year-old?*

"Chance, you're a marathon runner now."

The unattainable. I can feel that small frisson of excitement deep within me.

What is it all about, anyway, besides this love I feel for Chance and life, and the personal striving of the human spirit?

I know what I have passed on to her, and what she has returned to me. On the threshold of my story, I can open that door, if I want to.

I CALL BARRETT. "SADDLE THE IRISH HORSE."

Afterword

WHEN THE LONG DREAM ENDS, YOU SOMETIMES SELL THE BED. A new realtor finds a nice French couple who wants to buy the farm. I ask Barrett if the buyers will love it as much as we did.

"You bet," he says. "How could they not?"

"What about Charlotte? Will they love her, too?"

"Absolutely," he says.

"And her house?"

"Yes, yes, yes."

They demolish it.

Acknowledgments

My special thanks to Charlotte Fowble, who built our farmhouse in Upperco, Maryland. She is the footsteps, the laughter, the unexpected wind. Though she remarried, she never recovered from her first husband's death, with whom I imagine her very much in love. Life comes down to an illness, single misstep, buck, or swerving car. And then nothing is ever the same again. Her sadnesses are omnipresent at the farm. My ghosts remind me how much I am haunted and driven and instructed by the past and everyone and thing that have come before. The ghosts that guide me must eventually leave me, or I, them. I am learning to live without.

Charlotte hovers over my shoulder as I type this, wondering if it begins all over again, in a gingham apron, her red hair twisted into a bun, hoping to get a peek at a little immortality. Which I cannot promise anyone.

But I can promise you that is why we dream so hard—because everything is at risk, and nothing survives. Nothing, but these phantasms of memory.

I would also like to thank my children, who have put up with being the children of a writer for as long as they've walked this earth, and who I hope have become accustomed to being fair game. To my son, John, for his research into the historical origins of our farm, as well as for his artwork. Only I know how good an artist he is. My gratitude to the Baltimore County Historical Society for their help in researching Charlotte's family and the origins of our Maryland farmhouse. Many thanks to all my riding instructors who greatly enriched my riding life over the years. My indebtedness to Ashleigh McKown, who edited the finest of detail. And thanks to my other readers: Jack Stephens, Lisa Hayes, Mara Naselli, Mollie Stephens, and Anniebelle Quattlebaum. Thanks to Adam Robinson for his patience, precision, and enthusiastic guidance through the publishing process. Thanks to the editors of *5AM*, *Revolution John*, *JMWW*, *The Notebook*, *Muse/A Journal*, *The Evansville Review*, *Gargoyle*, and *Nimrod*, where some of the embedded poems first appeared. My special gratitude to Michael Downs, who read an early version of the manuscript and gave me the encouragement I needed to finish. Of course, my enveloping thanks to Barrett, who accompanied me every step of this journey and without whom the first draft would not have been possible. Most of all, my gratitude goes to my daughter, who was, is, and always will be the inspiration for this book.

About Julia Wendell

Julia balances the inner life of a poet with the outer life of an equestrian athlete. She is the author of seven book of poems, most recently *Take This Spoon* and *The Sorry Flowers*. She completed her first International Four-Star Event with her partner, Redmond, a Canadian Sport Horse, and went on to complete several additional Three- and Four-Star Events with Cavendish, an Irish Sport Horse. *Come to the X* is the sequel to *Finding My Distance: A Year in the Life of a Three-day Event Rider*. Julia lives in Aiken, South Carolina.